the Great Education Controversy

Your Schools

A critical review of education
1944 to the present day

the Great Education Controversy
Your Schools

A critical review of education
1944 to the present day

R.V. Bryant

© 2010 R.V Bryant

First edition published by Cambridge Academic, The Studio, High Green, Gt. Shelford, Cambridge CB2 5EG.

The rights of R.V Bryant to be identified as the author of this work have been asserted by him in accordance with the Copyright, Designs and Patents Act 1988.

All rights reserved. No part of this publication may be reproduced, stored in a retrieval system, or transmitted in any form or by any means, electronic, mechanical, photocopying, recording, or otherwise without prior permission of
Cambridge Academic at:
The Studio, High Green, Gt. Shelford, Cambridge. CB2 5EG

ISBN 1-903-499-54-2
978-1-903499-54-2

The contents of this publication are provided in good faith and neither The Author nor The Publisher can be held responsible for any errors or omissions contained herein. Any person relying upon the information must independently satisfy himself or herself as to the safety or any other implications of acting upon such information and no liability shall be accepted either by The Author or The Publisher in the event of reliance upon such information nor for any damage or injury arising from any interpretation of its contents. This publication may not be used in any process of risk assessment.

Printed and bound in the United Kingdom by
4edge Ltd, 7a Eldon Way Industrial Estate, Hockley, Essex, SS5 4AD.

Contents

1. Something is wrong with the education system.................................1
2. The 1944 Act and subsequent developments................................11
3. The Comprehensive School..21
4. Equality and individuality...33
5. The failure to produce a just discipline..43
6. The adverse effect of the uncontrolled delinquent.........................63
7. More recent thinking on discipline in schools and colleges..............91
8. Teaching and learning strategies..103
9. Vocational versus academic learning..115
10. Assessment: Tests, examinations and qualifications.....................125
11. The Curriculum..147
12. What is education for?..177
13. New schools and colleges...191
14. A new professionalism...207
Bibliography..239
Index..241

1. Something is wrong with the education system

Surely, after more than half a century of educational debate and the reforms of a variety of governments, there can be nothing wrong with the education system in the UK today. Yet, if everything is so rosy, as it is easy to claim, why do we see so much antisocial behaviour, disrespect for others, misuse of drugs and alcohol, teenage (child) pregnancies and the dangerously unforgivable assaults of the young on the young?

In the desire to encourage the development of self expression in the young we seem to have lost sight of the need for order, respect for others, a straightforward code of manners, clear boundaries to personal behaviour and the need for clearly understood sanctions imposed by teachers for misbehaviour.

Why do we have a system of intended child protection which causes adults to show such caution when dealing with young people that they cannot provide realistic care and enthusiastic instruction for those they are supposed to help?

Why do time consuming and restricting Standard Assessment Tests seem to result more in the labelling of schools as failures and in their closure than with any constructive effort to give deserved assistance where circumstances lead to poor results?

Why does the publication of inspection reports, which logically must result in institutions having their failures aired in public and with the consequent erosion of their positive ethos, seem such a good idea, rather than resources being quietly brought in to put matters right when problems are identified?

Why does the number of young people apparently excelling themselves in the public examinations go up every year while universities and employers complain about candidates' weaknesses in English and mathematics?

It is easy to convince ourselves that apparent rises in standards are real and of real benefit to those we educate, but have we fallen into the trap of accepting the unreal because we are expected to do so? Is what we have an unrealistic and frustration-breeding system in which people instinctively feel that what they are often expected to do is wrong?

Why do we press our teachers to develop and supervise school journeys and other out of class activities when we stifle them with health and safety requirements, allow them to be threatened by a culture of litigation and fail to accept that accidents will always happen?

Those working with children and young people today seem to be under greater stress, suffering more accusations of assault, accusations of incompetence, and threats of dismissal than ever before. Why, considering the introduction of so much in service training and mentoring through the appraisal scheme?

There is too little job satisfaction and far too many are looking forward to the day they can retire, evident discomfort of the workforce which is almost certainly linked to the present requirements of the system.

This is the state of affairs after more than half a century during which social reformers have been searching and striving for a system of education for all, linked with some kind of illusive equality of opportunity, which they believe will eliminate the disadvantages and privileges of class distinction. Through education the injustices arising from the environment into which a person is born shall be expunged for ever! Yet, while millions of pounds have been invested in the state education system, there remains considerable doubt about its achievements and considerable controversy rages over the ideals around which such a system should be built. The polarisation of debate around the political ideologies of the left and right has not helped, being reflected in the attitudes of the teachers themselves and their trade unions.

During the last decade or so there have been radical and controversial changes introduced by various governments ostensibly to raise standards. There has been revolution in school government, bringing parents and teachers into influential positions on governing bodies; and the introduction of the local management of schools has placed a large part of the responsibility for the running of schools in the hands of those governors. The chance to escape from local education authority control, by choosing grant maintained status, was abolished by Labour in 1998 but seen by some as being revived in their proposals in 2006: a hint of the vacillation and confusion in educational thinking during the last fifty years.

The introduction of the common-to-all 16 plus General Certificate of Secondary Education, National Curriculum and national testing programme, all imposed by the government, have largely determined what shall be taught and to some extent how it shall be taught.

The Technical and Vocational Initiative of the 1980s attempted to provide an alternative to the academic approach to the curriculum, teaching methods and assessment. This has included the promotion of teaching by negotiation, as opposed to the more traditional, and, it is argued by some, less meaningful, strategy in which teachers establish work schemes without reference to those they teach. A strategy which it is claimed alienates large numbers of students. The initiative has promoted the concept of assessment profiles, used in place of, or in addition to, examinations, where the student is subjected to ongoing assessment throughout the course and where attempts are made to record strengths in areas other than in the acquisition of skills and knowledge – for instance, there have been attempts to assess personal qualities, such as reliability and tenacity, and to include these in the student's profile. This in turn has led to records of achievement, school leaving student profiles in which everything positive the young person has achieved is recorded. These ideas were advanced further in the White Paper 14 – 19 "Education and Skills" published in February 2005 but never presented to parliament, for full debate and legislation.

City Technological Colleges and Academies have been established in some urban areas, with the promise of more to come, in an attempt to upgrade education in those geographical areas which are thought to be most disadvantaged by reason of their inner city location.

All of this is the outcome of a mass of relatively recent legislation, yet the arguments about the success or otherwise of the education system continue to rage, with the culmination, in 2006, of considerable political and emotional argument in response to the White Paper "Higher Standards, Better Schools for All" published in October 2005.

Those in commerce and industry still claim that they find new recruits lacking the knowledge and skills which they require. Young people fail to write proper letters of application, they present themselves as being illiterate. Engineers state that they find students unable to calculate. Researchers argue that reading standards have fallen, that standards in mathematics are lower than they used to be. Fewer young people are qualifying in the sciences and modern languages, areas of such great importance in the development of industry and commerce. Members of the public see the schools as causes of football hooliganism, increased vandalism and a growth in the number of delinquents.

Although it is always difficult to objectively evaluate such claims, the obvious conclusion is that there has been enough comment, discussion and debate to fuel the critics' view that there must indeed be something wrong and that the tax payers are not getting value for money.

It was during the 1970s that public dissatisfaction, echoed by the Department of Education, caused Prime Minister James Callaghan to initiate the Great Debate on education in his speech made at Ruskin College in October 1976. In particular, doubts were expressed about progressive teaching methods in primary schools and the inappropriateness of the secondary school curriculum. Subsequently national debate and consultation was promoted through nine regional conferences and Shirley Williams, Secretary of State for Education and Science produced the consultative document "Education in Schools" in 1977.

By 1979 the government had changed and the Conservative administration, also accepting that education was not producing the required results, set about introducing their substantial reforms in the 1980 and subsequent Education Acts.

But the debate goes on, with socialists and conservatives disagreeing with themselves and each other, not that there is a problem, but about the remedies. In the meantime, teachers have been bombarded with criticism and been required to develop and carry out a mountain of new procedures: it is claimed that their morale has never been lower and the old argument that higher salaries and more resources will cure the problem has been advanced with enthusiasm.

So who is right?

Could the root cause be found in the 1944 Education Act? Did it lay down the wrong foundations? Or is it more a question of development not keeping pace with the times? What was a major step forward in thinking in 1944 may now be at least irrelevant. In addition however deeply entrenched values having their origins in the immediate post war period may now inhibit the objective thinking required to develop an education system for the twenty-first century.

So how did the corner stones of post war education evolve? How did the early education reformers see and legislate for the needs of their time? Consider the lives of the ordinary citizen in the period before the 1914-18 war, when it was young children who entered the world of employment, a world generated by the forces of the Industrial Revolution. The power of steam built the mills and sank the mines where in general workers were compelled to slave long hours for little reward while their masters enjoyed the profits. The owners of factories and mines lived in large fine detached houses while the workers occupied the overcrowded close-lined terraces. Perhaps it was the more fortunate of the ordinary folk who served the well-off in their houses and gardens. They at least lived away from the danger, grime, dirt and noise of heavy industry. But it was only the rich who could afford to keep their children in the secondary or public schools.

Arthur Drew, born in North Wraxall, Wiltshire, into a country family of farm workers in the last quarter of the nineteenth century, was described by those who knew him as a clever boy, but he still had to leave school at the age of ten, in about 1880, to commence work as a gardener's boy. His brothers, who were described as less bright, never attended school at all and went straight into farm work as soon as they were physically able. But there is a significant fact here: they, and others like them who were not scholars, could find a place in life doing physical work. It may not have brought them wealth but it did at least give them a purpose.

The two Atkins sisters attended a school in Great Yarmouth during the 1870s when their parents, their father a railway worker, paid sixpence per week for their education, an education which, it was said, would enable them to gain acceptance in "good service". That is, to gain work as servants to the better off, but with families who treated them well. Again, service provided work and gave purpose to the lives of many who would have failed in the intellectual world: although their rewards would have been minimal.

Arthur Drew met Sarah Atkins in London, both in service, one as a gardener, the other a children's nanny. Was it their enterprising personalities which took them to the capital city? Was there something, somewhere, in their education which gave them this spirit of enterprise or was it some innate characteristic?

They married, moved to Great Yarmouth and had three children, each of whom died of diphtheria before the eldest was ten: a tragedy common at the time striking at both rich and poor. Dorothy Drew (eventually Bryant) was born later and not only survived but, in terms of health, thrived. By this time her father had surprisingly changed his trade to become a carpenter and frequently moved the family from one part of the country to another during his search for work in the mines and with building contractors. Dorothy was consequently educated in schools as far apart as Yorkshire and London and relates the story of an occasion when she had just moved into a new home and had been sent to buy bread and milk from the nearby shop. She was frightened out of her wits by the school board man who met her and demanded to know why she was not at school, instructing her to get herself there the following morning without fail. Was this a fear which is no longer generated by the present day welfare officer? Or was it the anxiety of a nervous child fearful in a situation where others would not be the least concerned?

Dorothy claimed that she was not clever and did not like school although reports described her as always very well behaved, quiet, and shy. She tolerated it but left as soon as possible in 1917 when she was fourteen to start work in a factory making geographical globes. It was there that she made friends who lasted a lifetime.

Sydney Bryant was described as a clever boy who spent several years in the top class but never worked seriously at his studies until his last year, when he realised the significance of school reports in the obtaining of employment. He officially left school at fourteen in 1916 although he had in fact worked on a milk round since he was twelve. He claimed that he was always getting into trouble: playing tricks on other pupils and teachers alike, he was made to sit at the front of the class where he was in reach of the teacher. When he was not clipped around the ear for his nonsense, he was given several strokes of the cane on his backside. It is appropriate to report that he never interpreted this as cruelty or abuse, but rather a justly deserved punishment for his bad behaviour!

He only started studying more seriously after leaving fulltime education. Working long hours as an electrician in a garage, he turned up at college after classes started covered in the black grease from a day spent in and under motorcars. In this way he gained qualifications in electrical engineering but never reached his full potential, in part, he argued, because the 1939-45 war prevented him continuing at night school.

Today his childhood would be classed as underprivileged: his father died when he was only six, he was one of a large family, and his mother was forced to go out to work to feed them. As the children reached school leaving age, if not earlier, it was imperative that they found work in order to earn money which supplemented the family income.

A moments' thought demonstrates that in many ways the lives of ordinary folk were vastly different then from now. Their opportunities were different, their expectations different. Working hours and wages were different. Life was different. But, in spite of these differences, the individual people were also different from each other: different in their abilities, different in their personalities. It is the significance of these differences that has too often been neglected, possibly because they have been perceived only as either good or bad qualities, instead of in terms of differing strengths to be used in life's different occupations. Furthermore, there has been a disastrous trend which has correlated success with elitism, bringing about a devaluation of meaningful qualifications.

Certainly, it was to be social disadvantage, rather than individual differences, which came to be accepted as all significant, and it is easy to understand why this was so.

Before 1800 education was provided on an ad hoc basis by fee-charging private schools, church charity schools and the grammar schools. The latter were established by various foundations to provide teaching in classical languages and evolved to become the traditional grammar and public schools. The first true education system was provided by the church and based on the monitorial scheme: a plan in which one teacher instructed a number of pupil teachers, or monitors, who then delivered the lessons to smaller groups of pupils. The founders, Andrew Bell and Joseph Lancaster, established the Anglican National Schools and Non-conformist British and Foreign Schools Societies for this purpose. The first government involvement was in 1839 when a committee was set up to administer the allocation of a small grant to these societies.

The next significant development came in 1870 when the Elementary Education Act created the School Boards, giving them authority to raise money on the rates in order to fund new schools which would supplement the church system. This was the birth of Elementary Education and Elementary Schools. The charging of school fees continued and whether or not attendance was compulsory was left to the discretion of the individual Boards.

It was little more than one hundred years ago, in 1888, that the County Council system of local government was introduced and ten years after that when they were given authority to raise money on the rates in order to pay for deserving elementary school children to attend grammar schools. This was not for all children and was not free. It was an education for those academically able children not already in fee charging grammar and public schools but whose parents could afford to support them.

Although the 1899 Education Act established the Board of Education, it was not until 1902 (the Balfour Education Act) that the local education authorities were set up, national regulations introduced for elementary and secondary schools, school examinations rationalised and a handbook produced for teachers. Even then it was expected that the government would not provide much more than fifty per cent of the cost.

Further encouragement was given to the notion that able children should continue in school when in 1907 local authority secondary schools became eligible for a grant if they made twenty-five per cent or more of their places free. In 1932 the special places scheme was introduced whereby parents of children selected for secondary education were charged according to their ability to pay.

In 1911 the compulsory school leaving age was raised to thirteen but the opportunity to remain at school until the age of fourteen depended on where you lived, the better off local authorities providing places while others could not afford to do so. It was also in this year that the Board of Education called for the provision of more practical and vocational work in the secondary curriculum, for science and art examinations to be reformed in order to encourage the teaching of new subjects and for more teachers with industrial experience to be employed. Was this a genuine desire to educate a realistic workforce, to provide an education according to the needs of the young, or a means of maintaining the class system? Certainly, practical and vocational courses came to be seen as inferior to, rather than merely different from, the academic courses provided in the grammar schools. Yet what is education for if it ignores the realistic requirements of industry and commerce: and the realistic ambition of young people to earn their living?

Grammar schools required pupils to attend until the age of sixteen and followed a clearly defined academic curriculum leading to the Schools Certificate Examination introduced in 1917, with, of course, compulsory games, largely rugby, football, cricket, hockey, netball and athletics.

Although there were undoubtedly children from less well-off families who had the intellectual ability to benefit from an academic education, the poor could not afford the fees required. Even if the fees were paid by means of a scholarship, the cost of keeping a growing youngster in school was prohibitive: they had to work in order to provide necessary income to help feed and clothe both themselves and other members of the family. In addition, there was a psychological factor which acted against some youngsters being allowed to continue with their education. Some parents could not accept that their children should be allowed to follow what they regarded as an easy life in school when they should be out in the real world earning their keep!

Yet, in the minds of the social reformers, because the public school system provided the route to the most influential positions in life and in salary terms the most rewarding employment, and because the grammar schools provided a further route into jobs seen in social terms as better than those in workshops and factories, an injustice was perceived in an education system which prevented the poor from having access to it.

Industry and commerce allowed a situation to develop in which those who did physical work were seen as inferior to those who worked with their intellect rather than promoting them as workers of equal status completing different but equally essential tasks. The situation was allowed to develop in which working hours in offices were shorter than those in factories. The working conditions of the mine or factory floor were clearly rougher, dirtier, noisier and more dangerous than those in the office. Furthermore, office work was allowed to bring greater remuneration and consequently a better standard of living and the route to this semi-paradise was via a secondary grammar school education.

In 1918 a further Education Act raised the compulsory school leaving age to fourteen and required local education authorities to provide advanced instruction for older or more intelligent children, including provision beyond the statutory leaving age. Fees for elementary education were abolished, playing fields and swimming pools were to be provided, plans were advanced for nursery education and an intention to introduce part-time education for 14- to 18-year-olds established. The Act encouraged local education authorities to experiment with different types of provision, leading to the introduction of Junior Technical, Commercial and Art schools in some parts of the country. Other authorities introduced Higher Elementary Schools, some had similar establishments which they called Central Schools and others Senior Schools.

Nevertheless, the grammar schools were still seen to have better resources than other secondary schools. They had better trained, better qualified and better paid teachers. They had smaller classes: groups of thirty while the elementary schools struggled with fifty or more in a group. They had more books and equipment, better accommodation and more specialist accommodation, including, for instance, science laboratories.

But the privilege of remaining at school until the age of sixteen, when friends left at fourteen, was a dubious one in the eyes of some of the children and a factor which should not be overlooked. It is inadequate to claim that all of those in the elementary schools would happily have remained in school for an extra two years, if only their families were sufficiently well-off. There are other reasons why children wished to escape from full-time education: sometimes originating from parental attitudes, where the type of education on offer may actually be seen as in some way inappropriate: or originating from the children themselves. There was an attraction in going to work, earning wages, being one among men and women and consequently feeling grown up and, to some extent, gaining an independence from parents. There was also the alternative of on-the-job training through apprenticeship training schemes. Schemes lasted until the apprentice reached the age of twenty-one and was, by then, well trained and well qualified for work in a trade – albeit restricted to the depressed apprenticeship wages.

But, in the developing social climate of the time, these factors were largely overlooked, the argument being that, given a fair opportunity to learn, all children would learn, and apparently learn the same things in the same way.

In 1922, in response to the perceived unfairness of the education system, the Labour Party introduced its policy of secondary education for all, with a proposed compulsory leaving age of sixteen. What did those who professed a dislike for school think of that? Did those who played and fooled about see the extra years of schooling as a waste of time? Was the socialist ideal to give all an equal opportunity through the same education, a grammar school education, and so remove class disadvantages? If it was, this was clearly an unrealistic goal.

Conversely, in 1923 Stanley Baldwin, the Conservative prime minister, argued that secondary education was not suitable for all and that to try to provide for everyone would merely lower standards. Others argued that only the gifted and intellectually able, who would supply the future leaders of industry and commerce, should be given secondary education. There was a fixation on the notion that secondary education was and would remain an academic education and that all could, or could not, benefit from it.

While there was a policy of providing grammar school places only for those with appropriate ability, a means of selecting those who would benefit was necessary and another area of conflict was born. Selection came to mean an evil division of young people into haves and have-nots, rather than a procedure for guiding those with different talents towards available options. The trouble was, of course, that too many people saw only the one option: a valued grammar school education or a less prestigious senior elementary school one.

By 1925 one in every eighteen pupils attending elementary schools was taking a more advanced course – that is, a course for older youngsters or for pupils perceived as being able to benefit from more advanced schooling, something more than the basic elementary school course.

The publication of the Hadow Report *"The Education of the Adolescent"*, in 1926, supported the notion that children are different and have different needs, stating that there should be four types of secondary schools: grammar, modern schools with a practical bias, modern schools with a mixed intake and elementary schools with senior classes. In addition it recommended that there should be facility for transfer between schools at twelve and thirteen and that the statutory school leaving age should be raised to fifteen.

The Spens Report published in 1938 helped to crystallise the concept of different schools for different children; advocating grammar, technical and secondary modern schools for this purpose. It was proposed that the compulsory school leaving age should be raised to sixteen. Grammar schools were expected to take fifteen per cent of the population. Technical schools were to be expanded and vocational courses further developed. There were proposals for the appointment for careers' teachers to advise young people on their choice of career. A foundation for a variety of types of secondary school was laid but was never going to be accepted by the social reformers.

The outbreak of the Second World War in September 1939 put a temporary stop to educational reforms. The raising of the school leaving age was abandoned among the more pressing preparations for evacuation of schools from target areas, although welfare schemes were established to combat rising juvenile delinquency which was thought to be the result of war time disruption to family life. But the spark of reform flourished to culminate in the Butler Education Act of 1944, devised and enacted by the wartime National Government comprising a coalition of all political parties.

2. The 1944 Education Act and Subsequent Developments

As the end to the devastating and world wide war approached, the government was able to turn its attention to the immense task of reconstruction. The disruption to society's traditions, as well as the destruction of much of its physical basis, provided the opportunity for change. In education, change was to manifest itself in the Butler Act of 1944 where the primary objective was to establish, for the first time, a free secondary education system for everyone. The concepts of primary and secondary education were established and it was clearly stated that there would be separate primary and secondary schools with a division at the age of eleven. Only in the case of the provision for the physically and mentally disadvantaged was it envisaged that all-age schools would exist.

The philosophy of the Act was based upon the simple notion that all schools should have an equal share of available resources. Premises would be equally good. The teachers equally qualified and equally paid. The maximum class size would be the same for all children; the provision of books and equipment the same for all types of school. Even the length of the school holidays would be the same. And, perhaps, it was this notion which led to the misconception: if the environment was made the same for everyone, all would flourish equally.

But this was certainly not the outcome of the Act, a matter which the Ministry of Education pamphlet number nine "The New Secondary Education" published in 1947, largely the work of the socialist education minister Ellen Wilkinson, clearly addresses. It promotes an education for all in which the individual child is placed first, a great variety of provision envisaged to suit different individuals but not different income groups, and where success is seen to be obtained through the arousing of the individual child's own interests. It was even stated that children must not be forced into an academic education which may bore them and cause them frustration simply because that education is thought to be more socially desirable.

The opening statements in the pamphlet emphasised the concept of no two children being alike, and that there should be different schools for different children. There can be no doubt that those who were motivated to bring about the great education reform of 1944 appreciated the need to provide different styles of education for different people. Variety was seen to be necessary, in the curriculum and in teaching methods, to cater for children with different aptitudes, being at different stages in their development and having different levels of achievement. There was an acceptance that such individual differences require different schools, and an assumption that it is right to expect some children to remain in school to a later age than others. But there was also the expectation that the different schools would carry equal prestige.

It was argued that the majority of children learn best through practical experience, and do best in schools which provide a good all-round education. The schools for this majority were referred to as modern schools where the curriculum would permit the pupils to sample a range of subjects and skills, and then to study those which they found most enjoyable. These became the Secondary Modern Schools.

Another group of children, it was claimed, were able to decide at an early age which career they wanted to follow, or displayed particular aptitudes: for example in science or mathematics or music and the arts. The underlying concept, that different people have different aptitudes, is still vigorously pursued in career selection today, in spite of the development of a common curriculum and leaving certificate. Such youngsters, it was surmised, would need specialised courses, and that these would be provided in Secondary Technical Schools.

Thirdly, another minority were identified in terms of their having abilities and aptitudes which thrive on books and ideas, and which appreciate an abstract approach to learning. These children would attend the grammar schools, and be expected to follow an academic course leading to external examinations at sixteen, and being likely to follow a similar but more advanced course into the sixth form, with eventual progress to university.

In spite of this three-school philosophy, there was an expectation that there would be similarities between the schools. All three would be involved in both book and activity learning: "the proportions in which these two ways of learning are to be combined should be determined by the capabilities and needs of the individual pupil". The existence of native ability, although a vague concept based upon intellectual ability and imprecisely defined special aptitudes, was accepted. Emphasis was placed on the idea that the child should work at those things in which it can be expected to achieve success and not be presented with subject matter which it cannot appreciate and which will only cause it frustration. It was also stressed that attention must be given to the whole child: to intellectual development, social, emotional and physical development and spiritual growth.

The provision of school libraries and timetabled library periods, during which every child would be taught how to use books for both entertainment and for the finding of information, were proposed. How many schools today still provide library periods?

How well has this initiative succeeded when a significant proportion of the population sees little use for books and there are frequent complaints of illiteracy among the workforce? It is all very well to point to the upsurge of computer aided learning, but the operator must first be proficient in basic reading and comprehension before being equipped to obtain the greatest benefits from modern technology.

Already in 1944 the significance of presenting material through media other than books was recognised. Schools were to be provided with cine projectors, film strip and micro-projectors, gramophones (the predecessors of the record, tape, and CD players we have seen in more recent years) and radios. It was even foreseen that television could one day be used to great advantage. But now of course, in spite of the existence of the Open University, schools broadcasts and educational programmes, a large part of the finance and technology applied to audio-visual presentation is invested in popular entertainment. What effect have programmes such as Grange Hill had on the ethos of the schools? The producer argued, when the series started, it was his intention to replace the old fashioned world of Billy Bunter with more realistic events from present-day school life, and there is no doubt that the storylines reflected the goings on in some schools. Many teachers, on the other hand, were quick to disclaim such happenings: they did not happen in their schools! Today, much of what appeared then to be unusual is now more commonplace, but how much has the real life-style drama been responsible for helping the exceptional to become the norm? What is the influence of the high powered advertisement? How many children have access to the video-nasties (now on DVDs) and the now common computer games? Where does the teacher stand in the face of such competition?

At the time of the Butler reforms, politicians were concerned with what they understood as education for good. They included the statutory requirement that each day should start with an act of collective worship, and the notion was promoted that each child should be encouraged to develop as a member of the community, learning citizenship, the workings of local and national government, the system of rates and taxes and the judiciary. But not politics, which some people today think can be taught objectively and without indoctrination.

It is the curriculum which defines the pupils' work programme and, in light of more recent initiatives, it is worth considering the views advanced on the matter in 1944. Quite clearly it was stated that the head-teacher has responsibility for the curriculum: the Ministry of Education did not lay down subject matter or the time allocation given to each part. The only requirement was the compulsory provision of religious instruction and the daily act of collective worship. The curriculum was in the hands of the professionals: they were acknowledged as the experts, trained in their discipline and consequently the best people to do the job. They were trusted with this responsibility. How things have changed!

Education was seen to be a partnership between the Ministry of Education, local education authorities, school governors and teachers. It is interesting to note that parents, members of local industry and commerce, and representatives of the community at large were not included.

With regard to the appointment of staff, the head-teachers of all schools were given the same responsibility for the appointment and retention of their staff as that applying to grammar school heads. The intention seems to have been that all head-teachers should have the responsibility for appointing, supervising and disciplining assistant teachers. There was a professional attitude to management which has since been replaced by a broader spread of responsibility throughout a governing body.

What has become known as the hidden curriculum was expected to play a large part in the social, emotional, physical and spiritual education of children. It was understood that not only the timetabled activities, but what is now often referred to as the ethos of the school, including the attitudes of the staff, would work towards this broad education. A moral tone should be established in the school, teachers encouraging pupils to treat others with courtesy and consideration, to be aware of the feelings of others and to respect their point of view. The way in which teachers behaved towards each other, as well as towards their pupils, was given importance. Yet in subsequent years there has been a welling up of militancy from the majority of the teacher unions, in which such professional attitudes have been subdued if not completely rejected. When teacher militancy was at its height, strikes closed schools for days at a time, selective strikes showed teachers walking out of school in the middle of sessions, dinner time supervision and obvious staff involvement were abandoned, causing discipline to deteriorate, valued school clubs and excursions were stopped and even public examinations threatened: all examples of teacher behaviour in which the needs of the young were placed second behind the demands of those who claimed to be professional educators. Such overt direct action, inevitably seriously disrupting the routine behaviour and learning of young people, must have adversely affected the ethos of schools. To argue that such actions are designed to bring long term benefits to the children is inadequate because for the young time is immediate and it is what happens at the moment which is all important in their education.

The significance of school clubs was recognised when in particular, it was argued that they help those with learning difficulties. Many teachers have observed the improved pupil-teacher relationships which develop during club and school journey activities being carried over into the normal classroom. There develops a greater mutual respect which brings increased pupil motivation and a lessening of the strains arising from confrontational discipline.

Little was said about the harsher discipline which was common in most schools at the time, but comments were made on teaching styles. There had been too much emphasis on written work at the expense of other activities. The child's curiosity was to be the main stimulus for learning and the teacher's job was to rouse this natural curiosity and relate schoolwork to real aspects of life. Children were seen as showing great enthusiasm and skill in the pursuance of a chosen hobby and this motivating force should be harnessed. It was thought that this eagerness could be applied to homework, where the youngsters were expected to become keen to collect and tabulate data, draw diagrams and make things. It is a fascinating fact today that such a notion is not only rejected by some pupils and parents but also by some responsible educators.

Science should play its part in directing this curiosity through the application of scientific methodology. There should be discovery through the consulting of sources, interpretation of information and the establishing of principles. Field work in history and geography should be used to further develop this principle of discovery and in mathematics the practical approach, through doing and measuring was to be advanced. All of this was a part of the general advice for the development of the modern school but with value for pupils in the other schools as well. It becomes clear, throughout the pamphlet, that the foundations, albeit often superficially defined, to much subsequent thinking, were laid down in the immediate post war years. Referring to the subject disciplines, it was said that sharp divisions between subjects were inappropriate, and this concept remains an area of contention today. Even subjects at university level now have different contents under the same titles, and similar contents under different titles! The introduction of new subjects and the redefining of the content of the more traditional disciplines have made this no less of a problem at school level. But some form of packaging of information is essential if learning is to progress efficiently. Perhaps modules, where smaller amounts of learning material are placed together, are a more useful way of handling subject content. A single module can apply to more than one subject: for example, the graphical representation of data, which is generally taught in mathematics, is probably taught again in science lessons and again in the geography class. It would be more efficient to teach the unit once and then to apply its techniques to the analysis of data in other areas.

The famous, or for some infamous, project method of teaching was promoted. The approach identifies a particular area of study and then draws upon several disciplines for its content. Its failure is illustrated by the geography teacher who had been involved in a project on the Trans-Siberian Railway only to discover that his pupils afterwards remembered such details as the number and type of wheels on the engines but nothing of the railway route or its commerce! Perhaps the failure lies in the whole being used in an attempt to teach the parts, when it would be more logical to teach the appropriate parts first and subsequently use them to investigate a greater whole.

The teacher in all of this was seen to be a supervisor and counsellor rather than as an instructor, and this is yet another aspect of education theory with its roots in the post war years, which still gives rise to considerable controversy. For instance, there is a move to introduce teaching styles in which individual learning programmes are negotiated between teacher and student, rather than imposed by authority.

With regard to the composition of teaching groups the mood at the time was to support the idea that children should be grouped according to their ability so that the teaching methods would be appropriate to their needs and the brightest not be held back by the less able: also enabling the slower learner to be taught in a different way, through the simpler presentation of subject content. This seems to be sensible stuff. Clearly, it was intended that children who found learning school subjects easy should be placed in one group, those with moderate learning ability in another group and the slowest in a third group. Unfortunately, such groups, referred to as streams, soon became boldly labelled top, middle and bottom, emphasising success and failure rather than mere differences in teaching strategies, and leading to the system being criticised for its divisiveness, denigration and perceived social injustice. Even in 1947, the reformers wrote of the social disadvantages of streaming, arguing that more able children actually gain from working with the less able, who in turn would be stimulated their brighter peers. A debatable point!

With regard to school leaving examinations, it was reported that a common system for all is not practical in an education system which sees the need for different pupils to be taught in different schools.

Alternatively, emphasis was placed on the keeping of individual records, where it was intended that the child's development and progress would be plotted throughout its school career, tests and teacher assessments being used to diagnose difficulties. Evidence relating to the young person's character was also to be included, then, on leaving school, a complete picture of the young person would be available for vocational guidance, fitting the candidate to a job. Again an element of post-war thinking demonstrates the origin of yet another more recent innovation: records of achievement.

Back in the refreshing idealism of the forties, an idealism in which all children would be surrounded by good books, pictures, decorations and good quality buildings, and all teachers raised in status to those working in the grammar schools, with equal pay, holidays, class sizes and expectations, the future looked good. The tripartite system of secondary education was in place and the roots of many of the theories and practices which were to dominate the sixties were put down.

In spite of the damage to and loss of school buildings during the war sufficient repairs and new building were accomplished to provide both grammar and secondary modern premises. The relatively new senior schools built during the 1920s and '30s, provided well constructed, pleasantly laid out accommodation but the older board schools, located in the inner urban areas, were hardly conducive to the fostering of new education. There also developed a type of building (consisting of such features as flat roofs, extensive glass areas in external walls and thin internal partition walls) which was susceptible to easy damage by both the weather and the occupants, leading quickly to shabbiness in appearance. But such physical handicaps did not detract from the efforts of education authorities to develop secondary education for all.

Grammar schools took more children from less well-off homes, relying on selection by ability rather than wealth, and secondary modern schools developed courses in keeping with the new philosophy.

Yet the enterprise of the 1944 Education Act and the philosophy of the New Secondary Education born out of it hardly advanced from the starting line before division of opinion developed an emotive controversy. The tripartite system did not satisfy the radicals' deep felt desire for a utopian social justice. They saw only division: the minority of grammar and perhaps technical pupils achieving the clean authority-commanding posts (while those from the private sector retained their stranglehold on the positions of real power) and the majority from the secondary modern pupils had no choice but to follow their destiny into the lower paid manual and clerical occupations.

A leading protagonist in the comprehensive school movement was Robin Pedley, one-time Director of Education of the Exeter University Institute of Education and in his book "The Comprehensive School" published in 1963, he comments that England was then an aristocracy, that is a society in which government is in the hands of the "best" people. He pointed out that the best people were formerly those born into wealthy aristocratic families but that the situation was changing to one in which those with ability were filling the influential positions, a fact supported by more recent surveys which showed the number of grammar school educated people in managerial and government posts. Such a society has become known as a meritocracy. He goes on to imply that the acceptance of this state of affairs does nothing to remove class barriers and consequently suggests a democratic form of government as a better way forward. Upon this oversimplified maxim rests the case for the one-school-for-all, and much of the underlying philosophy behind many current developments.

Such an oversimplification hardly seems to be worth consideration, but it is the simple uncluttered statement which is so easily understood and grasped at by those who seek straightforward maxims upon which to build their creed, and this statement is one of those. It lies at the root of much modern thinking on school government, working relationships between senior and assistant staff, teaching styles and child discipline. It places professionally untrained and inexperienced people in positions of authority on school governing bodies. It gives equal weight to the opinions of the newly qualified untried teacher and the long serving head-teacher. It places the child's immature judgements on a par with those of the professionally trained teacher in matters of curriculum and discipline. In short, it dilutes the authority of those who should know and gives it to those who do not know, with the result that decisions are made by compromise and the best solutions are to problems lost. If society is to flourish, we must surely accept that we cannot all be expert in everything and must rely on the professional expertise of others. Authority needs to be in the hands of those who should have the knowledge, skills and experience to make the best decisions, that is in the hands of the professionals. But not only have the pseudo-democratic ideologists succeeded in advancing their cause, the professionals have often let society down because they have been insufficiently professional. What is required is leadership by those with training, knowledge, skills and experience, the professionals, monitored by the elected representatives of the rest of us: a professional democracy.

For the extreme radicals in the 1950s and 60s, the development of the all-in-one, comprehensive school was the only route by which they could achieve their new idealised classless society. For many educators it was seen as a proper means of ensuring that all pupils received an equal opportunity to develop their true potential, while the existence of the grammar school prevented this. Whether or not the grammar school was doing a good and useful job came to be of little consequence. Grammar schools served an elite and had to go!

In the meantime, however, grammar schools continued along their pre-determined course, providing an academic education for those who could pass what was fast becoming known as the Eleven-plus Examination. Although the pass rate varied from one education authority to another, usually about twenty per cent of an age group was selected for a grammar school education. The significance lies in the fact that the remainder were not selected and came to be seen as failures, and this real or imaginary social rejection was greatly emphasised by those promoting their cause, until popular opinion hailed it as fact. It was implied that the eighty per cent not selected suffered permanent damage because of this apparent failure at the tender age of eleven. Pedley saw the situation as one in which different children were forced to attend different schools, and in particular, for those not attending grammar schools, children being labelled as inferior, a label which he saw as staying with them for life: sentiments which I do not believe to be true and which I certainly never experienced when growing up among a group of some dozen or so youngsters, only two of which attended grammar schools. But, by the time the enthusiasts had got their way, the poor youngsters had no alternative but to believe what they were told!

The division of children into different schools requires some form of selection to bring about their distribution and people came to doubt the accuracy or suitability of the techniques being used for this purpose. Some pupils selected for grammar schools were later found to be quite unsuited to the academic courses provided. Others, those from homes where books were in short supply, where language used was oversimplified and stereotyped, were not selected and yet eventually showed themselves to be capable of high academic achievement. Pedley commented on what must surely be accepted as the obvious: you cannot identify three types of youngster, each suited to one of three types of school.

But selection continued with the cultural or language anomaly being at least partially answered by the development of non-verbal intelligence tests, where candidates are given the opportunity to demonstrate their thinking abilities by comprehending relationships shown in complex diagrams and pictures rather than words or numbers.

But opponents were not going to have that! They argued that there was little evidence to show that intelligence tests forecast academic success, in spite of the fact that such tests were first validated by correlating pupils' scores with marks gained on traditional school tests. In other words, the tests were designed so that those who did well on traditional school tests also did well on intelligence tests. The perusal of different children's scores on the intelligence tests would therefore be expected to give some indication of the likely performance of these youngsters in school subjects. Furthermore, the fact that some of those selected failed in the later years of the grammar school overlooked other relevant factors such as personality and home pressures.

Education authorities did however develop Eleven-plus selection procedures which attempted to answer all of the criticisms. The objection that the results of attainment and intelligence tests taken on one particular day could be distorted by the child's circumstances or mood at the time was answered by consulting teachers' records and holding interviews with parents and children before the final decision was made.

But for some any form of testing became a social evil, seen only as permanently dividing those who shall succeed in life from those who shall fail, when instead they should be seen as a means of guiding each along routes leading to different personal successes. Indeed, it was fast becoming taboo to suggest that some people do not have the ability or abilities that others do! That is, in spite of the general acceptance that some people are more athletic than others, some have greater musical ability and some considerably more artistic talent, it becomes unacceptable to suggest that some are less able to comprehend intellectual matters than others. Failure in all of the special aptitudes is happily explained in terms of people not having that particular ability, and it does not matter one iota – but to suggest that children have different levels of academic ability brings forth a storm of protest with explanations given in terms of a myriad of social inadequacies which can be rectified if only the social conditions are perfected: a notion which seems to have its origins in the misconception that all are born with identical nervous systems with origins in the same genes.

Because those attending the grammar schools appeared to obtain the jobs which were better paid and had more favourable working conditions, while the majority were not selected for these schools, there would be overwhelming support from parents for a system which appeared to give all children access to the grammar school style of education. The system was of course the comprehensive school: demand for its introduction could not fail as the majority of parents saw it as a safer option for their children to gain entry to a good school, that is, in so far as their children were not certain to pass the Eleven-plus. Educators saw it as a more just application of resources which ensured a more equal opportunity for all.

3. Different comprehensive school systems in different areas

Although the concept of the comprehensive school was born out of the ideal that all secondary aged children should attend the same type of school, in reality local authority comprehensive school systems evolved out of necessity. For instance, the provision of secondary education for all in sparsely populated rural areas could hardly be brought about through the tripartite system. Up to 1944 such areas were served by small grammar schools, with only one or two hundred pupils, and all age village schools. The first were barely large enough to provide an adequate academic curriculum and the second were, by reason for the requirements of the Education Act, to become primary schools for pupils up to the age of eleven. Those eleven- to fourteen-year-old pupils not allocated to grammar schools consequently would have no provision. The obvious economic solution was for all to be housed in the enlarged grammar school premises, or, where this was not possible, in one new building. Such were the origins of comprehensive schools in places like the Isle of Man (with its own government), Anglesey and the former North and East Ridings of Yorkshire.

In Cambridgeshire the pre-war plan for adding adult centres to existing schools was further developed to produce the County College, a comprehensive community school for adults as well as all secondary aged pupils. Pedley was quick to recognise some significant positive characteristics in many of these rural schools. They frequently developed from established schools and were able to retain their deep-rooted positive ethos which had evolved in their relatively small communities where the children are known as individuals and as members of well known families. He also pointed out that the teachers were known to children and their parents in the social setting of local community.

There is something similar here to the spirit developed on the school journey and in the school club, albeit lacking the deep personal roots of the long established community. Unfortunately, this ideal has too often been either lost or never established. The positive long established traditions of both grammar and other secondary schools have too often been allowed to whither away or have even been deliberately destroyed, frequently because they have been seen as vestiges of grammar school elitism. Honours boards, speech days, school uniforms and prefect systems have been interpreted by some as objectionable hindrances in the search for equality.

In urban areas too there had often been closely integrated communities in which each member stood a very good chance of knowing each other and where the school teacher was a respected figure living within the community. These valuable social institutions have also disappeared, often the result of the well-intentioned clearance of poor quality housing found in the overcrowded developments of the Victorian industrial age and involving the destruction of established neighbourhood schools.

London's new comprehensive schools originated in this way: the capital, like so many of the country's urban centres, had been severely damaged by war time bombing. Many areas were destroyed or partially destroyed and could only be rejuvenated by clearance and rebuilding. With the political climate right for redeveloping these and other run-down areas, the stage was set for the growth of a new order.

Grammar and senior schools in the 1940s

As an eleven-year-old growing up during a world war I found myself, in 1942, a pupil in a modern senior school established in the relatively new London suburbs. The buildings, constructed in the late 1920s were low and spread out among playgrounds, playing fields and gardens. There were wood and metal workshops for the boys, and domestic science rooms for girls – separate provision being seen then as the way to satisfy the perceived different needs of young men and women.

On arriving for the first time the new pupils were marched up and down the playground for an hour or so, like new recruits to the infantry. The deputy head-teacher, who must surely have been modelled on the worst of regimental sergeant majors, directed this operation from his commanding position on a suitably placed table along one side of the playground. His discipline was rigid, expecting unquestioned obedience. Yet we observed that his attitudes were not supported by the younger class teachers, who mumbled disapproving comments while we marched up and down. In due course, it became clear that the head-teacher, a younger more recently qualified man, also held different views from those of his deputy. Attitudes relating to the educating of the young were changing.

Wrongdoers were still punished by being given strokes of the cane across their hands but the head-teacher was clearly trying to place more importance on rewards rather than on punishments: he promoted with enthusiasm his newly introduced scheme of "Commendeds". For good work, academic, practical or physical, teachers awarded the successful with pieces of paper emphatically stamped with the word "Commended". Yet in 1996 there were articles written by head-teachers and others who claimed that such reward systems were their new inventions.

Different comprehensive school systems in different areas

The curriculum was basic: English was divided into reading, recitation, writing, spelling, word study, comprehension, literature and composition. Mathematics consisted of mental arithmetic, mechanical arithmetic and problems. It was these basic foundation subjects which took up the greater part of the timetable while history, geography, science, nature study, hygiene, drawing, housecraft and handicraft, music, physical training and games, were taken as extras.

Multiplication tables were regularly chanted, mental arithmetic and spelling tested by questioning each class member in turn and reading practised by each reading aloud.

Every child's progress was assessed twice each year, by means of teacher administered written and oral tests. Totals were converted into percentages and ranked in order to produce class positions in each subject for each child. There were no inhibitions on the part of the teachers regarding those who must have inevitably found themselves towards the bottom of the tables. Such a position was merely interpreted in terms of the individual having to work harder!

As I managed an average sixth position in a class of approximately fifty boys and girls, I suppose, for me, things were going well enough – but I was not impressed. I was not excited by the teaching styles or subject matter in the lessons. The world of school was one of dull routine.

A year later I entered the grammar school and gained a distinct impression of being taught something for the first time. Just what this meant in the mind of a twelve-year-old is difficult to confirm. Did the less harsh regime of the new county school suite my personality and consequently foster my learning? Did the style of teaching impress me? Did the curriculum with its variety of subject syllabi stimulate me more than the narrower schemes of the senior school? Did a class of thirty cause my individuality to thrive, whereas in a crowd of fifty I faded into the background and went to sleep?

In the early 1950s, as a student and prospective candidate for the teaching profession, I completed three weeks teaching experience at the same senior school, by then flying its new secondary modern colours. I was still not impressed.

Those who some insist on labelling eleven-plus failures sparkled in my classes, responding to my very ordinary, if not awful, teaching with bubbling enthusiasm. My only problem was trying to keep the noise down!

Pupils in second year classes were equally excited but those in the third year slumbered into oblivion. They were neither excited by the material which they were offered nor enthused by the teaching styles currently in fashion. In the fourth year both boys and girls had only one objective, to leave and go out to work as soon as possible. They had no interest whatsoever in school studies and there was nothing I, or anyone else, could do to alter the situation.

The London County Council Comprehensive Schools

While I enjoyed my grammar school education, feeling sure that I had achieved much, my best pal, the lad living down the street with whom I had grown up, was one of those for whom the end of school could not come quickly enough. I recognised that intense academic learning was not for everyone!

It was this mixture of experience, albeit limited to that available to a young adult, which caused me to conclude that the existing school system was failing the majority of children. Consequently, I saw the new comprehensive school as a better way forward and deliberately chose to take up employment in September 1956 at a new London County Council purpose-built comprehensive school for boys.

It was an extremely well organised school for eleven- to nineteen-year-olds where its philosophy was promoted in such a way that it could not be challenged. The attitude, in simple terms, was that because it was a comprehensive school it was perfect.

I remember well the careers master saying to parents of third year boys at a parent's evening that, because their children were in attendance at this wonderful new comprehensive school, they each now had the chance of becoming bank managers. While struggling to teach the bottom of nine streams some very basic concepts in arithmetic, I was somewhat irritated by this claim. But even the suggestion of a more realistic prognosis was not permitted!

In order to answer the requirement that boys of different abilities, and even different social backgrounds, should be encouraged to mix – presumably in order to break down the class or cultural divisions – they were also organised into tutor groups. Tutors, assistant teachers with pastoral duties thrust upon them, were responsible for the welfare of about twenty boys whose ages ranged from eleven-plus to eighteen-plus who were otherwise taught in various streamed year groups. Tutor groups met twice each day for registration and once each week for a timetabled tutor period when the tutor could discuss individual matters with each of the boys in turn while the rest carried out private study: at least in theory. Thirty minutes or so each week to be divided between, at best, twenty boys, would give each a superficial consultation of one minute. If three boys were each given a more reasonable ten minutes, each boy could be seen once in half a term.

School uniform was compulsory, consisting of shirts of the approved colour, white, ties and blazers, as well as plain black shoes and grey socks. The well-ordered discipline is illustrated by the movement orders laid down for boys going to and from school assemblies. Each tutor group was led in line by its tutor at as near to the precise movement time as the school clocks would allow, each following a prescribed route from classroom to hall. It was decreed that the boys should enter the assembly hall with blazers buttoned and stand when the head entered and came onto the platform. At a staff meeting, one brave assistant teacher questioned whether the masters should also stand. The head's curt response questioned whether he thought that the staff should show respect for their headmaster – and the matter was decided without a further word being spoken.

In the upper school great emphasis was placed on boys gaining a good number of passes in public examinations, and on the numbers of boys who gained university places. It was as though all the pupils could now have the traditional academic type of education and would thrive upon it. It should not be overlooked, however that those who did not wish to, or could not, flourish in this relatively narrow field could leave at the end of the term in which they were fifteen. There was an escape route from the children's world of school into the adult money-earning environment of employment. No reluctant broad shouldered hostile adolescents remained in the place to lead a hard core of rebellious misfits. Consequently, judged on its organisation, its sound, albeit rigid, discipline and its good academic examination results, it soon became accepted as one of the best schools in London.

Conversely, another school in which I worked a little later soon began to illustrate the problems which would eventually become commonplace in large urban comprehensives. It was a huge glass and concrete palace with some two-thousand-three-hundred boys and girls between the ages of eleven and nineteen on roll. This immense size was the result of the fact it was thought necessary to have large numbers of eleven- to sixteen-year-olds in order to feed a viable sixth form – a sixth form which could offer a satisfactory variety of courses.

It became clear to me that, in order for the necessary learning environment to flourish, there would have to be a strict well-ordered regime to maintain order in such a vast conglomeration of young people. Yet the climate of opinion was growing away from such notions of imposed law and order towards the acceptance of the new liberalism.

In the older senior schools the teachers tended to teach a group of subjects to their own class – as for many years the primary school teacher taught a class rather than one subject discipline – with the children remaining in one room for most of the time. In the comprehensive school specialist teachers are based in their specialist teaching rooms and the classes have to move to the teachers. At the change of lessons, between four and eight times each day, hundreds of excitable young people will be on the move. This creates a major problem and it is necessary to have carefully planned movement orders, supervision and strict roll calls to ensure that all of the pupils reach the places to which they have been directed – in particular to monitor those who have every intention of avoiding classes at every opportunity.

Discipline in the early comprehensive schools

As in many of the new schools, discipline in my second London comprehensive was based upon the erroneous notion that all young people would quite naturally take proper advantage of the first class opportunities which the new system offered. The result was that there were always children roaming about the premises, even during lesson time, and there was little an individual class teacher could do about the problem. If a child, in such a huge impersonal establishment, was missing, was the absence genuine or truancy? Was he or she marked absent from school on the register, or merely dodging one or more lessons? Some teachers did not even notice when some of their pupils were absent, others tried to find out the reasons for the absence but gave up because the task took too much time from class teaching duties which they properly regarded as their major responsibility.

With such a loose control it is not long before groups of particularly antisocial boys and girls first roam, and then as their confidence grows, rampage about the school disrupting the lessons of others by variously shouting abuse through doorways and generally stampeding about the place. If this behaviour on the part of a minority goes unchecked, the vast majority of middle-of-the-road personalities claim greater freedoms for themselves and the behaviour standards of the school as a whole decline.

A major question arises as to how a firm but sympathetic control can be fostered in a large new establishment which comprises of hundreds of immature personalities. There are no established traditions – all situations are wide open to challenge. There are difficulties with inter-personal relationships. People relate to those they meet most frequently, they adapt their responses to meet the challenges of others. With numerous, hourly-changing circumstances and with no one adult firmly in charge of one group of youngsters, well behaved stable cohesive groups are difficult to establish. Conversely, the maladjusted, or those with behaviour problems, have the opportunity to come together in considerable numbers to reinforce each other's instability. Their behaviour declines. The vast majority then ask why they themselves should be denied certain freedoms and take liberties which society, for its own good, would like to discourage. Such a state of affairs could be seen developing in the 1950s. By the 1990s many people however showed amazement at the existence of the uncontrolled school, more of which is discussed in chapter 5.

Nevertheless, there was much good in the new schools. A large proportion of the teachers were extremely enthusiastic about their work. Apart from the routine learning in well equipped rooms with a generous allowance of resources, there were a hundred-and-one out of class activities which broadened the educational programme. There were drama and music groups producing public performances, art and craft clubs making all kinds of artefacts, and school journeys providing opportunities for travel which had never existed before. But the disciplinary problem was undermining all of this.

Streaming, courses and examinations

As in most of the early urban comprehensive schools, pupils in the London schools where I worked were placed in streamed classes. There were fourteen streams (teaching groups of about thirty children) in my second school, in each year, which were labelled according a code word which was supposed to disguise which classes were of top, middle or lower academic ability. But everyone, not least the children, did know! People do recognise their own abilities in relation to those of others, and accept their limitations – that is, until the education system insists that everyone should be academically clever!

In the upper school, from the age of fourteen-plus, courses replaced classes. The youngsters chose, with considerable guidance, courses appropriate to their perceived aptitudes, achievements and aspirations. Those most able, in the traditional academic sense, invariably ended up on a course leading to the General Certificate ordinary level examination. But there were also courses in, for instance, commerce and cookery, which led to appropriate examination qualifications, frequently administered by the Royal Society of Arts.

There were, however, those for whom there was no suitable school leaving examination. They gained no qualifications but could then leave school and obtain employment where they could earn a wage and feel grown up. There was no stigma attached to this, indeed, the facility to earn money was seen as a clear advantage by most young people. As they progressed through the school they behaved just like the children I had seen when teaching in the secondary modern school: they became less and less interested as their age increased. The comprehensive schools had not solved the problem.

The advantage of an enthusiastic and stable upper school

The early London comprehensive schools were organised on the eleven to eighteen pattern which included sixth forms. With those youngsters not suited to the academic style of learning leaving when they were fifteen and only the well motivated academics remaining to complete advanced level courses, the top of the school was dominated by a large number of people who were well disposed towards the system. For the most part there was a core of older well behaved and very talented youngsters at the top of the school to help uphold a good tone. They also helped the staff, being young adults about the place rather than children. Furthermore, their considerable skills led the school drama, music and sporting events; and a well received play, musical evening, or sports meeting does a great deal to enhance the reputation of a school.

Eleven to sixteen age schools

Not all local education authorities however accepted this pattern of development as that best suited to their areas. Some chose to establish a series of eleven-to-sixteen schools feeding one central sixth form college. This was a particularly attractive scheme in areas where there had been a well established grammar school of high reputation. Much of the criticism born out of the perceived loss of such a highly esteemed school could be minimised by showing that its excellence would be retained in the sixth form college.

Such a scheme also fitted nicely into the geography of clustered settlements. The eleven-to-sixteen schools could conveniently be established in the existing secondary school buildings located in the various sectors of a town or city, while the college could occupy a central site. Such an arrangement, at first sight, seemed to answer the comprehensive ideal of all from an area attending the same school at eleven – eliminating the anticipated division and supposed rejection of some pupils: an unrealistic concept, because rejection depends upon so many things. A child may be rejected by its fellows because of its uniqueness, because it stands out from the crowd due to its unusual home background, exceptional personality traits or even physical characteristics. Bullying of the scapegoat has not been eliminated from our comprehensive schools – in fact, it is often advanced as a major problem of our times.

With the removal of the co-operative, supportive sixth form student from the upper school, and the further raising of the school leaving age to sixteen, the senior classes in eleven-to-sixteen schools came to be dominated by the vast majority of the population who do not easily benefit from or accept academic teaching. This section of the population is also most likely to include a high proportion of youngsters with behavioural, as well as straight forward learning, problems. The implications on the tone of the school are obvious.

The neighbourhood school

The neighbourhood school, to which we are referring here, each school being in its own sector of the settlement, or neighbourhood, takes on the character of its environment. There are those areas which are favourably populated with comfortably-off, well motivated families, while there are other areas where clusters of disadvantaged families, and more recently some extremely antisocial families, live. Schools in the latter types of areas will therefore attract a high proportion of less well motivated and probably more antisocial youngsters. The upper parts of such schools stand a good chance of being dominated by poorly behaved young people who are opposed to school and react accordingly.

The latter establishments hardly begin to answer the social ideal of bringing together people from different backgrounds, and one attempt to answer this problem has been to bus children to schools outside their neighbourhoods – an attempt at a kind of social engineering. But who wants a lot of trouble makers dumped in their once peaceful nicely maintained area? Who among the less fortunate want to find themselves in competition with the more comfortably well-off?

First, middle and high schools

Yet another scheme has arranged schools into first, middle and high schools, where children between the ages of nine and fourteen attend comprehensive middle schools and those over fourteen all go to the comprehensive high school. In general, without the shadow of school leaving examinations influencing the curriculum, middle schools have tended to follow the pattern of primary schools, having less movement to specialist rooms and resulting in greater stability – but at what cost to specialised teaching, which it can be argued is of great significance for older pupils? The high school retains the advantageous qualities of the eleven-to-eighteen school without having to cater for needs of younger children.

Other problems arising from comprehensive reorganisation

Comprehensive reorganisation did not take place in all areas of the country at the same time. For instance, whereas London was leading the field with its crystal palaces in the 1950s, other authorities were only drawing up plans in the 60s and others even later. The regional differences observed before the war still existed – there was no national education system. Your chances, as a child, of being educated well, or not so well, even today depend upon where you live and that depends upon the circumstances of your birth – social problems which can not be resolved by a comprehensive education system.

Regional differences have, as would be expected, continued to be influenced by the relative wealth of local authorities. Londoners were fortunate. They had fine new buildings, although suffering from the oddities of architectural mania and fashion of the '50s and '60s, generous staffing ratios, a reasonable back-up from ancillary helpers, good capitation allowances, and grants provided for other activities such as educational journeys. Some areas never had these advantages.

Too often the needs of the new secondary education were merely interpreted as the same as those found in the older secondary schools. There was a refusal to recognise the new system as something quite different from anything seen before and therefore requiring quite different resources.

Before the 1944 Act, excluding the grammar schools, general education was concerned with providing children, not young adults, with fairly simple basic skills in language and arithmetic, and a kind of general knowledge in areas of history, geography and science: with the developing concept of teaching boys the crafts and girls domestic subjects. The concept has changed. Subject content has changed. The curriculum has expanded. Teaching techniques have developed from those requiring a blackboard, pen, pencil and ruler into multiple strategies using complex references and equipment. Young people, young adults, no longer children, are the object of the education.

Whereas one school secretary and one caretaker were sufficient to service the small more simply organised school they are certainly not sufficient for the large complex educational institutions which have developed since the war.

For instance: an office staff is required, a bursar with secretary, a receptionist, and at least one other; technicians to prepare and maintain the technical equipment; a nurse-welfare officer to deal with medical and social matters, both routine and emergencies; a librarian and assistant to service a fully equipped library on a full-time basis; and a staff, not just one caretaker, to supervise the general running and security of valuable premises, an obvious necessity even before the tragic invasion of schools by the highly disturbed and dangerous adults witnessed during 1996 and afterwards. The organisation of the new education is equivalent to that of industry and commerce. Can you imagine the managing director of any business having the equivalent size to many of our schools surviving with only one secretarial assistant to do everything?

A further problem with comprehensive reorganisation is related to inadequate buildings. There is argument now about the millions of pounds which local authorities are stating is required to maintain school premises. Many of these are of pre-war construction and others suffer from the inappropriate building standards of the '50s and '60s.

Many areas did not benefit from the construction of purpose-built premises (even though this was sometimes a mixed blessing due to the poor quality of the building) but had to make do with existing buildings, modifications and additions. Some new schools were actually housed in buildings separated from each other by a mile or more and a few even had sites divided by the constant roaring flow of traffic on a dual carriageway. New structures tacked onto old did not allow the efficient grouping of department rooms. For instance, I worked in one school where the workshops were at one end of the building and the drawing office at the other. In the same school there was no room large enough for a modern library and consequently the facility was housed in two smaller rooms twenty-five yards apart. Departments were forced to have rooms widely dispersed, with the problem of having to constantly transport bulky equipment over considerable distances.

It was argued by the critics that there would not be sufficient teachers, with appropriate qualifications, to teach according to the new requirements and to cater for the increased number of pupils. There was a shortage of teachers following the war and there does, it seems, to have been a shortage ever since: particularly noticeable in certain subject disciplines and certain geographical areas.

The problem of the inappropriateness of teachers' qualifications was also initially magnified by their limited experience: those who had been teaching successfully using academic strategies in grammar schools found it very difficult, if not impossible, to adapt to the needs of the less academic; those using different teaching styles in secondary modern schools found it difficult to maintain academic motivation with the abstract learners. It could consequently be argued that as teachers with secondary modern experience were by definition in a majority, academic teaching standards and academic discipline, the discipline of intense grammar school style of learning, also declined – no matter what was being taught.

Furthermore, some teachers enthusiastically welcomed the coming of comprehensive schools and deliberately set out to establish their careers in them; others, established in grammar schools or secondary modern schools had comprehensive reorganisation thrust upon them. They felt that they had been inadequately prepared for the demands which the new system would make upon them, but struggled to do their best. A minority reluctantly accepted the inevitable, tried to maintain the practices which they had followed in their previous schools, became frustrated and eventually abdicated their responsibilities. The first seeds of teacher frustration and low morale had been sown! Comprehensive School Reorganisation brought about a great upheaval and a loss of stability.

The **Great** Education Controversy

4. Equality and Individuality

British education has, for too long, been dogged by the bogey of equality. In efforts to give all, especially the least privileged, the best, policy makers have dogmatically entrenched themselves in the belief that difference leads to an evil elitism. Yet solutions to the problem of providing the best opportunities for all, the development of their strengths, will never be found if we refuse to admit the existence of, and cater for, vast individual differences within the child population. Some of these differences, possibly biologically determined, are difficult to accept and consequently there has been a marked tendency to account for differences in success predominantly in terms of socially determined factors. But human talents and capabilities are to a significant degree determined by nature and it follows that individuals achieve their greatest success in areas which lie within the field of their personal abilities. The successful athlete is born with the physical attributes which, when developed by disciplined training, bring success in sporting activities. There are those, on the other hand, who, no matter how much effort they put into their training, will never succeed beyond a moderate standard because their physical make-up is inadequate. There are other areas in which inborn attributes play a large part in an individual's success in an activity.

It is easy to accept that some have musical ability and some do not, that some have artistic ability while others display a complete lack of understanding of any kind of design and use the tools of the artist as though they were red hot irons in their hands, and that some have practical ability while others bring only a clumsiness equivalent to that of the bull in a china shop to anything demanding hands-on-skill. Yet it is almost impossible, and certainly political suicide, to suggest that some have intellectual ability while others do not. The major problem, of course, is that our society has allowed intellectual ability to command a prestige out of all proportion to other talents, particularly in schools and colleges.

The comprehensive school ideal has been based on a misunderstanding of individuality and has brought about attempts to produce an egalitarianism which is intended to minimise the misconceived evils of competition, elitism, privilege and divisiveness, consequently tending to stifle much of the good in human uniqueness.

Choice has been seen to lend itself to the grabbing of advantage by the most articulate and most determined, and has even been equated with privileges somehow unfairly obtained by an ill-defined middle class. But there is no such thing as a socially endowed middle class trait which automatically brings success. Some children from middle class families are successful in school and some are not. If anything it is an individual drive to make good which is the significant factor, no matter from which social environment an individual comes. This does not deny the significance of disadvantage: there are those born into such poor circumstances that, no matter what talents they may be born with, have no opportunity for development. And it is for this very reason that the education system must provide different environments into which children can move naturally and without prejudice.

The egalitarian philosophy denies the value of different schools, whether they are City Technology Colleges, Academies, Trust Schools, those which have opted out of local education authority control, or those in the independent sector. It has led to dogmatic attempts to teach children with greatly varying abilities and talents in the same classes, the abolition of teaching according to intellectual ability, practical ability, and previous attainment, and to the imposition of a closely defined common curriculum from the age of five to sixteen.

In order to combat the perceived undesirable aspects of failure, elitism and divisiveness, what is required is an infinite variety of provision to cater for individual differences, not restriction and narrow limitation. Individuality needs to be fostered while understanding that it is what each individual brings to society that enriches that society. Educational developments should be concerned with providing different styles of schools and colleges each having a different ethos; centres of excellence in different disciplines; centres where specifically directed training takes place; specific schools of religious teaching; and provision for both boarding and day students.

The nature of individuality

Individual differences manifest themselves in the way individuals behave. Teachers are quite able to recognise those children who display cleverness in classroom learning and those with friendly lively outgoing natures. They also register the presence of those who present the opposite characteristics, and their reactions to the children will be influenced by these perceptions. Yet there are hosts of other individuals who display less outstanding characteristics and they can so easily be overlooked.

Theoretical studies of individuality have developed under two main headings: those concerned with intelligence and those concerned with personality. Indeed, the study of intelligence may be regarded as one aspect of the study of personality but has developed from the work of Alfred Binet in France during the early nineteen hundreds as a discipline in its own right. It is easy to understand why this is so because the work is concerned with looking at differences in learning ability as they apply to the traditional classroom situation, and was originally intended to help with identifying children with special educational needs in order that these needs could be more efficiently addressed.

The other aspect of the study of individualism has been concerned with traits such as sociability, friendliness, forcefulness and many others which together are referred to as the personality.

Intelligence as an indicator of individuality

There developed among psychologists an idea which defined intelligence as the ability underlying learning, which individuals could have to a greater or lesser degree. For teachers, such a concept appears to offer a neat way of classifying young people according to their ability to learn from school lessons, and to provide a sound foundation for allocating them to courses which best suit their needs. Intelligence tests were invented for this purpose.

The first, compiled by Alfred Binet and Theodore Simon, the Simon-Binet test, dates from 1905 and was developed in order to identify those children thought to be feeble minded so that they could be given special education. Binet and Simon thought intelligence developed with age and compiled lists of items which most children could understand at different ages in their growth. Subsequently, other children tested on the scales could be shown to be below, the same or above the average for their age group.

A simple, neat convenient tool was developed to compare a child's intelligence test score with those of others. By comparing an individual's score with the average score for different age groups it is possible to report the result in terms of a mental age. In other words, a child with a score equivalent to the norm for seven-year-olds is said to have a mental age of seven. This may or may not agree with the child's chronological age. In order to compare mental age with chronological age on a linear scale, Binet and Simon developed the concept of the intelligence quotient or IQ which is defined as the figure obtained by dividing a person's mental age by his chronological age and multiplying by one hundred. Clearly, if the mental age equals the chronological age the quotient is one hundred and this figure provides a base line from which an individual's performance can be assessed. Those of us growing up before, during and immediately after the Second World War were therefore subjected to intelligence testing and labelled with our IQ.

But this was not the original purpose of the system. In the first instance, it was recognised that an individual's IQ was a score obtained from one test on a particular day and was not necessarily a measure of an ability fixed throughout a lifetime. It was intended to be used as a rough guide for identifying those who needed help and was certainly not intended for placing all children in rank order.

Intelligence as a fixed ability dependent upon inheritance

Almost immediately however the system was hijacked by those who regarded the IQ as fixed and dependent upon inheritance. A notion which evolved from Francis Galton's work on intelligence levels in families reported in his book "Hereditary Genius" in 1884. He showed that children from families with intelligent parents were themselves intelligent and concluded that intelligence was therefore an inherited ability.

The idea was reinforced by the American Goddard in 1912 when he published his studies on the Kallikaks. A member of this family conveniently produced two lines of descendents, one described as a descendent of a feebleminded barmaid and the other of a respectable Quakeress. He showed that the descendents of the barmaid developed into feeble minded degenerates, while those of the Quakeress became respectable members of society.

Today it is easy for us to question what all of this has to do with the ability of an individual to learn, when it is so plainly obvious that the living conditions for the failing branch of the family would hardly have been conducive to learning whether they had ability or not! And surprisingly again, one offspring of the feebleminded lady was institutionalised and was found to improve. The conclusion: it was good for the feebleminded to be institutionalised! It is over simplified generalisations such as these which have helped to undermine any possible usefulness of the concept of intelligence. After all, it is plainly obvious to any teacher that there are children who can learn with ease, those who learn with difficulty and those who find it almost impossible to learn at all. Any system which helps to clarify this situation should be welcomed.

Multiple intelligence

There is, however, an obvious objection to the notion of the existence of a single ability to learn, or one kind of intelligence. It is quite clear that different people learn different things easily or with difficulty, apparently depending upon whether or not they possess the necessary specific talents.

Spearman examined this aspect of intelligence by submitting the scores of different people on different items to factor analysis. In simple terms this entails inter-correlating the scores obtained by large numbers of people on as many test items, which are thought to measure intelligence, as possible. Resulting clusters of correlations are then examined mathematically in order to identify the factors which define the clusters. Using this technique Spearman identified one common factor which he called "g" or general intelligence and other specific factors "s". General intelligence, he supposed, was driven by some biological feature of the brain and was therefore dependent upon inheritance, while the specific factors depended upon learned skills, a notion which today seems, to say the least, to be oversimplified. It is not necessary to enquire further than to ask whether the athlete is aided by the inheritance of a favourable cluster of genes.

Thurstone, in 1938, defined a number of independent primary mental abilities: verbal comprehension, verbal fluency, number, spatial visualisation, memory, reasoning and perceptual speed. He then developed tests to measure these variables in order to produce individual ability profiles.

P E Vernon (1971) further developed this approach to the definition of intelligence to identify two specific clusters: one involving verbal skills and educational ability (presumably as it applies to traditional academic learning) and the other involving spatial and mechanical abilities.

More recently, in 1985, Gardner developed a theory of multiple intelligence, postulating seven unique abilities, each having its origin in a particular area of the brain.

He identified linguistic intelligence which manifests itself in the ability to read, write and understand speech – a significant concept for the teacher, because it is so easily observed that some children seem to develop expertise in these areas so much more easily than others, and because success in subsequent learning depends upon the early development of language skills. If such intelligence is dependent upon a specific brain function which some individuals possess in greater degrees than others, it is very clear that its recognition is significant in order for there to be a development of other modes of teaching for those lacking this ability.

A second intelligence in Gardner's theory is musical intelligence, displayed in musical appreciation, composition and performance. Although it is generally recognised that some people have musical ability and others do not, the ability to appreciate the sounds of music seems very different from the ability to compose scores and play musical instruments.

Thirdly, there is mathematical-logical intelligence which is displayed in numerical calculation and logical reasoning: which may explain why some individuals are better at calculation than others.

Fourthly, he identifies spatial intelligence which relates to the ability to find one's way. An aspect of intelligence which perhaps explains why some people are good at map reading, geometry, surveying and allied activities, and why, for instance, others show a talent for artistic presentation.

Body-kinaesthetic intelligence is another of Gardner's variables displayed in movement dexterity and consequently in sport, dance and similar activities. Clearly, there are those children who are graceful and co-ordinated and those who are clumsy, always knocking into things and almost completely useless at playing ball games.

His last intelligences, the interpersonal and intrapersonal, seem to relate to those characteristics which have more usually been associated with personality. The first relates to the ability to interpret social signals and predict their outcomes and thus lies behind our relations to others. The second relates to the understanding of oneself.

Critics argue that Gardner ignores the significance of social factors interacting with the various intelligences he defines but his purpose has been to explain different mental abilities in terms of activity within specific areas of the brain and does not detract from the possibility that social influences interact with the various intelligences to produce observed behaviour.

There is an attraction in all of this: a temptation to identify a neat system in which there are underlying abilities, which we all have to a greater or lesser degree depending upon our biological make up, for instance intellectual verbal skills, special mechanical abilities, number skills, logical reasoning ability, and the ability to remember and reason, which seem to depend upon inheritance, and other skills which we learn through our experiences of life. Teachers will be quick to identify children whose achievements can apparently be explained by reference to such a system. And the identification and categorisation of what a child can apparently do or not does have useful implications in devising subsequent learning programmes.

There is a tantalising reality attached to the various classifications of intelligence. There are similarities and areas of overlap, as though there is a truth to find if only the entwined threads of overt behaviour and underlying biological mechanisms can be untangled. Unfortunately, uncertainty and conflicting evidence have been used as reasons for decrying the whole concept of intelligence and even for opposing the application of tests for the purpose of educational guidance. Out of all of this has come the hostility to selection of individuals for different learning programmes and, in particular, the hostility to selection for entry into different types of schools.

There is a tantalising dilemma: common sense, apart from any research evidence, insists that people are different, but the concept of social justice seems to get in the way of finding practical solutions to educating people differently.

Each of us is unique, with a unique personality, including unique abilities and unique strengths in those abilities. Each consequently has different aspirations, different strengths and different potential. The thinking behind the 1944 Education

Act recognised individual differences but subsequent developments failed to find an acceptable way of catering for those differences. There has been a failure to break out from the restrictions of all must have everything, ending up with a mundane sameness.

Government White Papers: "14 – 19 Education and Skills" and "Higher Standards Better Schools for All"

More recent thinking has attempted to answer the problems arising from individual differences by using the concept of equal worth. The Secretary of State advanced the notion that all young people should be regarded as being of equal worth *(14 – 19 Education and Skills, Secretary of State, paragraph 3)* but, in reality, people do not have equal talents and people are not consequently valued equally. There is much work to be done in the bringing about the valuing of people more equally.

Certainly any education system should, as the White Paper implies, enable each individual to develop his or her potential, and it recognises individual differences, particularly those associated with motivation through vocational training. But there is more to solving the problem than the mere provision of vocational opportunities. Poor motivation can be tackled through individual counselling of young people and their parents but not necessarily solved!

The significance of the individual personality

There is more to people than their ability to learn, whether we see this as an intelligence or a complex of many different forms of intelligence and strengths in those intelligences. People are characters. It may be argued that young people are in the process of forming their characters but there are underlying aspects of personality which play a large part in the determining of character. Teachers generally recognise such traits as quiet, friendly, withdrawn, aggressive, a loner, easily led, a leader, shy, confident, unreliable, immature, attention seeking, nervous and so on. It will be the most socially acceptable or the most disruptive who will be noticed most while the vast majority will merely jog along and, possibly, be given less attention than they deserve. Their true potential may not be recognised and their achievements may fall short of their best without anyone being any the wiser.

Some teachers are very good at recognising individual differences and at responding appropriately to them. Others are not. Strategies are needed for helping all staff to appreciate differences among their pupils and students: for instance, the application of sociometric techniques and personality rating scales, which indicate how people see each other and themselves. It is possible to illuminate patterns of friendship or hostility which may otherwise go unnoticed and be disregarded, to see where the young people undervalue themselves and where interpersonal relationships may be causing problems.

Caution is of course required when looking into what may be seen as the more personal aspects of the personality. Abilities, intellectual and other talents, are generally recognised and more or less accepted by teachers, parents and young people. Taking notice of individual traits of behaviour is not always seen in the same way. Indeed, with the individual freedoms and rights which it has become the custom to bestow on our young people, to suggest some personality traits are unacceptable may lead to a charge of denying human rights.

The head-teacher of London comprehensive school where I started my career recognised individual differences and established the tutor group system in order to provide some individual counselling for his pupils. The system was inadequate, but the approach was an initiation of what is needed. The more attention is given to individual differences, the more individual counselling becomes essential, and this is expensive. One case may take up an hour. There may be parents to see. In a class of thirty, someone will have to find thirty hours of consultation time. And how frequently will this be necessary? How many times will the consultation take place in the week, in one term, in one school or college year?

The classroom teacher has the primary duty to teach, not to counsel, with the exception that day-to-day conversation may be a part of this. Otherwise, the classroom teacher should be using strategies to help manage classroom behaviour and to identify where specialist help is required, but not to give in depth or specialist help.

The White Paper "14 – 19 Education and Skills" emphasises the need for vocational courses because a significant section of the upper school population rejects the traditional academic-school orientated education. This is recognition of individual differences and the proposal for personalised learning programmes, including personal development, further emphasises this recognition. The approach, however, appears to be directed towards those with obvious learning difficulties or who come from underprivileged backgrounds.

If personalised learning programmes are to become a teaching strategy, a great deal of pupil-student guidance will be necessary, and this is expensive in terms of teacher-class contact time, preparation time and marking time. Add to this the time required for normal guidance and extra counselling for those with special needs and the demands on time become even greater. Specialists; small group tutors, individual tutors, educational counsellors, those trained in behaviour modification, educational psychologists and others; are required as well as the traditional classroom teacher, if these responsibilities are to be realistically carried out: and, if this is the case, the whole school-college staffing structure needs to be changed to include a variety of specialist as well as classroom teachers.

The White Paper recognises the need to cater for individual needs *(the summary chapter 3)*, the concept of people maturing at different ages *(the summary chapter 2)*, the existence of people with different talents and aptitudes *(6.1)* and the differences in the achievements of people of different class, gender and ethnic background: seeing these differences catered for by the use of a variety of teaching methods and environmental provision, personalised learning programmes, small group teaching and individual counselling. In the drive for vocational education there is a hint of different schools satisfying different needs, but also of all schools providing the same things! It is expected that schools will provide *much of the extended vocational provision (7.14)* although it is understood that all schools will not be able to cater for all vocations *(7.26)*. Specialist schools have been encouraged to develop, a system of Academies has been introduced and the concept of Trust schools has been advanced, suggesting that schools should develop along different lines, offering different curricula and developing their own unique ethos. This is a large step in the right direction, given that there are necessary refinements to make.

However, the one-school-for-all lobby sees selection and its evils in all of this.

5. A Failure to produce a Just Discipline

For any teaching style to succeed, for any education system to be successful, a first requirement is that the learning environment should be calm, well ordered and secure. The learner needs to be a member of a cohesive unit in which positive standards of behaviour, including a study discipline, are actively promoted. Unfortunately, too many institutions, particularly among the comprehensive schools, are disrupted by the coarse, rough and even delinquent behaviour of a dominant maladjusted minority.

Failing Schools

In 1996 this matter was brought to a head as a great brouhaha exploded into the media relating in particular to the Ridings School, Halifax, where the National Association of Schoolmasters Union of Women Teachers threatened to take strike action unless a number of disruptive pupils were either expelled or disciplined. The union alleged that one female teacher had been punched in the face, a male teacher had had a lighted firework thrown at him, and that another had been punched and stoned to such an extent that hospital treatment was necessary.

During the previous summer term the union had been involved in a dispute at the Glaisdale School, Nottingham, where a disruptive thirteen-year-old pupil was eventually expelled. It had also threatened strike action at the Hebburn School, South Tyneside, unless a disruptive boy was removed from the normal teaching situation. During the following autumn term, members of the same union at the Manton School, Worksop, Nottinghamshire, refused to teach a ten-year-old boy. The school was subsequently closed by the headmaster on the grounds that the safety of staff and pupils could not be guaranteed.

The Ridings School was closed by the Local Education Authority on Thursday 31st October when members of the NASUWT retired to the staffroom, refusing to resume teaching until action was taken against pupils involved in various incidents of unacceptable behaviour. Mr Mike Tomlinson, at that time the leader of the inspection team sent into the troubled school at the beginning of that week, outlined the events witnessed by his team the previous day. At 11am a senior teacher was observed manhandling a disruptive pupil from a classroom. During the lunch break corridors in the school were described as race tracks as behaviour became dangerous. None of the staff were on duty. The inspectors stopped one boy attacking another and after the lunch break were unable to persuade pupils to return to lessons. By 1.40pm they advised the head-teacher that they considered that the school was becoming out of control.

The specific incidents alleged to have precipitated the union action on the Thursday include a fourteen-year-old boy fondling the breast of a supply teacher in front of a class; another teacher being hurt when a fourteen-year-old girl had slammed a door in his face; another needing to go home after being pelted with books; and a fifteen-year-old boy having gone home hurt after being hit on the head by a video cassette thrown at him by a girl pupil. In addition, a group of previously expelled pupils were causing trouble on the playing fields.

Some observers were quick to accuse the NASUWT of deliberately giving the question of pupil disruption a high media profile in order to promote its policy of ensuring that such pupils are removed from the normal school situation. Some saw the campaign as an effort to boost union membership figures and there can be little doubt that the publicity, in which the NASUWT were shown to be taking action in support of teachers under stress, would promote the union's image. It would, however, remain to be seen whether a majority of teachers would support this way of doing things. The point is that the situation should never have been allowed to develop in the first place.

It is quite clear that, during the days of crisis, immediately before the closure of the school, the teachers were not doing their job. It is impossible to run a school when teachers remain in the staffroom and it can be argued that the union concerned put the majority of pupils at greater risk by withdrawing their supervision. It is also clear that many teachers were exerting no positive influence over the pupils even when they were in the corridors and classrooms. The question is: why not?

Nigel De Gruchy, then General Secretary of the NASUWT, argued that management was at fault. Although admitting that some teachers may have been incompetent in the given situation, and for various reasons, it was, he argued, the responsibility of management to solve this problem. His duty was to look after his members. He also stated that all of the teachers had been good teachers, presumably implying that it was the circumstances at the Riding School which caused previously good teachers to fail.

The Ofsted inspectors reported that teaching was unsatisfactory in some two-fifths of the lessons, in some lessons little real teaching or learning took place. Some of the teachers, they concluded could not control their classes. Relationships between staff and pupils varied, in some cases being very good but in others being strained or confrontational.

During breaks and lunchtimes inadequate supervision allowed bad behaviour to flourish. Attendance and punctuality were poor, the school apparently not knowing where all of its pupils were. Those in the school were not always in lessons, while others stayed away without proper reason. It was claimed that the management systems for monitoring and following up such absences were inadequate.

Consequently, poor teaching by failing teachers, lack of proper supervision of pupils, weak management from the head-teacher and other senior staff, inadequate oversight by the governors, and the failure of the local education authority to act were all blamed for The Ridings failure: failure arising from a school passing out of control, through a failure of discipline not only among the pupils but also among staff.

The inspectors clearly found a lack of structure and authority, yet this seems incredible. A presumably senior and experienced teacher was appointed as head-teacher of a newly opened school formed from the amalgamation of two already disadvantaged and failing schools. Surely those who had this responsibility made their choice wisely? Or had new government legislation, which took much of the authority away from the professionals and placed it in the hands of politicians, parents and others not trained as educators produced an inadequate appointment? If the head-teacher did not exert an authority over her staff, then the staff could have little authority over the pupils. But there is the possibility that the head-teacher had no authority because she was not allowed to have any, a situation which has grown out of the post war search for a new participatory democracy, about which more is said in chapter 14 (A New Professionalism).

Where the appointed leaders, whether they are leaders of the staff or the pupils, exert no authority, others fill the leadership gap. The bullies and thugs among the children hold sway in the streets outside the school, in the playgrounds and corridors and in the classrooms. In the staffroom the most forceful teachers' union, the one prepared to use militant strategies to advance its policies, undermines the leadership of those appointed to run the school by imposing decisions and actions upon its members over and above the authority of the senior staff.

Yet the possibility of a school getting out of control has been evident for many years and the question must be asked: how have the situations which encouraged militant trade union intervention been allowed to develop? Warning signs were evident as early as the 1950s.

Being concerned about the influence of a minority of pupils upon the tone of the larger comprehensive schools, in 1971 I wrote a small article, based upon personal experiences in the third newly established London Comprehensive School in which

I worked. This was published in the *Times Educational Supplement* on 18 June in answer to claims that mixed ability teaching groups were advantageous in bringing together pupils of different abilities and social backgrounds, each helping the other in the learning situation. I made the point that there existed both "good" and "bad" mixed ability classes, the "bad" or difficult groups being "caused by the interaction of a few maladjusted personalities contained in them". I recalled a second year class (aged twelve plus) in which there was a boy "liable to fly into rages, an unstable girl and yet another who provokes the other two into open hostility". In a group of thirteen-plus children there were two maladjusted boys who constantly fought each other and argued with the teachers. "These disturbances are frequent, demanding upon the teacher's time and disrupting for the other pupils. They cause the development of wrong attitudes to both academic work and behaviour. Furthermore, these pupils are not without influence outside the classroom."

The article continued: "In any large school which takes pupils of all abilities there will be a significant number of these maladjusted pupils. (In a streamed school they tend to be placed in the lower groups which then become very difficult to teach.) They will tend to react against the establishment in many ways. They may refuse to do homework, dominate the less aggressive children, damage school property and cause disturbance in the neighbourhood.

"The relatively permissive atmosphere of our modern schools permits these youngsters to dominate the majority of well balanced boys and girls. It is surely necessary to take some action to control the influence of the maladjusted few, or do we wish them to run *(and I should have said "ruin")* our civilisation for us?"

More recently we have observed the growth in the number of uncontrolled schools, labelled under the new inspection regime as failing schools.

Less dramatic in its impact is the general lowering of standards of behaviour across all schools, a fact that is often denied because an admission can be interpreted by those outside schools, who are unable to comprehend the true nature of the problem, as the failure of teachers to do the job they are paid to do. To admit to having problems often encourages others to label a school and its staff as failing, subsequently creating further problems through the destruction of any positive ethos which it previously maintained. The general decline in standards is demonstrated by noisy unregulated movement about school, an increase in swearing, decrease in the application of good manners and increased loud uncouth behaviour and vandalism both in school and in the neighbourhood. All of this is due to the inability of schools to enforce a code of socially acceptable behaviour. In a society where some influential commentators actually demand freedom from all restrictions, a freedom in which each individual is to be allowed to seek his or her own happiness without reference to anyone else, the imposition of a disciplined structure is actually undermined by the constant challenges made using human rights legislation.

The elements involved in school control

The internal elements which come together in the day-today running of a school to promote or undermine its discipline are, at least superficially, easy to identify. There are the pupils with their infinitely varied personalities and home backgrounds, there are the teachers with their differing personalities and teaching styles, there is the management team with its mix of personalities and educational philosophies.

More difficult to unravel is the complex interaction of these elements with each other. Furthermore, these elements do not work in a social vacuum, there are intense pressures exerted from outside the internal environment of the school, the external elements. There is the governing body with its notions and prejudices on how things should be done, there are the parents who display interests ranging from nil to complete domination, there is the local education authority confined by legislation but guided by its political leanings and there is the national government which constructs the legislative framework in which the executors work.

The interaction of the internal elements with each other, within the framework established by the external elements, determines whether or not a school will be seen to be successful or unsuccessful within the parameters defined by the external elements.

Michael Rutter and his team, reporting the findings of their research into secondary schools and their effects on children in "Fifteen Thousand Hours" in 1979, comment on the interaction of factors within the social make up of a school which come together to produce a social climate, which they call the ethos of the school.

They refer to the ethos of the school which they describe in terms of the coming together of values, attitudes, and behaviours which the school promotes giving the place its particular character Consequently there appear to be schools which are in many ways similar but which have a greater or lesser success according to the ethos produced by the interaction of what they call school processes or the social organisation of the school which produce the teaching and learning environment involving both teachers and pupils. That the team refers to both staff and pupils is significant because it recognises two elements which react together: if the experiences of the pupils are good they reflect back a positive mood or spirit which in turn provides good experiences for the teachers who then provide more good experiences for the pupils and the process snowballs. But the opposite can be the case. If the pupils reflect back a negative mood, the teachers' experiences are bad, fostering feelings of failure and despair. Of course, a positive cycle can equally be broken by poor quality teaching – the pupils not being given good experiences in the first place. In situations like that at the Ridings School, the teachers' union sees the cycle broken and standards lowered by a dominant and aggressive group of disruptive pupils. But the inspectorate argues that the breakdown of a positive ethos cannot be due to the pupils alone, the teachers must have been at least in part to blame.

Again, at the Ridings, a new school formed from the amalgamation of two other schools where it appears that there was no great positive ethos in the first place, the new school did not, or was not able, to establish a positive spirit from day one.

It is worthwhile asking whether or not the Rutter investigation sheds further light on this situation. The results of the study certainly suggest that there are significant processes which may be at work in a school which correlate with positive outcomes. For instance, taking a simple case, in schools where a good level of the use of the library was reported there were good examination results. But it is not certain that one is a cause of the other. In this case both scores could be the result of there being a high proportion of academically able youngsters or youngsters from highly supportive homes in the intake.

The school processes in the Rutter investigation were seen in terms of the extent to which the academic side of education was emphasised, teachers' actions in the classroom, the nature of the relative application of rewards and punishments, whether or not conditions in which the pupils worked were pleasant and comfortable, the degree to which the children were able to participate in and take responsibility in the life of the school, the stability of teaching groups, the stability of friendship groups and staff organisation.

The main finding was that the make up of the school's intake correlated with the pupil's success or otherwise, especially in relation to school attendance and delinquent behaviour. On the other hand, the children's behaviour in school was found to be related to the school processes, and far less with the child's personal characteristics, his home background, or the nature of the intake.

Perhaps there is no surprise in the finding that academic success was a related to school processes but examination success correlated with the pupil's ability, and that success or otherwise was related to the child itself, the nature of the school's intake and the school processes.

The most significant link with delinquency was the academic balance of the school. The child's ability level was also important but equal to that of the parent's occupation. The significance of the school processes was far less. That is to say that what went on in the school, the way the school was run, did not exert any great influence on the delinquents, nor presumably on the potential delinquents, who for the most part are the most unmanageable part of a school population.

The implication, according to Rutter, is that peer group influences were serving to form the youngsters' behaviour. Clearly, the group culture becomes more influential than that of the school. These people are hostile to school. It may consequently be argued that if the proportion of delinquents or potential delinquents in a school population is sufficiently high, their influence becomes dominant while that of the school processes in minimal. So, although the Rutter findings strongly support the notion that schools do influence the progress of their pupils, they also explain the failing school. This reasoning could explain the situation at the Ridings.

Schools having a higher academic emphasis had a lower number of delinquents. In simple terms therefore it might be claimed that because those schools emphasise academic learning, they motivate their pupils better, those pupils are well integrated into the school, and there are fewer delinquents. Or it may be the case that schools with a higher intake of delinquents cannot motivate their pupils using the academic approach and consequently try some other strategy: at worst failing to motivate their pupils at all and displaying examples of lessons in which no positive teaching takes place.

Then again, should not the academic emphasis in Rutter's study be seen in terms of a wider school purpose? The positive school process sought after is still learning but not necessarily academic learning. It could be learning through the mastering of practical skills, thus capturing the interest of the less academic, including those already displaying delinquent behaviour and those who may, if left unmotivated, become behaviour and delinquent problems. Delinquency is shown to be associated with low academic ability and it is therefore logical to suggest that a different school process from that of academic style teaching is required to motivate these pupils.

It is important to provide a variety of teaching and learning styles if a school is to have a chance of building a positive and thriving ethos in which the whole spectrum of personalities is thoroughly involved.

Such a conclusion, even in 1979, was not new because it is well documented in the work of social psychologists that groups take upon characteristics of their own and develop norms; and how individuals are under pressure to confirm to those norms.

Clearly, schools are social institutions and will be subject to these forces. Much of the work of social psychologists however has been completed on small groups and schools, even the smallest, are quite large by these standards. In large institutions there will be a much greater possibility for subgroups to form: indeed, it will be inevitable because human nature only enables the individual to form a limited number of relationships. In the case of the failing schools, such as the Ridings, it is a particularly dominant subgroup, or number of subgroups, which have become all influential and prevent the formation of a positive ethos. Instead, it is the negative aspects of group behaviour which take over.

It can be argued that it is quite possible for the same school, with the same inputs and the same outputs to be seen as successful, judged against one set of parameters, yet shown to be failing when judged against a different set. This is a question of priorities (governed by the political fashion of the times) and during the years since the Second World War these priorities have changed. In attempting to find reasons for the apparent growth in the phenomena of failing schools changes in these priorities and their influence on the various elements of school discipline must be considered. An example of such apparent opposite situations is where academic qualifications are either seen as all important or not important at all. In the first instance a school would be judged as successful if its pupils gained a high number of "O" and "A" level examination passes, an essential ingredient for success on government league tables. In the second case emphasis may be put upon pastoral care, and so long as the pupils are seen as happy, well mannered, confident young people, apparently positively occupied in some way, that school would be judged successful. Before the coming of league tables, many schools with a large number of low ability and problem children were able to gain this kind of success. But it can still be asked whether pastoral success alone is an adequate success. After all, a school is a place where the learning of knowledge and skills, and the development of aptitudes, are an essential part of its purpose.

The significance of the maladjusted pupil

It has already been noted that at the Ridings School at least some of the teachers saw difficult pupils as the major factor in the failure of the school. Others did not entirely accept this.

Yet it must now surely be conceded that the uncontrolled deviant has been allowed to thrive and the reasonable majority suffer the injustice of seeing the persistent and serious rule-breaker go uncorrected and unpunished while they are reprimanded for their minor transgressions. Consequently, they rebel and claim more freedom for themselves, disregarding the rules which uphold the structured society in which each can have optimum freedom without interfering with any other. Simple things such as caring for text books, taking pride in the layout of written work, arriving in class with the required equipment and applying good manners, come to be of little consequence when it is known that others are getting away with truancy, vandalism, bullying and even criminal activity. With the growing disregard for rules the school becomes less and less controlled: the teachers are no longer respected as worthy leaders, the worst of the young people run amok and even the quietest, mildest personalities need to develop a superficial harsh nastiness in order to survive. They must adopt the declining standards of the peer group or become its victims, subjected to bullying, withdrawing into themselves, developing a fear of school, reinforcing their own insecurity and in the most tragic circumstances, taking their own lives. The decent become the victims and the school ethos declines.

Standards in society then decline as young people enter the adult world never having learnt the wisdom of self-discipline: they seek instant gratification of their needs, no matter how antisocial those needs may be, too easily resorting to aggressive behaviour, both verbal and physical, and seek pleasure in such acts as wanton destruction, drug or alcohol abuse and, recently, actually seriously attacking and injuring any bystander they happen to come up against for no other reason than personal excitement. They disrupt, vandalise and are delinquent, leading pseudo-exciting lives of self destruction when their energies should be diverted into constructive occupations. They are left free, the law somehow unable to curb their excesses and they lead others into their way of life. They cause a great deal of inconvenience to the law abiding citizen and cost society a great deal of money.

This is the tragedy of the antisocial and is leading to the growth of an anarchic, hostile social class, for which, although it corresponds to a considerable degree with deprived groups, deprivation is not the simple straightforward cause.

In so much of the above there has been an emphasis on the situation in the large secondary schools, although many of the underlying principles also apply to primary schools, and it must be recognised that problem children are frequently problems before they reach the age of eleven. Where eleven-plus entrants formerly came as innocent, anxious, children, frightened by the prospects of initiation into the realms, mysteries and rituals of secondary education, they now come more and more as self-centred horrors, clothed in the armour of self survival acquired from the buffeting experiences of eleven years of neglect. They have been forced to find their own ways through the turmoil of life, with little protection, little guidance, rare discipline and immediate self gratification. And the infant and nursery teachers will tell the same story about their entrants at four and five.

There has consequently developed a core of wild untrained personalities, where wilful, self centred, naturally aggressive temperaments have never been trained, coming into schools to cause disruption in even the youngest age groups. There has developed a situation in which teachers have no authority and dare not discipline a child in case they are accused of abusing the young people. It is only necessary for the least reliable child to make such an accusation and the teacher's word accounts for nothing. There are children so sophisticated and lacking childhood innocence that they will use this weapon to get their way and to seek revenge for any real or imaginary ills which they may harbour.

Different discipline for different pupils

Although a situation has arisen in which a minority of maladjusted young people have been identified and aggressive youngsters often dominate schools, there are other pupils for which a strict discipline is not appropriate.

A harsh raised voice will terrify one child into a trembling silence, another it will cause to giggle nervously, and yet in another it will cause a hostile defiance. These various reactions will depend first upon the nature of the child, second on its upbringing and third on the circumstances at the time of the rebuke. The circumstances include the structure of the institution and the defined bounds within which the taught is expected to operate, the previously developed interpersonal relationships between the teacher and pupil, and also the mood of the culprit at the moment of rebuke. It is therefore important for the teacher to recognise and understand the individual personalities of those being taught so that appropriate individual responses to misdemeanours can be applied: different reactions being required from the teacher in order to control different children.

In the big school, with frequently changing teaching groups, a response appropriate to each individual is far more difficult to achieve than in the small school where one teacher remains with one group of children for most of the week. But there is also the fact that some teachers are better at assessing such individual characteristics than others. It is possible that those with the sharpest skill in this field make the best potential teachers. They can rapidly assess the nature of any event in relation to the characters of those responsible and immediately produce a reaction, harsh, humorous or otherwise, which demonstrates a fair control. Some teachers can learn strategies, using, for instance and as mentioned in the previous chapter, sociometric and other psychometric techniques, to help them with the task; but others seem to find such judgements beyond them, always producing the wrong response and inviting challenges to their leadership by others in the group who see the injustice of the situation. Perhaps the latter are among those who should not attempt teaching as a career.

A significant aspect of the need to comprehend such individual differences is the essential skill of recognising the abnormal personality. Because critics of school discipline have been able to argue that it is mischievous youngsters, rather than those who are seriously maladjusted, who are beyond control, they have been able to deny the existence of serious problems, blaming teachers for the breakdown of discipline and avoiding any search of more appropriate remedies. There should now be no doubt that there are young people in schools and colleges who demonstrate abnormal behaviour more serious than was previously thought possible. One reason for this is the erosion of the authority of the adult. The problem child has never been made to conform because certain theories of child rearing have been grasped at and put into practice without a full realisation of the consequences. Such strategies have been applied to all without consideration of individual differences. A first requirement is the recognition that normal disciplinary procedures may have no effect on the maladjusted but this is an insufficient reason for not applying them when working with normal children. A clear distinction needs to be made between the discipline of the normal and the treatment of the abnormal. This question is considered further in chapter 6.

The teachers

Some strongly believe that it is the teachers who are the major factor in the decline in pupil behaviour: it is easy to claim that they are not doing their job properly. But can this claim be upheld?

When the education system expanded in the 1950s and '60s, staff shortages developed, bringing about a watering down of teacher quality.

Some teachers were promoted to senior posts when previously they would have been considered insufficiently experienced: the young, inexperienced, and even those with few academic qualifications, were employed in order to fill vacancies. The scramble for posts of responsibility and the drop out of those who found they could not cope, led to rapid staff turnover adding to the breakdown of sound interpersonal relationships between teacher and student. Training establishments, called upon to produce more and more teachers, accepted inadequate students and then excused every weakness in an effort to pass out a sufficient number of bodies to meet the demand. More recently, with the coming of falling rolls and decreasing budgets, the most experienced staff have been allowed, if not encouraged, to retire early and very recently it has even become economically sound to replace expensive long serving teachers with cheaper newly qualified inexperienced staff straight out of college. The long earned respect and established wisdom of the experienced teacher has been replaced by the untried enthusiasms of the young and new. The mistake of cultivating over familiar teacher-pupil relationships is not recognised until mutual respect is lost and irretrievable, and the consequences of untried teaching methods are not fully appreciated before classroom management has failed. The result has been to further increase instability and decrease the quality of both instruction and supervision.

Children and young people placed together in a building need constant supervision, they need the guidance of mature adults to temper their immaturity. When the building has more than a thousand occupants, the need is greater and more complex. Yet supervision has been relaxed rather than intensified. The traditional notion of children being expected to be silent and stand still on the sounding of a whistle, so that they can be given further instructions, has been rejected. The idea that they should line up in their class groups, so that they can be directed to enter the building in turn, has been replaced by a free for all scramble.

Teachers have become less willing to complete supervisory duties. They are reluctant to station themselves about the building before the pupils enter, at best working within the confines of their own rooms or, far worse, preferring the cosiness of the staffroom. That pupils should be greeted coming into the building, and late comers checked, seems to be a completely foreign concept among some staff, or if not completely rejected, it is someone else's responsibility, not theirs. Too many fail to emerge from their classrooms to supervise movement in the corridors at the change of lessons and some move about the school blinkered, walking by the most antisocial misbehaviour. They fail to realise that to ignore misbehaviour anywhere is to send a message to the culprit that the teachers do not care, that it does not matter. Too many see their job as being only within their own classroom walls and even there expect someone else to maintain order for them.

A more contentious responsibility is that of the supervision of pupils going to and from school and of those roaming aimlessly in the vicinity of the school during lunch breaks.

Teacher militancy

The attitudes and campaigns of the teachers' unions to improve working conditions have not helped. For example, in their efforts to give teachers a lunch break, they place the freedom of the teacher before all else. It was of no consequence that schools require supervision at lunch time and that the best people to do this are the teachers themselves. The unions took the view that others must take on this responsibility, that teachers must be completely free from all duties. They have also challenged the need for their members to complete duties before and after school, in each case reinforcing the message that the teacher does not want to know about what is going on outside strict and limiting working hours.

The consequence of a lack of cohesion in a school staff

If the teachers' associations are really looking for a better education system, rather than destroying much of what was good and worthwhile through the militant refusal to carry out responsibilities, they should seek to enter into careful negotiations for the drawing up of a contract of employment which would prevent the exploitation of the teacher while ensuring that all of the traditional duties are carried out. This would of course be the professional approach to the problem and, if achieved, would remove the facility of causing disruption by direct action, a strategy which some ideologists would not accept.

The changing nature of the secondary school population

An obvious, yet too often neglected, change in the nature of the secondary school population is that there has been a move away from a situation in which most young people over the age of fourteen joined the adult world of work to one in which they remain in a school environment. In practical terms, this means that they are no longer in an adult culture and are not subjected to the discipline of the adult workforce. Instead, they remain in a situation where they, the immature adolescents, are influenced mainly by themselves and the teachers find themselves trying to lead groups of young men and women who have the physical capabilities of adults but the emotional development of the teenager. Not so long ago, secondary education was for the minority who were intellectually able, following an academic curriculum towards academic qualifications which would give access to employment or university. Motivation was, in general, good but where youngster, parent or both, did not support the ethos of the school, the student could choose to leave or be expelled. There was no hard core of reluctant and antisocial learners. Today there is a form of compulsory secondary education for all but one in which a majority find no realistic purpose: more than ever now that even a good collection of ordinary level passes at sixteen fail to earn a place in employment. The school leaving age has been raised twice, first to fifteen and in 1973 sixteen without making proper provision for the majority of learners for whom the academic approach is not suitable. Today there is an expectation that young people should remain in education until they are eighteen and that the majority should continue further learning in universities.

Present day secondary schools, with their movement of pupils from one specialist room to another up to eight times each day and where groups are forever changing as their members follow different course options, are not only larger but far more flexible than earlier institutions and offer greater opportunities for the deviant to play truant and become involved in unchecked disruptive or delinquent behaviour.

Changing attitudes towards children and children's rights

Resulting from the zealousness of various ideologists, carried away by their misconceived desires to either help the underprivileged and abused child or impose their dogmatic views of childhood upon society, there has evolved a situation in which parents, professional carers and educators have been forced into unnatural relationships with children.

For instance, a mother of a ten-year-old boy and nine-year-old girl, a mother from what the sociologists would call the working class, with a husband frequently away from home working as a long distant truck driver for an international chemical firm, spontaneously demonstrated some of the absurdities of our present adult-child relationships as seen through her own eyes.

With other mothers, she witnessed small children coming out of school half dressed, with buttons undone, trousers forced onto legs the wrong way round and shirts and blouses flowing in the wind. Seeking an explanation of their children being allowed to leave the building in such a state they were given a threefold explanation. The children had changed clothes for games, and presumably stripping garments off and putting on simple shorts and shirts was well within their abilities. Afterwards, however, they were not able to dress themselves properly. The teachers explained that they could not help because they were not allowed to touch the children!

The same caring parent also referred to the absurdity of infant school teachers not being allowed to reassure the timid child by sitting it on their knees while having story time. There must be no love or affection shown lest it be interpreted as sexual abuse.

This ordinary adult, one who is not professionally trained to work with children, showed disbelief at finding her child supplied with a written list of his rights. And pressure groups, social workers, administrators and lawyers are quick to emphasise their view that children must have and know their rights, being in a position to challenge what they may see as a denial of such rights.

Surely someone living in cloud cuckoo land devised such a concept, or is it merely the interpreters and executors who have misused the good intentions? They deny that they have, of course, so what are the grounds for suggesting that they are wrong?

Firstly, children are children, with the perceptions and understanding of young immature beings. They neither see nor comprehend events in the same ways as adults and it is therefore futile to present them an adult system and expect them to be able to use it in an adult way.

Children need protection, not a list of rights, or if you insist on being politically correct, they require one overriding right: to be loved, cared for and taught in a stable family environment. This is not a right which needs to be spelt out to children, hoping that they will understand its complex meaning and be able to recognise and challenge situations in which they are being mistreated. A child is not mature enough to understand, it is not within the child's experience, body of knowledge, and its mind is not sufficiently developed to interpret such adult terminology. If they have this right, they take it for granted, continuing to grow well adjusted and happy, but still rebelling against the bounds which a civilised society imposes upon them because their young natures demand immediate satisfaction of immediately perceived needs – but not necessarily needs which the individual should have satisfied or which society should accept. A child is a demanding, testing being, learning the bounds of socialised behaviour.

Where a child does not have the basic right to a good and satisfactory upbringing, it does not know this and it does not help for an adult to tell the child so. Children grow up accepting what they experience. For some, a drunken father and sickly mother is the norm, and to tell them that they are not being given their basic right is meaningless. The instability of such a family, to them, is understood and is preferable to a strange unknown. So it must be for adults and society to know what rights a child should have and to interpret and uphold those rights.

The undue influence of pressure groups

There can be little doubt that differing ideologies relating to how schools and classrooms should be organised have led to confusion among teachers over how they should react to changing requirements. Even when an individual is quite clear, albeit intuitively, about how things should be done, confusing expectations from teacher training establishments, colleagues and the inspectorate have led to their insecurity. Yet two of the requirements for a school to be effective, according to research carried out by the University of London Institute of Education and reported by its Director, Peter Mortimore in *The Times* of 13 February 1995, are that there should be "clear discipline" and "shared vision and goals". Confusion on the other hand, no fault of individual teachers, leads to the deterioration of standards among both staff and pupils. An educational establishment needs a clear structure and bounds within which teachers and taught can operate efficiently.

Management styles, teaching methods and relationships between pupils and teachers have been seriously undermined by the influence of minority pressure groups and enthusiasts. In relation to pupil discipline, driven by their ideologies, they have challenged the use of corporal punishment, physical restraint, detentions, extra work, whether it is purposeful or routine, and even objected to the forceful use of the voice, until the teacher is left with no means of commanding authority. But, of course, there is an underlying principle here. There are those who deny that a teacher should be an authority figure and who, equating authority only with an unpleasantly harsh autocracy, deliberately set out to destroy this form of leadership.

The question arises: should a teacher be in a position of authority or not? A question asked and answered according to various strongly held beliefs by theoretical educators and teachers alike. A comprehensive collection of these beliefs is outlined in the book *"Discipline in Schools"* edited by Barry Turner and published by Ward Lock Educational in 1973. The publication is a collection of essays written by writers holding various opinions and attitudes which extend from the traditional views of the one-time headmaster and Member of Parliament, Sir Rhodes Boyson, to those of the ultra-liberal school of A.S. Neill, given by the then headmaster of Summerhill. The article by John Watts, then principal of Countesthorpe Community College, Leicestershire, gives a very good insight into the thinking of what might be described as the democratic school of discipline in which the teacher is certainly not an authority figure but a mere facilitator and participator in the education process.

Watts argues that because society has changed, so must education change and the old traditional ways of doing things can no longer apply. The pillars of traditional education, in Watts's view, were the existence of a recognised and manageable body of knowledge and an accepted code of values. These he sees as being handed down to submissive, unquestioning youngsters by power wielding teachers, that is, teachers demanding an unquestioning obedience and relying on the sanctions already mentioned to ensure that obedience. But even where the teacher is the accepted authority figure, teaching is not like that illustrated by Watts. The degree of authority demanded and of democratic participation invited varies with the personality of the teacher, the nature of the class and the social climate which changes from day to day.

Furthermore, there is a body of knowledge and skills which can be given to others via a whole range of teaching strategies. Teachers, from those working with first year infants to college lecturers, are trained graduates and a large part of their training includes the learning of a body of knowledge and associated skills which are frequently, for convenience of handling, called subjects. All teachers do not have the same knowledge, different adults will have some of it and children start school with a little or any of it. The teacher is there to help the student, young or old, to acquire the knowledge he or she already holds and understands. To claim that there is no body of knowledge or that, if there is, it changes so rapidly that it cannot be passed on, is utter nonsense.

The second pillar of the traditional education, a uniform code of values, no longer exists, according to Watts. In this he is at least partially correct and a result is that while youngsters wallow in the confusion of not knowing what is right or wrong, society suffers the results of their anarchic behaviour. The democrats develop their argument to suggest that schools should not attempt to impose their own code, a code foreign to the young people, but rather abdicate their position of authority and accept the standards, or lack of standards, which come to them. But, like the failure to pass on the knowledge and skills investigated and substantiated by our forefathers, this is also a failure to educate. The fact that there is no common code does not mean that one is not needed. The converse is the case: educators should be working towards the establishment of a common code of values for application in schools.

Watts and others do not accept this as the way forward. They see teachers as largely middle class, and holding the middle class values of thrift, stability, self denial, permanence and respect for authority, which were applicable to the selective grammar school model of education and which the majority of comprehensive school pupils do not hold. The fault is to claim such values are only applicable to a middle class, when many traditionally working class folk also claim to uphold such values. Furthermore, to claim that because a sizable minority do not subscribe to such a code is insufficient reason to argue that there are no worthwhile values which it would be reasonable for all to adopt.

The critics of this concept prefer to seek a new utopia. They seek a discipline which somehow evolves from the adoption of a different curriculum and of different relationships between teacher and the taught. The curriculum, they argue, is neither to prepare an elite (i.e. those passing through the traditional grammar school) nor to provide qualifications but somehow evolve from the whole population entering the school. How this ideal can possibly by divorced from the means to qualify for a job is difficult to comprehend as this is the only reason which gives meaning to education for most people. However, taking this as their starting point, the innovators go on to say that the teacher is neither the main source of knowledge nor selector of problems to be solved. Instead, he or she becomes a facilitator, helping the learner to formulate his or her own problems and providing techniques for problem-solving. In this way, it is argued, the learner chooses and learns to respect the choices of others and comes to respect a group authority and social discipline which somehow evolve to bring about co-operation. It is assumed that this will be a good discipline, if not the best discipline, but there is another possible outcome and that is that there develops the discipline of the most dominant personalities in the teaching group. Watts sees the development of co-operation in matters related to the curriculum as subsequently bringing co-operation to the social aspects of the youngster's lives.

So at Countesthorpe in the early 1970s, the traditional school authority was abandoned: there was no required dress, no given regulations, other than a refusal to accept antisocial behaviour, and no areas of the premises exclusively for the use of the staff. First names were used by all and the head-teacher and staff were given the same voice as the pupils, a false situation in which there is responsibility without authority.

A final comment on this form of discipline is that it is a system which its protagonists autocratically impose upon their schools or classroom! Within the education service there are those who passionately believe in its perfection and those who see it as only producing anarchy. Many have been convinced that it will lead to a better world if only they can introduce it and, like so many educational theories, its strategies have been attempted without fully understanding the implications. Somehow many educators have come to believe that the introduction of the newest enthusiasms is essential for success and there has been insufficient genuine evaluation of the new before well-tried traditions have been swept away.

Sanctions

Corporal punishment has been equated, in the emotive language of the militant protestor, with cruel beatings and floggings equivalent to an eighteenth century military discipline. This emotive interpretation of what was once a legitimate sanction has been developed to include even the gentlest of slaps, until adults have been placed in the absurd position where they dare not touch a child for fear of being charged with assault. Yet, as mature and compassionate physical restraint has been rejected so untamed aggression among the young has become more of a problem.

To detain a child after class hours has become, in the eyes of some extremists, associated with denying a basic human right, akin to false imprisonment. Even where it is accepted by parents and governors as a reasonable sanction, some teachers refuse to accept its supervision as any part of their responsibilities. The imposition of extra work or some routine exercise is similarly regarded by some as punishing the staff as much as the culprits. After all, teachers have to set it, collect and check it, and this is now seen as extra work, no longer a traditional part of the teacher's job. A less teacher-selfish explanation of the rejection of the sanction is to claim that the work itself is time wasting and more likely to discourage a learning discipline than to encourage it.

Even the raising of the teacher's voice to give a firm instruction is frowned upon in some circles as being an unnecessarily autocratic act, and this touches upon a primary philosophical problem.

Certainly, where traditional sanctions have been removed, alternatives are found to be long winded, consuming hours of time. For instance, the short sharp shock of corporal punishment has been replaced by long counselling sessions during which a youngster is determined to stick to his or her position, no matter how obviously wrong it is, and equally long periods are subsequently spent trying to demonstrate to a parent how wrong their child is. The situation has developed in which the school has become more and more like a court of law, where the misbehaviour is inevitably denied by the culprit and must be proved, requiring several teachers to be brought to testify as it were – a ludicrous situation in which the blatant rogue always tends to escape unrepentant and unpunished – while in the training of the young it is essential for the wrongdoer to be seen to be promptly brought to task.

A more realistic philosophy needs to be adopted and a code of practice agreed – including a definition of expected acceptable behaviour and procedures to be adopted when a pupil fails.

The **Great** Education Controversy

6. The adverse effect of the uncontrolled delinquent

People might be forgiven if they believe that juvenile delinquency is nothing to do with the ordinary school. Many teachers will claim that they have enough to do preparing lessons, encouraging the majority of ordinary children to learn and marking pupils' exercises without becoming involved with law-breakers who they may regard as clients for the social services, the police and the courts. They would, in the simplest terms, prefer the delinquent young person to be taken out of their field of responsibility. But the dividing line between the behaviour of the normal mischievous child and the maladjusted is not distinct and the maladjusted problem child becomes the delinquent only when brought before the court. He or she will no doubt be involved in antisocial behaviour before conviction and this behaviour will impinge upon the school. Furthermore, the question must be asked: is the task of the school solely to educate young people in the knowledge and skills of subject disciplines or does it have a broader responsibility? If the latter case is the true aim of education, there is much work to be done in order to tackle the problem of juvenile crime, and it has already been shown in Rutter's work that school processes have little influence on the delinquent pupil.

As the head-teacher of a mixed comprehensive school situated in a northern town, and having a large proportion of its intake coming from underprivileged families, I soon discovered that, whether the school wishes to be involved in the question of juvenile delinquency or not, the delinquent pupil cannot be ignored, because he or she invariably exerts a considerable derogatory influence on the ethos of the whole school.

In the 1990s numerous cases of exceptional child delinquency made headlines in the national press. For instance, a headline in *The Times* of Friday 3 November 1995 read "He is cunning, evil and beyond control". The article was referring to a fourteen-year-old boy who it claimed ran two gangs and was responsible for seventy-two offences. At a recent court appearance, the boy admitted twenty burglaries. The article stated that the only course of action which the court could take was to place the youngster in local authority care. From there he absconded and continued his career of crime.

The boy dominated both younger and older associates. Detective Inspector Tim Wilson was quoted as saying "He has an aura of authority about him and he is the one in charge." The boy's insolence is illustrated by his response to police questioning: he repeatedly sang "No reply, no reply, no reply" to the soccer chant of "Here we go, here we go, here we go". "We arrest him, charge him and recover stolen goods. But that is where our involvement ends".

They boy's father, a 38-year-old unemployed miner, was quoted as saying : "We've tried everything we can do to keep him out of trouble and now he needs to be locked up in a secure unit because he is completely out of control."

As far as school was concerned, the boy stopped attending when he was thirteen, despite his father taking him and even sitting with him. Subsequently he should have been attending a special school but rarely did so. He showed no fear or respect for the court, knowing the workings of the system and recognising that it had no means of restricting his freedom. His grandmother reported that his parents threatened to "wallop him" but the boy merely retorts with threats to report them to social services for abusing him.

It was as early as the mid 1970s when I drew the attention of the local education authority, social services, magistrates and police, to the danger of society's failure to deal positively with young law-breakers. Although such problems are few, the trouble they cause is out of all proportion to their numbers and I witnessed too many examples in my school.

One thirteen-year-old boy, let us call him John, was transferred from a neighbouring school, his mother citing difficulties with travelling and having a younger child in the school as reasons for the move. But his records showed him to be an unstable child and largely out of control at home: indeed, he had already been brought before the juvenile court and had been made the subject of a supervision order.

Almost immediately he had to be reprimanded for smoking on school premises and his response was to swear at the teacher concerned. His parent was requested to come to school and, following discussion, John settled down and demonstrated a reasonable standard of behaviour. Three months later, however, he was called before his Head of House to explain a morning's absence. It transpired that he had again been brought before the juvenile court to answer charges involving some £480 worth of stolen property, some seven or eight other offences being taken into consideration. The court returned him home on bail. To the child, already the subject of a supervision order, this did not indicate a serious disapproval of his behaviour. He had gotten away with it again. The following day, with two other boys from the school, John broke into further properties and stayed away from home until found by the police a week later. This time he was detained until his court appearance in three weeks' time.

It was decided to place John under observation for four months, during which time he would live with a relative in a different part of the town but continue attendance at the same school. Consequently, other pupils interpreted the situation as that of a boy who had committed serious crimes being let off and subsequently followed his example, truanting, staying away from home and becoming involved in law-breaking activities.

In another case, a pupil, Gerald, with his younger brother and another pupil from the school ran away from home. A little later he broke into the school overnight and stole money and dinner tickets. As this was an offence against the school and came to involve numerous pupils, I spent a great deal of time investigating the matter. Stolen dinner tickets were being exchanged for meals in both of our dining rooms and during all sittings! It became clear that pupils had bought tickets from Gerald at a much reduced price. As the police were investigating the break-in to school, although knowing perfectly well who was responsible, the school did not take direct action against Gerald, having been advised by the local authority that to do so was to risk the legal situation of double jeopardy. That is punishing a culprit twice for the same thing.

While conferring with a constable on the matter of Gerald's break-in to the school, the boy came to my office to explain his version of the situation, to head off trouble! On observing the policeman he ran off and was not seen in school or at home for many weeks. He went to an east coast resort where he broke into numerous properties, coming to the notice of the police in that town.

At the start of the new school year, he returned to school and we were suspicious that he was the culprit who had broken into the building during the holiday. After a few weeks, he again broke into school overnight and the matter was placed in the hands of the police, with charges being brought. However, while awaiting his court appearance, he stayed out at night committing further burglaries and taking two other boys with him.

The school frequently worked with Gerald's parents, listening to their problems and offering advice, as well as trying to bring the boy to improve his behaviour at school, but neither the mother nor the father were able to control him. Clearly, the good relationship between a youngster and his parents, where adult supervision of the child is maintained through a developed mutual respect, had broken down – if it had ever been achieved in the first place. Gerald was clearly a youngster who was beyond the control of his parents, but left to run wild by those agencies in society which should have been taking positive steps to prevent him causing so much trouble for everyone, and working towards achieving his social adjustment.

The concept "being beyond the control of one's parents" needs to be reconsidered and strong meaningful procedures need to be put into place to deal with children so placed.

Another case involved Martin, who had also been transferred from another school at the request of his mother who complained about the disciplinary procedures at that school. It was clear from discussions with Martin's previous head-teacher that he had been a considerable problem. As in other cases the transfer brought a short improvement in behaviour but this did not last. Martin frequently truanted and when present caused problems for his teachers. During one period when he was absent from school, the parents of other children complained that he was bullying their youngsters, attempting to coerce them to truant. Martin's mother attended school for discussions and these matters were thought to have been resolved. But a few days later, the boy came to the school gate during school hours, not intending to attend lessons and stood smoking. The Senior Master went to the gate and attempted to reason with him, asking him to put the cigarette out. Martin's response was to swear at the teacher and run off.

A letter was sent home requesting that his parents bring him to school. There was no reply and consequently the School Educational Welfare Office was requested to call at the home. The response was that the parent would not come to school and nor would Martin. As the child was already a subject of a supervision order, the appropriate supervising officer was informed of the situation. Further letters were sent to the parents, but no reply was received. Eventually Martin's father came to see us and yet another fresh start attempted. However, after two weeks reasonable attendance the boy ran away from home, committing various delinquent acts.

Martin was eventually apprehended by the police, charged with his new offences, and returned home. The following week he came to school but stayed out of lessons, damaging door handles and light switches, having brought a screwdriver with him for this specific purpose. When tackled about his behaviour he ran out of school.

It seems so obvious from cases such as these that there are a significant number of young people who require placing in secure accommodation, first to prevent them interfering with the normal rights of the majority and, secondly, so that they can be placed in a face-to-face situation with properly trained and experienced adults for the purpose of diagnosing their problems and continuing their education.

The responses from the various agencies, answering my criticisms of the apparent failure of society to deal properly with such children, give some indication of why the juvenile discipline and training system fails.

The police stated "that the role of the police in society is to keep the peace and prevent and detect crime and that punishment and treatment of offenders does not come within our responsibilities". How true, but how restricting this is. Within the brief of crime prevention, there is the possibility of establishing Juvenile Liaison Schemes and I called their attention to those being operated by the Essex and Devon forces at the time.

Social services responded to my observations by pointing out that in their Social Enquiry report they had recommended that the boy needed to be placed in a controlling environment, and expected a Care Order to be made, going to the trouble of finding at a Community Home. But the juvenile court rejected this advice and returned the child to the Community.

The subsequent response to my correspondence from the Clerk to the Justices was both lengthy and informative, pointing out the restrictions which limited the powers of the magistrates and calling attention to the numerous newspaper articles complaining of these restrictions and giving juvenile courts greater powers.

The Children Act 1989, the Criminal Justice Act 1991 and subsequent amendments and additional statutory instruments were presumably Parliament's answer to such criticisms.

At the time of writing in 1977, the Clerk to the Justices explained the limited powers available to the Court, following the introduction of the Children and Young Persons Act of 1969.

Apart from dealing with comparatively trivial offenders by means of fines and discharges, the Court had available three viable alternatives: detention centre (maximum three months), committal to the care of the Local Authority and committal to the Crown Court with a view to borstal training.

Committal to a detention centre was further restricted by the requirement that there shall be a vacancy. The reality reported by the Clerk was that, in the case of a juvenile detention centre (that is taking youngsters up to and including the age of sixteen), this is a relatively rare occurrence. It somehow seems incredible that whether or not a disturbed youngster, in need of care and supervision, will be placed in secure accommodation depends upon the unlikely chance of there being a vacancy. This was at a time when the previously existing approved schools, which provided a reasonable answer to such a need, were being closed down and their buildings disposed of.

Committal to the care of the Local Authority involves transferring parental rights from the natural or legal parents to the Local Authority for all purposes, including the decision of where the juvenile shall live and how he is to be made to attend school.

This power of the Local Authority, invested in its social services department, is very significant. It is the social services who were given the responsibility of dealing with socially maladjusted and delinquent youngsters.

Committal to the Crown Court with a view to borstal training was a restrictive power designed to meet the needs of juveniles who required a long period of training with a view to their being rehabilitated, and was not available to the Magistrates.

A further power which was available to the Magistrates was an order requiring the youngster to be under the supervision of either the probation service or the Local Authority for up to three years.

Clearly, in the 1970s, there was a reluctance to grasp the nettle and to attempt, through a coming together of the agencies involved, to find a solution to the problem of the wayward youngster. This is understandable in so far as each felt that their authority was limited or annulled by counteractions of others. Meanwhile, the problem of the wrongdoer increased. Youngsters stealing cars and taking younger children with them became a commonplace occurrence. The danger to themselves and others is obvious, particularly where they or innocent bystanders are killed. Burglaries by the same young people go on while more are encouraged to follow them into a life of misconceived excitement and adventure. And as I write today our society is dogged by the fashion of carrying (and regrettably using) knives.

So how have we come to find ourselves in the in the position where there is a significant problem and no adequate means of dealing with it?

Early responses to delinquency

Society's attitude towards juvenile delinquency has changed. There has been a change in attitude towards the general discipline of the young, change to the way in which a young person is seen or not seen as responsible for its actions and changes in the use of various sanctions or treatments in an attempt to divert the young from pursuing antisocial behaviour.

In the early days of the Industrial Revolution, the practice of employing families, as opposed to individuals, the kinship system, meant training and discipline were family affairs. It was generally accepted that the father, as head of the family unit, was responsible for its discipline and children were regarded as his property. It was for him to hand out punishments according to his own philosophy in response to misbehaviour.

As far as the work place was concerned, the Factories Act of 1833 changed this situation. The working hours of children were limited and the responsibility for discipline of children at work was transferred from the father to the foreman. Consequently there began a necessary establishment of statutory requirements for dealing with children and eventually there developed schemes for compulsory schooling and for the protection of the young from abuse through the use of the workhouses and children's homes.

Previously, in 1785, the English Solicitor General found that nine out of ten offenders hanged were below the age of twenty-one. In the early nineteenth century, young offenders were detained in prisons. For instance, in 1817 the Second Report of the Commons Committee on the state of the Police in the Metropolis reported, for the previous year, that the Clerkenwell new prison held 399 delinquents aged between nine and nineteen. The attitude taken to such offenders was harsh. Boys imprisoned for petty theft were imprisoned for a short time and then flogged before being released. As they had no money, no means of feeding themselves, it is likely that they would re-offend simply to stay alive. Transportation to the New World colonies was a sanction of the time, but not for those under fourteen who were detained in the convict vessels (hulks) anchored in the Thames estuary. John Capper, in charge of the hulks in 1831 reported to the Select Committee on Secondary Punishments that the youngest prisoner was aged only nine and was incorrigible. Some were unable to dress themselves.

It is quite clear from such evidence that the problem was as much one of neglect and destitution as of crime, and this reminds us of the street children of the present found in countries such as Brazil and Bulgaria.

The Parkhurst Act of 1838 allowed the old military hospital on the Isle of Wight to be used as a prison for boys between ten and eighteen years of age. But in the mid-19th century the same laws and punishments applied to children as to adults, they could be imprisoned, flogged and hanged for the same offences.

The reformer, Mary Carpenter, complained about the use of leg irons, armed guards, whippings, and solitary confinement in a regime in which boys became so desperate that they would break out, plunder and even kill. They were certainly not reformed and Mary Carpenter called for the setting up of Reformatory Schools not only for young offenders but also for others of the "Perishing and Dangerous Classes"! As the working classes were seen as performing only manual work, the Industrial Schools were established to provide training and to develop skills for this purpose.

Reformatory Schools, with the purpose of reforming bad behaviour, were eventually established in 1854, being run by voluntary bodies and supervised by the Home Office.

The difference between the delinquent and the destitute was recognised. In the first case the youngster was seen as responsible for his conduct with a consequent need for reform in a Reform School, while in the second the problem was one of his status in society for which he could not be responsible and thus requiring a caring solution provided by the Industrial School. In reality there was little difference between the regimes of the two establishments and an emphasis on what the children had done, rather than on who they were, predominated.

The courts first began to deal with children as separate from adults in matters of property, making judgments in the interests of children when intervening between parents and children in property disputes. However, the law was not used to protect children from abuse or neglect until after the Prevention of Cruelty to Children Act of 1879.

Also, although in the early part of the nineteenth century, children under fourteen years of age were on the one hand presumed incapable of committing a crime, it was considered that, after the age of seven, if they did offend then they must be held responsible. Only the very young and the mad were supposed to be incapable of understanding right from wrong. The street children of the latter half of the nineteenth century, those claimed to be out of control by their parents and those known to associate with criminals and prostitutes, were sent to Industrial Schools to be reformed rather than punished. There was developing a two-fold recognition of children's problems, those seen as welfare problems and those seen as criminal.

The Children's Act of 1908

The 1908 Children's Act abolished imprisonment for children under fourteen years of age and established the first juvenile courts, but all children, whether seen as in need of help or as wrongdoers, were dealt with in the same way, under the same court orders and sent to the same children's homes. The question of whether to punish or treat remains unsolved today. Although it is clear that there are children who by reason of their circumstances are clearly in need of support, they may also have committed crimes for which punishment may be seen to be necessary. Where a child is abandoned, has run away from home or lives in a family situation which is quite unsuitable for the young and where no delinquency has occurred, the welfare solution does seem to be a proper one. But there is a further development of this line of thinking which claims that the cause of juvenile delinquency is to be found solely in poor social conditions and that the only necessary response is therefore a welfare one.

Depending upon the seriousness of the situation, the first juvenile courts could discharge a case, impose a fine, place the child on probation or remove it from its home to board in a reformatory school or industrial school.

The Children and Young Person Act 1933

The 1933 Act brought about the appointment of justices having a particular interest in children, furthering the distance between adult and juvenile courts. Reporting restrictions were also introduced and the justices were to have regard for the welfare of the child when making decisions. A statement which was to have a greater impact when reinforced in the Children's Act of 1989 and the cause of unhelpful developments arising from a confused understanding of what really is "the best interests of children".

Approved schools were introduced to replace reformatories and industrial schools, but were often housed in the same buildings. The schools could be run by local authorities or private persons and were subject to inspection by the Home Office.

They were boarding schools to which children could be sent by the courts for periods of up to three years and to which they could be recalled during a subsequent two year period: a system which, in my limited experience of it, had advantages and worked reasonably well. But this was not the view which came to be generally accepted!

The Criminal Justice Act of 1948

The Criminal Justice Act of 1948 introduced the idea of the short sharp shock for young offenders aged between fifteen and twenty-one for whom a long period of compulsory residential training was thought to be inappropriate, but who did not respond to fines and probation. Detention centres were established to house such offenders and their regime was to be strict, with an emphasis on physical activity, drill, physical training and manual labour.

The Act abolished the use of corporal punishment as an option available to the courts, and stated that it should not be used in borstals or detention centres. However, the punishment continued to be used in approved schools until the 1960s.

A third introduction made in 1948 was the Attendance Centre to which offenders aged between ten and twenty-one years could be sent for hourly or two hourly sessions for a total of 24 hours. The sanction operated during the young person's free time and activities included inspections for general tidiness, physical training and instruction in useful skills.

Other developments before the 1969 Act

Further measures designed to combat juvenile delinquency were introduced in the 1950s and '60s, before the significant changes brought by the Children and Young Person's Act of 1969.

The Children and Young Person's Act 1963 raised the age of criminal responsibility from eight to ten years and emphasised the need for providing help for families and youngsters where there were signs of developing delinquency.

Juvenile courts could make Fit Person Orders which transferred parental rights and responsibilities to a guardian, most frequently the local authority. The local authority would then place the child with foster parents, in a children's home, in a boarding school for the maladjusted or in an approved school.

Probation Orders, laying down conditions for the supervision of the delinquent for a period of up to three years, were introduced. The conditions included reporting to the probation office and being visited by a probation officer. The child was also expected to abide by any other conditions stipulated by the court, such as living in a particular place and undergoing psychiatric treatment.

A breach of a probation order could lead to further sentencing and the committing of a further offence while on probation could lead to two new sentences, one for the original crime and another for the further delinquent act.

Socialist thinking in the 1960s

Two White Papers outlined the thinking behind the Children and Young Persons Act of 1969. The first, of 1965, "The Child, Family and Young Offender" was the outcome of the recommendations of the Committee on Criminal Policy chaired by Lord Longford, and the second, "Children in Trouble" 1968, was intended to answer criticisms aimed at the 1965 recommendations.

Delinquency was seen as a normal part of growing up and criminal proceedings were thought to be inappropriate in most cases. It was claimed that the law as it stood dealt with offenders from the working classes, while middle class youngsters were dealt with outside the courts, either in school or by the psychiatric services: an interesting observation in the light of present experience where schools are shown to be unable to deal adequately with problem children. Delinquents were also seen to be in need of help and guidance, that is treatment, without the stigma of an appearance in court. The causes of delinquency were dogmatically accepted as child neglect and lack of proper training, and consequently capable of being identified and treated. It followed that punishment was not an appropriate course of action. This required the role of the juvenile court to change to one of seeking professional help for the treatment for the young offenders. In turn, therefore, the courts were seen as inappropriate places for this purpose and it was recommended that they should be replaced by "family courts". It was suggested that "family councils" be established in which the child, family and social workers came together to discuss the treatment of the offender. As evidence could be disputed by the different parties and agreement prevented, it was further suggested that there should be "family courts" to resolve these matters.

Parliamentary debate illustrated a division of opinion on who should have authority over a child's liberty. The political left was proposing that the social workers should be placed in a position of finding suitable treatment for the wrongdoer. The political right, the probation service and magistrates argued that it was undesirable for social workers, those outside the legal profession, to have authority over a child's future.

There is something in the notion of keeping the young out of criminal court proceedings, but the alternative requires a summary judgment from other professionals and in the present climate, in which people have been encouraged to turn to the law to solve their problems, with its reliance on legal proof and suing for damages, it is difficult to see how such a situation could be achieved.

The Children and Young Persons Act 1969

A main aim of the 1969 Act was to reduce the number of children being brought before juvenile courts and consequently the committing of an offence was not to be sufficient reason for bringing a child before the court. The intention was that referral should only become necessary when agreement as to an appropriate course of action could not be reached between the social workers, parents and child. Furthermore, authority was given to social workers to implement and vary court decisions.

A new concept, Intermediate Treatment, was introduced to provide places of temporary residence, attendance or participation for periods no longer than one month in each year. The thinking was that the scheme would introduce an offender to a new environment or new activity which had not previously been available to the youngster.

The false reasoning here is immediately clear. Although such action could be of value to genuinely deprived children from caring but underprivileged families who had aimlessly drifted into crime, it completely overlooks the reality of the situation. Too many delinquents have developed lifestyles far beyond this point. They come from families where hostility to authority is deep seated, where their parents are themselves delinquent or adopt casual and inconsistent attitudes towards reasonable behaviour. A failure to remove a delinquent from such an environment will prevent any adoption of new more acceptable patterns of behaviour, even if the child has the will to change.

A complete change of environment for a meaningful period of time is surely essential for any behaviour modification to be achieved.

Places to which children could previously be sent for such treatment, then approved schools, were merged with other residential homes and called community homes. In reality, many were closed and their buildings sold, the delinquent being returned home, or to another residence within the environment of home and school.

Court Orders committing youngsters to approved schools or into the care of a fit person were replaced by Care Orders in which parental rights were transferred to the local authority, namely to the social services department of the local authority.

Both during the drawing up of the Act and afterwards, serious disagreements between the political left and right hindered the establishment of a sound programme for the improved treatment of young delinquents, and a change in government in 1971, from Labour to Conservative, resulted in aspects of the Act not being implemented. Criminal proceedings against those under fourteen years of age were not stopped, the minimum age for borstal training was not raised from fifteen to seventeen, and detention and attendance centres were not phased out. Juvenile courts continued to operate as before. The number of custodial sentences rose during the 1970s but with the closure of the approved schools it became obvious that there was inadequate accommodation of the type which could provide the conditions required for the teaching of improved behaviour patterns.

There developed confusion about what should be done. Differences between the ideological approaches of the various agencies involved, the social services, the police, the magistrates, and between individuals within these bodies, resulted in little co-operation and as complaints relating to what appeared as a growing problem of antisocial juvenile behaviour within society increased, each blamed the other for any difficulties.

Ideology rather than reasoned thinking continues to prevent an objective assessment of the juvenile delinquency problem and the setting up of humane, yet efficient programmes for dealing with the youngsters who cause so much disruption in their environments. Evidence to the House of Commons Expenditure Committee given in the Eleventh Report 1975 (The Children and Young Person's Act 1969 Vols. I and II) illustrates this situation extremely well.

The National Council for Civil Liberties saw the causes of juvenile delinquency and consequently measures to combat it in the social and physical environment.

The Justices' Clerks Society said that the lack of distinction between the child in need of care and the child as an offender deprived the magistrates of the power to protect the public.

The British Association of Social Workers thought that the Act was a step in the right direction.

The Magistrates Association recognised the problems associated with crime control versus the care of the child and were particularly concerned about the undue problems caused by apparently hardened street-wise young criminals. And that was in 1975!

The subsequent White Paper published in May 1976, in attempting to please all sides, pleased none. The problem of identification of two types of offender, the majority for whom treatment according to the child's circumstances and needs was appropriate, and the hard core requiring a different approach, was not achieved. It seems doubtful that, indeed, such a division can ever be achieved: the real problem being that wrongdoing needs to be answered by a very clear disapproval and only afterwards followed by a search for reasons and remedies.

Juvenile court magistrates were given power to recommend what actions should be taken in a case but different views, different basic philosophies, between magistrates and social workers made this a meaningless exercise.

Detention centres continued to exist but due to ideological opposition on the part of some professionals involved in cases they were not properly used.

The Criminal Justice Act 1982

The White Paper "Young Offenders" 1980 proposals included the re-introduction of a number of detention centres with tough regimes on the one hand, and the need to reduce the number of juveniles held in custody by using community based schemes on the other. It was accepted that juvenile offenders who could be diverted from the criminal justice system at an early stage in their offending were less likely to re-offend than those who become involved in judicial proceedings.

Subsequently the Home Office encouraged the police to use cautioning methods, defining national standards for their application and accepted the use of multiple cautions in cases where such a procedure was thought to be appropriate.

The Act itself shortened the duration of the detention centre sentence from between three and six months to between three weeks and four months. Imprisonment for under twenty-ones was abolished and borstals were replaced by Young Custody Centres where offenders could be detained for between four months and one day and six months under Young Custody Orders. It was intended that such sentences should only be used if no other action was possible, but it transpired that magistrates used their powers to commit offenders to borstals rather than detention centres.

New requirements were attached to supervision orders.

Tim Newburn, quoting Gelsthorpe and Morris on page 138 of "Crime and Criminal Justice Policy", sees this legislation change from the treatment of the young person's needs, personal responsibility and oversight by social workers to decision making by the courts, with the child viewed as a juvenile criminal.

Subsequently, money was made available to support Intermediate Treatment programmes as alternative to custody and with recommendations that work with persistent offenders should be co-ordinated by inter-agency committees.

The Children Act 1989

In this Act, the Care Order, created in 1969, was abolished following criticism from magistrates that it failed to put children where they could be controlled. Yet statutory recognition was also given to the need to avoid prosecution.

The Act intended to put children's welfare first and protect them from harm, seeing the children's homes and families as the best place for them to grow up, linked with the attempt to minimise interference in family life. Local authorities were then expected to provide services for children in need, working together with them and their parents. It is perhaps this legislation which has led social services into the position where tragedy is allowed to happen, because they are possibly unsure of when to intrude into families when the children's best interests are not for them to be kept in obviously unsuitable environments.

The Criminal Justice Act 1991

The objectives of the 1989 Act were further developed in 1991. Juvenile Courts became Youth Courts and their jurisdiction extended to include seventeen-year-olds. But a prime factor was the reminder to those sentencing young people, of the intention advanced in the Children and Young Persons Act of 1933 that courts must have regard to the welfare of children and young people. Together with the check list of items intended to give further guidance with the interpretation of this sentiment, the legislation has reinforced and overdone the concept of children's rights.

The Act made available to magistrates new sentences: fines, community sentences and custody and introduced a new scheme for post custody supervision. The maximum duration of a sentence in a Young Offenders Institution was reduced to twelve months.

Chief probation officers and directors of social services were together made responsible for making local arrangements to provide services to the youth courts.

So, by 1991 intentions were clear: to keep children out of court proceedings as much as possible, to put the welfare of the child above all else but to have heed to the problems caused by the most hardened delinquents.

Criminal Justice and Public Order Act 1994

Following repeated public concern over the apparent ability of some young offenders to repeatedly create havoc in their communities, the concept of the Secure Training Order was introduced by Secretary of State, Mr Kenneth Clarke. These orders were first intended to apply to twelve- to fifteen-year-olds, but this was changed to those between twelve and fourteen, and also to those convicted of three offences for which imprisonment would have been appropriate and who had proved unwilling or unable to comply with supervision within the community.

Five new secure training units were built to house those committed, each unit holding forty young people: the maximum sentence to be two years, half of which should be served in custody and half in the community.

Such legislation has been criticised as being a return to an emphasis on punishment in dealing with juvenile delinquency, but there remains, among some of the executors of the legislation, motivation to avoid punishments. There remains confusion, and amidst the confusion, problems associated with the serious misbehaviour and delinquency of the young are not being solved.

The need to establish some principles

There is a need to re-consider what is or is not being done to remedy the problem of juvenile delinquency and to do this some primary principles need to be established. But there is nothing new in this! Indeed, Morris, Giller, Szwed and Geach attempted this very same exercise in their book "Justice for Children" published in 1980. At that time they were respectively lecturer and research assistant at the Institute of Criminology, University of Cambridge, barrister in the Middle Temple, London and research officer for a local authority social services department in North London. Their argument centred upon the notion of diversion, diverting the young from appearance in what were then the juvenile courts, because they saw reactions to delinquency doing harm rather than good. In particular, they claimed that the system generates a labelling process, so that offenders become labelled as criminals, go on to live up to their name and then become hardened in their delinquent ways. Consequently, they proposed that only the most serious juvenile crimes should be referred to the juvenile courts, other misbehaviour being dealt with informally and welfare matters being brought before a family court. However, although their conclusions provide an appropriate response to serious delinquency and welfare matters, they fail to provide meaningful solutions for less serious, but nevertheless significant, misbehaviours.

Furthermore, much of their thinking, which they apply to welfare problems, has subsequently been used in dealing with the lesser misbehaviours with the consequence that such wrongdoing is not treated as wrongdoing at all. This is a primary error because children, who are still developing their personal codes of behaviour, expect reward for good behaviour and punishment for bad.

In their discussion of diversion strategies, they oppose the need for removal of children from home, claiming that a child is best off with its parents except in exceptional circumstances. Yet, in any consideration of delinquent and other serious misbehaviours, it is quite clear that the child-family relationship is, to say the least, unsatisfactory.

There is also the question of who shall have authority over children, particularly where removal from home is involved, and with this the involvement of the law and lawyers. Too many street wise youngsters have learnt to use the law to the advantage of their misbehaviour. The defence lawyer's task is to show that the accused is not proved to be guilty, not to seek the truth, and this is not the way to help children and young people develop a sound sense of responsibility, because they too frequently get away with their wrongdoing, developing instead a contempt for authority. What is needed is a route which encourages owning up to the truth, the showing of remorse and a genuine effort on the part of the wrongdoer to get things right.

The discussion that follows therefore takes a somewhat different line from those given in "Justice for Children".

The delinquent and society

A first principle, whether it is considered that delinquency merits punishment or treatment, is to accept that steps must be taken to protect others from the offenders' dangerous, damaging and costly behaviour. The protection of the rights of the decent, socially well behaved majority must be a priority, even where this means that the basic freedom of the offender is restricted.

Juvenile delinquents, whether they become involved in assaults, vandalisms or burglary, disregard the right of others to live in a secure danger free environment. They do not respect others or their property. Consequently, this principle is, on first consideration, likely to be widely accepted. But as soon as it is realised that there is a need to be quite precise in defining when behaviour really does impinge upon the freedom of others, the acceptance is not so straightforward.

In "Justice for Children", page 38, the perception of behaviour is seen as a significant factor in dealing with wrong doing. The authors take the view that there are too little objective criteria on which to judge behaviour and that the decision-makers consequently use subjective criteria when making their judgements. As a result, judgments are made as good or bad not because they are objectively so, but because of the personal view taken by those making the assessments.

There is some truth in their claim that wrongdoers are, at least sometimes, judged not on their behaviour but by people's perception of them. While it may be true that those who appear well mannered and well turned out are perceived more favourably than ill mannered scruffs, irrespective of their wrongdoing, there surely is general agreement on what are the worst forms of behaviour.

The question is of course: how far can one rely on people's judgements when determining a child's future? I remember overhearing a heated argument in the staffroom of a comprehensive boy's school in the 1950s during which a boy's housemaster described the pupil as the laziest and least co-operative youngster he had ever come across. Another master was challenging a reference which the housemaster had written referring to the pupil in these terms and was very adamant in his view that the comments were unfair and untrue. How could two experienced, professional teachers hold such opposing views about the lad? The solution is easy to find. In the first instance, as well as being the pupil's housemaster, the teacher who made the judgement was also the boy's games master, and the boy detested games, thus behaving accordingly. The other master echoed the views of the academic staff, in whose classes the boy was most co-operative, industrious, and successful!

But to suggest that in general children's behaviour is judged as maladjusted, delinquent or wrong, simply in terms of adults' personal values and beliefs, is not helpful. There are clear cut examples of behaviour which in a civilised society are wrong. Unfortunately, there are those who believe in the ill-founded notion that each individual should have the right to find happiness without reference to anyone else, apparently, even where the achieving of that happiness interferes with the freedom of others. They do not seem to realise that practising such a philosophy must lead to anarchy.

To suggest that professionals, such as teachers, social workers and the police do not objectively know what is or is not acceptable behaviour is to claim that proper behaviour can not be defined, a fashion from which society needs to rid itself. Examples of unacceptable behaviour are well understood and accepted: for instance, it is wrong to break into other people's houses; to break into, drive away and smash cars; and to knock someone to the ground and kick them senseless – among many other things!

What is more difficult to decide is the degree of wrongness attached to the behaviour and to take different appropriate actions to deal with the different wrong doings. There are, however, two concepts which help with this.

There is the concept of frequency of action. It can be determined whether the offence is a first, having the chance of being a one and only misdemeanour, or whether it is one of an established pattern.

There is also the concept of seriousness of action. It can be determined how serious the offence is in terms of its consequences, the cost of damage done, the value of property stolen and the gravity of injuries to people attacked.

Finally, under this heading is the necessary acceptance of the concept that the protection of the majority requires that action be taken to show society's disapproval of wrong behaviour and that this may well include curtailing the freedom of the wrongdoer.

The juvenile delinquent and the school

The principle arising from the last statement above is therefore that those who offend should not be allowed to go unpunished because to allow them to do so is to promote a feeling of injustice among the majority.

Problems for the school resulting from the unchecked behaviour of delinquent pupils arise where the behaviour adversely influences other pupils. Many young people by reason of their age and development are examples of immature personalities, their personal codes of behaviour are not fully developed and they are consequently easily led into antisocial acts. The least mature are at greatest risk.

The presence of a known delinquent in a class depresses the positive ethos of the class: just as the maladjusted pupil disrupts the learning discipline, so does the delinquent, but not always through direct classroom misbehaviour.

Even one serious and apparently unchecked delinquent pupil in a school can cause other pupils to display restless behaviour. They know the culprit has done wrong and they expect a reaction on the part of the school which shows a clear disapproval of the wrongdoing. Where an obvious delinquent appears to remain unpunished, their own understanding of justice is damaged. It is the young in particular who have a strong sense of justice and where justice is not seen to be done they react unfavourably. As they are learning the necessary rules and etiquettes of social living, they become confused and fail to adopt appropriate behaviour strategies. That is, they remain or become, to various degrees, antisocial themselves.

Where there is more than one delinquent pupil the problem increases, not least because the troublesome come together to form influential gangs, a feature recognised in the tragic circumstances which culminated in the death of the headmaster, Mr Laurence. The gangs are influential in the neighbourhood outside school and bring their disruption onto school premises, frequently those of neighbouring schools where they have never been pupils themselves but where they see the challenge of rival groups. For some youngsters, individual delinquents become their heroes and gangs their model way of life.

Children beyond the control of their parents

The principle here is that a child who is out of the control of its parents needs to be placed under another's control for both the good of society and itself.

Apart from the obvious display of delinquent behaviour, involving such acts as assault, burglary and vandalism, there is other behaviour which results in sufficiently serious problems, creating dangers to the public and the child, that it merits society's intervention.

This behaviour results from the youngster being out of the control of its parents. It may be that the parents do not exert control because they cannot be bothered, do not know how to, or because they are hostile to any form of authority, either seeing nothing wrong with their child's behaviour or even encouraging it. These parents do not co-operate with the school in its attempts to divert youngsters from trouble. Some even protect their child from the positive influence of school discipline by opposing its recommendations and even go so far as to transfer their child to another school where they hope there will be less hassle.

The youngster may stay away from home, living on the streets or with others in a position which is likely to place the child in danger of further corruption. The young person is in need of care and protection. It is likely that such a youngster refuses to attend day school, even when escorted from home and supervised when there. Complete supervision in the normal school is neither possible nor desirable.

For such cases there must surely be a compulsory provision which takes the youngster out of its neighbourhood and places it under secure supervision somewhere else. There also needs to be different residential supervision for those who present different behaviour problems aimed in particular at preventing the spread of criminal know-how from the established sophisticated delinquent to the less initiated.

Objections to this principle are found in the views of Morris *et al*, "Justice for Children" page 38, where they claim the concepts of 'being beyond control' or exposed to 'moral danger' are not objectively defined: that whether or not a child's development is being prevented, the child neglected or is beyond parental control is objectively clear. They point out that different interpretations can arise from parents' different views on child rearing practices and that these depend upon ideologies concerning the roles of children, men, women and families in society.

They also claim, (p127), that middle class practices are judged as good while working class practices are seen as bad: another fashion of our times and an absurdity which implies that there are no general standards of behaviour applicable to all, an insult to caring, well-ordered working class families.

What this type of reasoning implies is that society cannot know when a child is beyond control or in danger, but common sense dictates that such conditions are recognisable and definable. For instance, I was recently told of a child who refused to live at home. Investigation demonstrated that the parents objected to their daughter staying out during the hours of darkness and late into the night. The child's reaction was to leave the family home and to take up residence with a girl friend.

Neither attended school regularly and subsequently both girls took themselves off to another district to live with the friend's sister. There they came into contact with prostitutes.

The girls referred to were aged fourteen when these events took place and, although the parents wanted help to control their daughters, the authorities seemed to take the view that there was nothing they could do. Such notions as the girls' own views being important and their wishes being paramount seemed to settle the issue. Yet it is quite clear to those with relatively simple views of life that the girls were both out of control of their parents and in moral danger. The tragedy is that progressive thinking, involving a political correctness, prevents otherwise supportive agencies from doing anything about the situation.

This fashion is further demonstrated in the judgment of the court that it is not important for a parent to know that its child is seeking the use of contraceptives, is pregnant or may even be seeking an abortion.

These circumstances have arisen from the acceptance of thinking such as that expressed by Morris and her colleagues which, in turn, has become enshrined in the Welfare Principle of the 1989 Act.

Morris states on page 128: "Every child must have the basic right of remaining in his own family unless there are compelling reasons which justify his removal".

The reasoning continues. This basic right is only to be overridden if there is proof of the child coming to harm, or breakdown of child-parent relationships. Even with proof, Morris is opposed to removal from home.

A badly misbehaved child can create havoc in its home, in its school and in its home environment and still claim its basic right to live at home where it can continue with its antisocial behaviour. The child's basic right is given priority over almost everything else. Only in cases of serious criminal behaviour does this seem to be superseded by other priorities and even then there is a shortage of appropriate residential places for a child to go.

Yet is it possible to define when a child is beyond the control of its parents and when it is in moral danger. The real difficulty arises when the depth of the problem is considered. Leaving home on one occasion, following a heated argument, may demonstrate a temporary state of defiance towards one's parents and be a temporary example of being out of their control but it is not sufficient evidence to prove a long term problem. On the other hand, it could be just as dangerous to the child: it need take only one opportunity for a child to meet up with paedophiles and procurers of prostitutes and to come into immediate danger.

The concepts of frequency of action and seriousness of action help to answer these problems. Whether or not the child frequently runs off after arguments, frequently defies its parents' reasonable requests and instructions, and where it runs away to, are significant factors in trying to determine 'beyond control' and 'in moral danger'.

Action may be required in the crisis situation and there is legal provision for this. Longer term provision is required where the behaviour is more serious and or more frequent. There is provision for this to happen, but there is a reluctance to act because of the difficulties arising when applying the Welfare Principle.

It is not sufficient that the Residence Order provides a simple caring situation. Where the child has run away, the caring situation must be a secure one and one in which assessment, diagnosis and remedial strategies can be carried out.

School authority

The principle that schools be given authority to discipline delinquent pupils whose behaviour impinges upon the school and to be given responsibility for transferring the pupil to a special day or residential school.

Where delinquent pupils have an adverse effect on other pupils, schools need the authority to take some action, even if the ultimate decisions relating to the young person's future have to be taken by the court, using accepted legal processes. If a school is to be seen to have any influence over its pupils this is an essential element of its disciplinary processes. At present, the use of exclusions and expulsions is the only sanction available but these, at best, merely transfer the problem to a special day unit.

A facility which would help schools is an ability to transfer delinquent pupils to a special school while calling for psychological and social reports to be prepared. It is important that the parents and the child should understand the reasons for this action and see it as a means of upholding discipline but also as a course of action designed to help the youngster to fit into normal society. Such action could be a means of diverting young people away from criminal proceedings and of avoiding the stigma (or in some cases the prestige) with which court proceedings are associated.

Where a child is in conflict with its parents, or beyond their control, the placement should be residential.

Clearly, subsequently there needs to be a body of professional people, including representatives of the school who then decide on further action, including a programme of education and treatment, to effect an improvement. Such measures require the provision of suitable daytime and residential accommodation, facilities which do not exist.

Where the child is the subject of a court appearance, there may be conflict between school and court discipline, the school being expected to do nothing while awaiting the court's judgment. As a court appearance can be a lengthy time after any crime is committed, the school appears to be doing nothing and its inaction encourages others to accept the wrongdoing as unpunishable. There develops a social climate in which the badly behaved can claim they can do as they like and the school can do nothing to stop them. A facility such as that above would overcome this difficulty.

Schools and potential delinquents

The principle that schools should not only be given the authority to take action where maladjustment, potential delinquency or delinquency is evident but that they should also be given the resources (professionally trained people, time, space and equipment) to diagnose and treat problems where it is possible for them to do so.

Ideally schools should be in a position to identify potential delinquents and be able to do something to stop the further development of the problem: yet a combination of circumstances makes this difficult. As seen already, a child's parents may refuse to co-operate with the school. The child may frequently transfer from one school to another and procedures initiated in one place can be lost, overlooked, or deliberately ignored. There is a conflict of interests in this: some people will see a fresh start in a new school requiring a clean slate and deliberately refuse to consider previous events. Transfer from one school to another without more positive steps first being taken to diagnose the causes of and find solutions to the behaviour problem is not a sensible solution. It does not work and merely puts off the day of reckoning.

In addition, but by no means least in importance, is the lack of resources available to a school. With its main purpose of teaching skills and knowledge, schools have not been provided with the resources to diagnose and treat the problems of the maladjusted pupil, whether the maladjustment is demonstrated in relatively minor antisocial behaviour, potentially delinquent behaviour or full-blown delinquency. Yet, if only given the authority and the staffing, schools are ideally placed to do this work.

Parent-child relationships

There is a principle that it is not necessarily in the best interests of a child for it to be kept in the family home when it has reached a crisis situation, such as committing serious delinquency or being out of control, but rather that a crisis should provoke a removal of the child from the home and its environment for assessment, diagnosis and treatment.

This is clearly the opposite of the currently held views which have already been discussed above.

Relationships between a child and its parents are complex, having developed over many years through the experiences of constant interaction with family members. Where the youngster has reached the stage of being beyond control, these family interrelationships have broken down to such an extent that they will not be rectified in a short time. Things have reached crisis point and a crisis reaction is required. Time is needed to analyse what has gone wrong, what is wrong and to devise strategies which will hopefully build new relationships. At such a point in the child's development a removal from the crisis situation, the home and its environment, helps the individual, its parents and society. Society sees something being done. The individual recognises that its faulty behaviour will not be tolerated but also learns that he or she is to be helped to recognise the problems and to put them right.

The need for an immediate response

This involves the principle that action is taken immediately following antisocial behaviour for it to be meaningful and effective.

In our dealings with juvenile offenders, in spite of many good intentions, society fails to protect its victims, help the parents or treat the child.

When a youngster is clearly seen to commit an offence, an offence clearly recognised as such by the youngster as well as others, and there is delay before he or she is reprimanded, the impression is that no one cares and that the culprit has got away with it. The delinquent's antisocial behaviour is reinforced. An immediate response is essential.

Appropriate responses

The principle here is that responses to antisocial behaviour should be appropriate. For first time or trivial offences, the sanctions should be minimal but for serious offences they should be markedly more restrictive. The concepts of seriousness and frequency of action need to be developed and applied.

This is in keeping with the recommendations in "Justice for Children". Because different courts have been shown to use different sanctions for the same offences and because youngsters feel that it is not fair when they see others who have committed similar offences to their own being subjected to more or less severe sanctions than themselves, Morris suggests the principle of proportionality of sanctions, that is sanctions for juvenile offenders should be proportionate to the seriousness of the offence(s) and not be linked to the person committing the offence.

One aspect of the failure of society to combat juvenile delinquency is the inappropriate action which is taken against potential delinquents or where delinquency is trivial. For instance, shopkeepers may not take appropriate action against shoplifters, possibly because they see prosecution as cumbersome and more trouble than it is worth, and because there is no alternative.

I am reminded of the occasion when I was in charge of a group of difficult children at a field study centre. As a part of their course they were trusted to go out into the local areas to buy cards and gifts for parents and friends at home. Unfortunately they became involved in taking what they wanted without paying for it and the local constable was called by the shopkeeper. He in turn eventually called for me. He explained that he could see no point in charging the youngsters, by the time they came to court they would have forgotten what the fuss was about and the offence would only result in a discharge in any case. Such action, he claimed, would merely reinforce the youngster's view that they could do as they liked and get away with it. "I would have taken 'em to the station," he said, "and given 'em a good 'iding, but they won't let me do that today. But you can. So I hand the matter over to you to deal with."

Action against repeating offenders has frequently been shown to be insufficiently meaningful. No matter from which theoretical standpoint the question is approached, seeking punishment treatment or care, the public is not protected and the young person not deflected from the course of antisocial behaviour.

After repeated delinquency, while awaiting another court appearance and judgment, insufficient action is taken to ensure that a youngster does not get into further trouble.

Loss of respect for authority

Another matter which needs attention is the loss of respect on the part of the delinquent for those in positions of authority, not only parents but also schools, welfare agencies and the courts. If there is only contempt shown for these agencies, their attempts to improve the young person's place in society cannot succeed.

The law should be used sparingly but when it is used be used with all seriousness and solemnity, and its sanctions should be emphatic and meaningful. For this to occur there needs to be clarification of and a change to the application of the Child Welfare Principle.

Belief, ideology and dogma

There are a number of factors involved in the study of and consequent legislation for delinquency which arise as much from individually held beliefs as from anything else. For instance, are the causes of delinquency found solely in the social and physical environment? Surely not. The individual mental state of the offender reacts with the environmental circumstances at the moment to produce the delinquent behaviour. Human beings have different natures, personalities or temperaments which are to a large extent dependent upon inherited features, the nervous system, the brain and the genes.

Some may well be disposed to mental break down more than others and are consequently more likely to show disturbed behaviour or maladjustment. There are those who keep doing wrong although they know what they do is wrong and that they will be caught and punished as a result.

Another factor which causes problems when trying to decide how to react towards juvenile offending is that of the criminal age of responsibility. The question is asked: when does a child become responsible for its actions? However, a more useful approach would be to ask: if the child is not responsible, then who is? Someone has to be. Society cannot permit offenders to run wild.

The fashionable attitude of the moment is to talk of children's rights and to emphasise the necessity of listening to a child's opinions and taking notice of them. This is now enshrined in law as the Welfare Principle, the Children's Act 1989 but it is enshrined in confused thinking about what constitutes a child's welfare and what constitutes the "best interests of the child". To allow the young to have their own way, creating havoc and coming into danger is not in their best interests. The law, or those who interpret it, emphasise keeping the child in its home, in its neighbourhood, when it is clear that it should be in secure and supportive accommodation elsewhere.

Who shall have authority over a child's freedom?

Under normal circumstances a child's freedom is regulated first by its parents but also by members of the extended family, and, from the day that the child is first put into the care of another, by carers and teachers. If all goes well, there is a gradual process by which the child takes on more and more responsibility for itself and so develops greater independence in its decision making, that is greater freedom to run its own affairs.

In the discussion here, however, the arguments are not to do with a normal, or what is seen as a successful, course of development but, instead, a situation in which the process of growing up has gone wrong, where the child presents behaviour problems and delinquency.

Morris *et al*, in chapter four, page 49 onwards, first point to the continued failure of our society to solve these problems and then quite rightly claims that conflict between ideologies has resulted in confusion, blocking the making of progress. They add to this their claim that little is known about the causes of criminal behaviour and that treatment does not work, going as far as to say that the treatment may even adversely effect children.

Consequently, Morris and her colleagues conclude that change is necessary in the way we deal with delinquents and that a large part of this change should be a policy of diversion, that is diverting youngsters away from courts.

It is plainly obvious that society has allowed certain youngsters to develop contempt for the most serious authority, the law. Therefore they should perhaps be diverted from it. But of course there are various elements of the law with which delinquents may come into contact. There are the police, the courts, and the processes of law.

Once children with behaviour problems see that their wrongdoing has to be proved and that a good lawyer can show in a court that there is insufficient proof for a conviction, the young learn that they can get away with their antisocial behaviour although they, their peers and some adults know that they have done wrong. This breeds contempt for the law. So I am referring not only to the appearance in court but also to the legal processes which are then precipitated.

What is wanted from our wrongdoers is the owning up to mistakes made, remorse shown for hurt caused, effort made to make amends, and effort shown to improve subsequent behaviour so that it reaches acceptable standards.

Morris *et al* continue (p53) to show that few can claim that they have never committed a crime but that most have been dealt with informally by neighbours, parents, schools and employers, implying that there are many ways in which society shows disapproval and that pursuance through a court system is not always essential or the best route to follow.

The writers claim (p54) that diversion removes the stigma and negative aspects of appearance in court. Surely there is however evidence that on the part of some at least that appearance in court is seen as a prestigious qualification or treated with contempt. But prior to the reaching of this state in their lives the process of legal intervention may create this state of affairs.

The youngster sees itself as delinquent, therefore acts as a delinquent and is seen by others as always delinquent.

So far so good! But society has encouraged people to use the law. We are fast becoming a society which is ready to sue anybody who seems to fail or cross us. Those who might wish to operate some informal approach to misbehaviour cannot do so because they are repeatedly shown to have no authority by the emphatic application of the law. For instance, it would appear that it is easier for a responsible, caring adult to be charged with assault than for a delinquent's behaviour to be contained. Teachers in particular have been placed in a position where they are frightened to discipline antisocial pupils. They have had their traditional sanctions taken away, in particular corporal punishment, a sanction which is immediate, very indicative of disapproval and yet quickly enabling forgiveness. Now a mere tap can be interpreted as an assault.

There is the reluctance to apply the law to youngsters lest they become labelled delinquent and subsequently find their behaviour more difficult to change, but also a failure to recognise that some authority over those who fail to show socially acceptable behaviour is essential. It is not sufficient to suggest informal strategies for dealing with the wrongdoers unless those responsible for operating the informal strategies are given authority to back up their responsibilities.

One relatively recent innovation is the juvenile bureau, derived from schemes pioneered in Canada and the USA in which potential delinquents and those in which the delinquency is not serious are dealt with by an especially established bureau.

In Scotland the responsibility for diversion from court has been vested in the reporter who attempts to distinguish between the "normal delinquent" and "problematic delinquent", between the "normal runaway" and the "problematic runaway". But why set up these special bodies, who will not know the child and its circumstances, when there exists an already well established system in which a major task is to know the children, the schools?

Morris et al (p56) claim that the juvenile bureaux system has resulted in greater social control. So the argument has developed from diversion away from the court to diversion from social control but, where there is no self control, there must be social control.

It is the job of the police to detect crime and apprehend the offenders, and those whose misbehaviour takes place outside the home and school will inevitably come into contact with them. This is more so today than in earlier decades because responsible adults who would have played their part in the disciplining of the young are now prevented from doing so for fear that their actions could put them in the wrong.

Morris (p56) however points out the reaction of the police to offenders can depend on the seriousness of the offence but also the age, sex, turn out, family background of the child and on the street this becomes an emphasis on attitude and appearance because they have no other criteria available.

Given that the most serious offences must be brought before a court of law, the course of police action in these cases is clear. But what should happen where lesser offences have been committed, if we are seriously to attempt to divert youngsters from the court and the law?

The police already have the authority to visit the home, make judgments, to take no further action or to caution the offender. But their knowledge of the offender will be superficial. So who outside the home will know the child? Surely the answer is plain: it is the child's school. It is in school where the youngster is known by several or more adults and it is there where examples of the child's general behaviour will be recorded. This knowledge will not be superficial but be based upon a period, often lengthy, of contact with the child and its family. There is a very good chance that the school will know if the offence is out of character, whether or not the child has been led by others or is an instigator, whether or not there are problems at home, and the nature of such problems. It will certainly know the views and reactions of the offenders peer group and stands a far better chance of finding out the truth of a matter than any court. Schools are very well placed to deal with problems referred to it as well as those it comes across in the course of its traditional duties but they require both authority to act, vested in the head-teacher, and the resources to carry out the responsibilities.

It must be remembered that some parents are unco-operative, even hostile, and that the only course of action is for them to be brought to face authority. It may well be easier for them to do this in a school situation, where there has hopefully been a building of relationships between home and school over a number of years, but the head-teacher still needs the authority to require parents to come into school in cases where they are reluctant to do so, a situation recognised in the Education White Paper of late 2005.

If schools are given the authority to become a major agent for the diversion of the young from the court and its legal procedures a number of areas of responsibility need to be defined.

Firstly there are the geographical areas in which it is expected that schools will have jurisdiction: on school premises, including out of normal school hours, on the route to and from school, and in the environment of the school and home.

Secondly there are types of misbehaviour, with degrees of seriousness, to define.

Thirdly it is necessary to define a range of reactions which the school can employ, from the traditional setting of extra work and detentions, through procedures for making amends for wrongdoing and attendance at special schools, to referral to court if all else has failed.

The development of such a scheme would place the major responsibility for counteracting misbehaviour among the young where it should be: with the extensive agency established to educate the young, the education system, the schools.

7. More recent thinking on the discipline of young people

For many years there has been a reluctance to face the problem of the poor behaviour of young people in schools, colleges and neighbourhoods. Although in 1945 discipline of young people was not seen as a great problem, there can be no doubt that it has become one. The Government, in 2005/6 was brought to recognise this by the actions of school teacher trade unions and public opinion, and has responded in the White Papers "14-19 Education and Skills" and "High Standards, Better Schools for All". There is the clear statement "that there must be zero tolerance of both serious and lower level discipline and behaviour issues." *(Higher Standards, Better Schools For All 7.5)*

So what is being done?

On the question of truancy

One aspect of the indiscipline-delinquency problem among young people is truancy, unauthorised absence from school, and the government has spent a considerable amount of money advancing schemes to tackle this matter.

The White Paper "14-19 Education and Skills" points to the coincidence of truancy and delinquency, suggesting that if you cure the truancy problem then you reduce delinquency; but there is a danger of over simplifying this relationship. Obviously, if a young person is confined to classes in school, he or she is not able to commit delinquent acts outside school during school hours, and incidents of bad behaviour outside school, among those of school age, are known to increase during school holidays.

Truancy however is not the cause of the delinquent behaviour which, demonstrated in acts of vandalism, bullying and disruption in school, is still in evidence when the young person is in attendance – to the cost of the school and the rest of the pupils in it.

On the question of failure in school

The White Paper *(9.17)* recognises many factors which coincide with a young person's failure in school. But they are not the causes of the failure. There is a complex of interacting factors at work and a reluctance to see that there might be an underlying problem other than poor social conditions. It is far too easy to see low family income as the cause of many of the problems. It is not. Many families, during the last 100-150 years, have been financially poor, living in overcrowded (very often squalid) conditions due to the circumstances into which they have been born. Many have not been antisocial, delinquent or neighbourhood trouble makers. Helping these families to overcome their disadvantages is the route to the social justice which the White Paper so rightly seeks to achieve but curing the problems of vandalism, delinquent behaviour, opting out of education and so on is a different question.

Financial assistance

Financial assistance *(9.16)* is essential to help those wanting to improve their learning, who are well motivated and behave in a proper fashion, but come from families where there is genuine hardship. Equally, such assistance should not be allowed to take on the characteristics of a bribe to encourage the poorly motivated troublemaker to make a nominal appearance in education institutions. There must be real evidence of full-time effort and commitment being applied to the chosen course and of appropriate personal behaviour. Failure to comply with such simple straightforward conditions must result in the withdrawal of the financial assistance. If this is not done, social justice is undermined. If it is seen that anyone, no matter how antisocial, can have free handouts, this will be seen as grossly unfair by those who conform and this in turn undermines the social climate of decency that one is trying to encourage.

Personal support

The personal support suggested *(9.17)* is essential for those with serious personal problems: learning difficulties, antisocial behaviour and delinquency. Where the problem is one of failure to learn and where antisocial behaviour and delinquency are not serious obstacles to learning, this is a matter for the educational institutions. Personal, individual, support will still be necessary but this is expensive to provide. Where antisocial behaviour and delinquency impinge upon the good order of the educational institution, the individuals concerned cannot be helped in those places and should attend elsewhere. As is previously explained, allowing seriously delinquent and antisocial young people to remain in normal education seriously disrupts the freedom to learn of the vast majority and prevents this majority from going about their lives in a peaceful secure environment. The good ethos of the institution is destroyed. This is not social justice.

This problem is now generally understood and accepted, with the sanctions of exclusion and permanent exclusion being employed. It is the intention to extend the use of parenting orders in an attempt to make parents take reasonable responsibility for their children's unsatisfactory behaviour in school and to supervise their children doing school work during the first five days of an exclusion with the imposition of fines on parents if their excluded children are found out in public during school hours. Similar sanctions against parents have been imposed in cases where their children are persistently found truanting from school.

Although such actions urge conscientious parents and those able to carry out their parenting responsibilities to take action, they are of no value in tackling the young people who are out of the control of their parents or where the parents have abdicated their responsibilities and show no sign of accepting them. This is why the government truancy campaigns which cost so much money fail to bring the desired improvements. It is in these cases where there is likely to be constant bad behaviour and delinquency of the kind previously outlined. For young people coming into these categories a residential school place is essential, where security and education go hand in hand.

Again, although government expects head-teachers to make off-site provision available for young people excluded for more than five days and the local authority to provide places for permanently excluded youngsters, the need for more and appropriate residential placements is not considered.

The Government Entry into Employment Programme

The Entry to Employment programme *(9.19)* needs to be seen as helping those who genuinely deserve helping and not as help for the delinquent or disruptive student when this support is denied to those who work hard and behave properly. Such a condition does not detract from the notion that the delinquent and antisocial need help: the assistance needs to be seen to be given in exchange for their expected improved standards. It must be seen that they are expected to, and do, conform to usual and acceptable standards of behaviour, that they are willing to attempt improvement. Failure to do so undermines the very social justice which is being sought after.

Behaviour in schools

The Government now accepts that unacceptable behaviour in schools has become a significant problem. It has become more disruptive. Learning requires a calm co-operative ethos in which to thrive. The disruptive individual influences the behaviour of the group in which he/she is placed, he/she may command the attention of individuals within the peer group, and may gain the admiration of individuals within the peer group. The group may adopt the behaviour patterns of the disruptive. This influence of the disruptive on others will depend upon: the strength of the personality of the disruptive youngster; the degree to which the group ethos can convince the majority that the behaviour of the disruptive is unreasonable and unacceptable; and the number of disruptive people within the group. The proportion of disruptive young people within a class, school or college is a significant factor in the quality of the educational provision which an institution is able to provide. There is a level at which the disruptive element becomes dominant.

Disruptive behaviour and social background

The incidence of disruptive young people is seen to coincide with certain social conditions, in particular with growing up in dysfunctional families; but not all disruptive individuals *do* grow up in obviously dysfunctional families and/or poor social conditions; not all of those who grow up in dysfunctional families *are* disruptive. There must be personal factors involved. That is, factors particular to the individual person, factors having their origins within the nature of the individual; for instance, a tendency to dominate others, to disregard the existence of others as individuals different from oneself, and perhaps a susceptibility to drug/alcohol addiction. The part played by factors peculiar to the individual can easily be, and often are, under estimated and it is folly to disregard this truth. Such people will find it difficult if not impossible to improve their situations via *classroom instruction*. They need individual specialist help. Where the disruption is shown to result from environmental factors such as inadequate parenting, behaviour therapy (as opposed to medical help) may improve the situation; but they will require *individual* supervision and training from an educator. They should not be the responsibility of the classroom teacher who is concerned primarily with teaching knowledge and skills to those who present normal behaviour.

Proposed provision for individuals with behaviour and learning problems

A large part of the White Paper 14 – 19 Education and Skills was concerned with re-engaging the disaffected in education through vocational courses. Chapter 6.38 and the Executive Summary note 17 sections 2, 3 and 4 recognise young people "who face serious personal problems" and the solution advanced is to offer *"significant work-based learning, probably amounting to two days each week; leading towards a level 1 Diploma; and on to a range of further options including Apprenticeship"* : but this will not eliminate the problems presented by disaffected possibly delinquent youngsters, they will continue to go their own way – although it is a significant step in the right direction for the non-academically motivated and well behaved young person.

In Chapter 9 note 17 it is said "we will make sure that young people at risk receive effective targeted support to help them to overcome barriers to learning. The Connexions service has had some success in beginning to reduce the size of the NEET group."

A code of conduct for pupils and students

We have reached a position where the normal reasonable authority of the educator needs to be re-established, and the White Paper accepts this. A code of expected behaviour is suggested and this is satisfactory in so far as it recognises a part of the problem but its coverage is not sufficiently extensive.

With the decline of traditional values and the growth of multiculturalism, we need to have agreed a multicultural code of behaviour for young people in schools and colleges. The code needs to be mutually agreed, nationally recognised, multicultural, and be backed by legally defined sanctions. The reasonable everyday application of these sanctions needs to be generally unchallengeable. In this way authority will be given back to those in charge of pupils and students.

Another reason for the redefining of acceptable standards is that Society's expectation of young people's behaviour has changed, encouraging unconformity and challenge to tradition. This has led people to question why they should follow rules with which they do not agree. When challenged, *some* can see reason but *others* cannot. Young people are inexperienced, they are learning how to react to circumstances and require firm guidance. They need to have boundaries and expectations defined, and need to have these boundaries and expectations upheld.

Expectations also change from one institution to another: consequently there is a need to define and agree universally acceptable expectations which safeguard the freedom of the individual while not disrupting the freedom of others. Some of the areas where expectations need to be clarified are: dress, behaviour towards staff, and behaviour towards each other. There are unacceptable actions which must be stated.

Areas in which the behaviour of students is the concern of educational institutions

There are three areas in which the behaviour of young people is of concern to educational institutions: in the classroom during class time; about the school before and between lessons, in toilets, in the corridors and within the grounds; and in the neighbourhood when coming to and going away from school. Any code of behaviour needs to define standards for each of these areas.

For instance, in the classroom situation: pupils should attend all lessons unless specifically excused from doing so. They should arrive on time; should not enter any classroom without the permission of the member of staff in charge; and wait quietly and in an orderly fashion by the door. An element of "lining up" may be essential in a large and busy establishment as corridors should not be obstructed. On entering the room they should go to their places quietly and without causing aggravation.

When in class they should pay attention to the member of staff, expecting to listen to descriptions, explanations and instructions, carry out instructions, and expect to carry out the tasks which they are given to the best of their ability. When needing to attract the attention of the member of staff when in a large group, that is in a normal class size group of say 20 to 30 young people, they should expect to raise a hand and not their voice.

When homework is set this should be completed on time. They should bring those items of equipment reasonably expected to be supplied by them for the appropriate lesson: for instance, a pen, the usual textbooks and notebooks, and PE and games clothing.

Failure to comply with expectations

Lapses in good order will occur and young people must be expected to recognise their minor misbehaviour and apologise for their indiscretion. Children in particular, but young people too, need to be constantly reminded of the need to comply with simple rules in order for group activities to continue in an orderly fashion. Lapses will inevitably occur and need to be corrected without over reacting, the expectation being that an apology followed by the correct behaviour will be forthcoming. Some will repeatedly fail and will need constant correction but so long as apologies and correct behaviour follow all is well. Some will deliberately, but not aggressively and disruptively, challenge the rules and there needs to be accepted sanctions which the teacher/lecturer can apply in these circumstances. Unfortunately, some come with no intention of complying with the rules and instead disrupt the good order of others. These must be removed from the normal classroom situation.

Movement about the school or college premises

In a school or college there is regularly movement of large groups of young people from one part of the building to another. Outside the classroom there is no single member of staff in charge of a known group of young people, classroom restrictions do not apply and supervision is loose. Under these circumstances young people are more likely to become unruly, to disregard the rules of reasonable behaviour and to challenge authority. Those with a mind to congregate and adopt a mob culture can easily do so.

This problem, apparent in all schools, has become greater with the increase in the size of educational establishments. More disruptive youngsters are present. More congregate together and encourage each other in their disruption. Conversely, there are fewer teachers who will recognise and know the culprits. The close inter-personal relationships found in the smaller schools are not possible. It is possible for those with the will to get away with bad behaviour because they are not recognised by the duty staff and there are more places in which to hide or to get into mischief. Putting matters rather crudely, mob rule reigns and the school will become out of control.

Moving to and from school or college

The situation when people are moving to and from school or college, and when moving between one institution and another, is similar to that of movement within the institutions boundaries. The young people are free from restrictions and can lapse into unruly, often antisocial, behaviour. The general public will notice and be inconvenienced by any bad behaviour and, in any case, society does not want to encourage or allow what has become known as loutish behaviour to flourish. It is therefore desirable that the school or college should be able to take action against people who behave in this way and who consequently bring the reputation of their school or college into disrepute when they are travelling to and from educational institutions.

In February 2006 the Government announced that it would give the legal right to teachers to discipline pupils misbehaving on their way to and from school.

Aggression on the part of young people

Young people are learning what is, and is not acceptable behaviour. Some come to school and college having learnt and accepted what is reasonable, others have not. In any case, arguments and brawls between young people are not new. They can be a fiery lot!

The point is that brawls will occur and tempers will be lost. Youngsters' behaviour can and does sometimes become that which is completely beyond the bounds of reason (albeit momentarily) and does not respond to the spoken instruction. They will need to be separated and/or removed physically from the situation and it must be made quite clear that, under these circumstances, a member of staff can use reasonable force to right the problem without any fear of being accused of abuse. This will need to include the physical restraint of the person, a point which is now supported by the government. In addition in the case of violent behaviour it is recommended that the school involves the police and in serious cases should permanently exclude those involved. *(7.38)*

There is also the question of spoken aggression to consider. Abusive language should not be tolerated. Reprimand and apology in cases of minor slip ups resolve the problem but there are those who are habitually and deliberately abusive. They too must be removed from the class (again without fear of the teacher being accused of wrong doing). It is very likely that these young people will also be physically aggressive.

Repeated serious physical aggression on the part of a young person in the school or college and on the way to and from the institution must result in the permanent exclusion from that school or college. (Incidentally, there still seems to be confusion about terminology and definitions when excluding young people from an educational establishment. The old term "expulsion" seems to have been replaced by "permanent exclusion": there are therefore the categories of short term exclusion, longer exclusion and permanent exclusion, the definitions of which could still be more precise.

The carrying of weapons

It hardly seems credible that it should be necessary to raise this matter in relation to educational establishments but we have allowed a culture of weapon carrying to develop in our country and witness the results in the far too regularly reported stabbings and shootings which now take place. Apart from the fact that such a culture needs to be eliminated, the carrying of weapons can certainly not be tolerated in schools and colleges. It must be made quite clear that the *carrying of anything with the intention of using it as a weapon* will result in a full investigation into the circumstances surrounding the incident in which any such item comes to light, with the expectation of serious consequences to follow.

Where the item is quite obviously a weapon (a knife or gun for instance) the police should be informed and the young person isolated until he or she can be removed and excluded from attendance. There are no circumstances when any weapon should be brought into schools and colleges. An understanding of this situation is illustrated in the White Paper: where they say head-teachers will be given authority to search pupils for knives and other weapons *(7.5)* Should this also include searching for other items, for instance, in cases where there is strong suspicion that the young person has drugs in their possession or some stolen item? Searching children, instructing them to turn out their pockets, used to be a common act on the part of teachers, and so it should be for those in positions of responsibility and authority in schools and colleges.

There should be no question of double jeopardy in this matter: being punished twice for the same offence should not come into the equation. The school or college needs to be in a position to take immediate action and what may happen subsequently as a result of police investigations regarded merely as a continuation of the same case.

Sanctions

The need for sanctions is now recognised at government level, with the acceptance and implementation of recommendations made in the report by The Practitioners' Group on School Behaviour and Discipline published in October 2005. In the White Paper "Higher Standards, Better Schools for All" there is stated the intention to give teachers the legal right to discipline pupils including the right to restrain pupils using reasonable force but there is also the expectation that schools will establish a clear set of rules and sanctions.

In addition the White Paper *(7.38)* makes special reference to bullying suggesting a number of sanctions which should be applied including the removal of the youngster from class; withdrawal of privileges; detention; in particular, the removal of the privilege of being allowed to take part in school trips or sports which are extra-curricular; and excluding the child for a fixed period.

Furthermore, the involvement of the police is recommended in cases of violence with permanent exclusion of the pupil where there has been extreme violence.

There was also a move to investigate how far a National Behaviour Charter would be helpful, for clarifying the rights and responsibilities of pupils, parents and staff in the matter of encouraging good behaviour *(7.22)*.

However, there is no sense in producing a code of conduct if its requirements cannot be upheld: sanctions are essential. As school and college rules are likely to range from the routine (such as being required to carry a pen to class) to the extremely serious (such as those relating to assault and the carrying of weapons) sanctions need to be devised which are appropriate to the level of the misconduct. It is unfortunate that traditional sanctions such as the setting of extra tasks and detentions have been challenged, creating a situation in which the culprit can break the rules and go on to defy reasonable authority by refusing to be sanctioned. Some parents have condoned this defiance in their children. Even such simple school-only sanctions such as the above now need to be given the support of law because the law has been used to challenge their use. But it is unfortunate that an educational institution now needs to be given legal backing to the right to award certain sanctions in order for it to be quite clear to everyone that properly defined and reasonable rules must be upheld.

There should be levels of sanction. There needs to be those which all teachers can use: the setting of extra work and detention come to mind and could be used in the relatively straightforward maintaining of order in the classroom and around the school or college premises.

At a more serious level there is hostile aggression or deliberate vandalism. These matters need to be dealt with by the head of the establishment and those senior staff appointed to deal with such incidents. Sanctions should then reasonably include the requiring of parents to attend a meeting, giving the school or college the status of a court of law in this matter. Such a court could consist of the head-teacher, the chairman of governors, another teacher and a parent representative from the governing body. The aim of such a court should be to see justice applied. As a sanction the appearance before such a court should in itself be seen as a serious matter but further sanctions need to be available to demonstrate that serious misbehaviour will not be tolerated.

In the case of exclusion there is at present a provision for there to be an appeal against the school's decision. The authority of the school is open to challenge and in our society, where there has been an increase in the tendency to turn to the law to solve problems, is open to legal challenges. In cases of school discipline this is not helpful, encouraging the belief that, so long as you are clever enough or have a sufficiently clever lawyer to represent you, you stand a good chance of getting away with your misbehaviour. When a matter of school misbehaviour is investigated the outcome depends upon the ability of staff to call upon young people to show the culprit to be wrong. This can be done when the investigation is concerned with seeking the truth and is not a matter of legal argument about what might, or could, have happened in some hypothetical case, thus casting doubt on what did happen and ending with the denial of guilt. The point is, in a school or college population, the young people do know what happened in such cases, they know the truth. If the truth is not discovered and appropriate sanctions for wrongdoing not applied, they easily see injustice. Injustice breeds a contempt for rules and, indeed, for the law, and this is not sound education. Lawyers should not under normal circumstances be expected to become involved in matters relating to the internal discipline of schools and colleges.

In the case of unruly behaviour, a period of isolation from the normal environment may be considered, with extra duties of some kind required to be carried out of class hours. Where damage has been done the school or college must be in a position to require the culprit to pay a reasonable sum for repairs. Educational establishments need legal authority to do this.

In cases of financial hardship perhaps some system whereby the culprit is put to work to earn the appropriate money can be devised. Parents must understand that the educational establishment has the legal authority to take action and that their co-operation is expected.

In the White Paper the government confirmed the headteachers' power to permanently exclude pupils for serious misbehaviour (even for a first offence) and changed the exclusion appeal procedures in an attempt to treat more equally the interests of the pupil and the school. Is this sufficient?

The sanctions of exclusion and expulsion should be instigated by the headteacher and appeals only be allowed to the school court. There should be no other over-ruling authority, although it should be quite clear which circumstances will lead to these sanctions being applied.

Accusations made against teachers

The law has become unfairly biased against teachers accused of improper conduct. Any child, no matter how unstable, unruly or delinquent is given the unchallengeable right to accuse a teacher of anything. The teacher is immediately punished by being suspended and disgraced. In other words, teachers are treated as guilty until proved innocent and this situation further undermines their reasonable position of authority They cannot be expected to continue working under these terms.

Headteachers and senior staff, and governors too, should know the school staff. They should be working closely together as a team. They know each other. They know whether or not the accusation is likely to be serious or merely the invention of a vindictive child and/or parent.

Much more consideration should be given to the substance of such accusations, and the known character of the accuser, before what has become the over-zealous hand of the law being allowed to take charge.

Given that all are subject to human weaknesses, headteachers and their staffs, with their governors, are responsible people who should be trusted. Internal investigation could sort those victims of false accusations from those where accusations have substance. Such matters, for instance, as touching a child on the arm or shoulder during some disciplinary action, the physical restraining of the unruly or the pulling apart of fighters, should not be regarded as an assault by the teacher.

A change of attitude is required.

8. Teaching and learning strategies

There is a temptation to argue that; if only we could get the teaching right, instil the right enthusiasm, include the young people in the decision-making regarding what is taught, the poor behaviour, the inconsiderate destruction; the problems of bullying and delinquency would be solved. It's not true, of course, but equally, teaching and learning strategies do make a difference!

In any educational discussion there is nearly always an argument about old and new teaching methods, but without a clear definition of each. There is the time-distorted memory of our own teaching days, its enjoyment or otherwise, and a consequent feeling of success or failure. It is likely to be those who were successful who place value on the old, but what detail can they recall? Not only has time elapsed, but what they saw and were subjected to, they saw and experienced through the eyes of a child.

It is likely that many of us were taught in groups of thirty or more, each sitting in rows of double desks and receiving a great deal of information from the class teacher who stayed, for the most part, at the front of the class and made frequent use of the blackboard.

Before this idea is pursued further, a word or two about classroom furniture is not without significance. We sat in rows: the older ones amongst us in dark wooden contraptions in which a double-desk and seats were firmly joined together by stout ironwork. These units were heavy and almost immovable. Seats were hinged to the back support and had to be folded up in order for us to stand. Desks sloped towards the seated and had sockets into which inkwells fitted; usually with a sliding cap to cover the ink container. And incidentally, one or two of our number would be designated "ink monitors" with the duty of collecting ink cans and filling the wells at the beginning of each week.

The graffiti artists of the day carved names, hearts with arrows, and other things, with penknives – a long and laborious exercise. In any case, the tough dark wooden tops did not damage easily. And, as we had most of our lessons in the same room sitting in the same place, the chances were that we would be caught committing our vandalism.

In the new schools, from the 1950s onwards, someone somewhere decided that new furniture should replace this heavy serviceable stuff. Light tables, light in colour and weight, replaced the heavy desks. Individual light chairs with bowed, sprung wooden legs replaced the fold-back benches. Everything moves so easily: it can be rattled and clattered by accident or intent to produce a cacophony of sound reminiscent of bedlam. The teacher's job had in one stroke been made at least a little harder.

Firstly there is the din to contend with, but secondly, those who wish, can now rearrange the layout of the room. Instead of having neat uniform formal lines and rows of desks, there can be untidy, scattered, informal groups amongst which chairs can be discarded like so much debris, providing obstacles around or over which each of thirty young imps can scramble or fall. Again, the teacher's job is made more difficult – the informal scatter is not so easy to oversee as formal rows.

Of course I have overstated the case: informal groupings can be supervised, so long as the teacher is positioned in such a place as to see at a glance what each youngster is doing. No table needs to be out of sight, hidden behind or even near some bookcase, cabinet or screen. But the situation is more complex than in the traditional classroom and extra effort must be made to ensure that constant supervision is taking place.

It was also in the '50s that monsieur Biro invented the ball-point pen, that instrument of sculpture which can impress a host of messages and designs into the new soft-wood or veneered desk tops, side or chair back. There were great battles fought to keep this weapon out of school – it ruined handwriting and left dirty smudgy blots across the page – but progress and improved designs demanded that it become the modern writing instrument.

Eventually someone else invented the felt-tip pen, the paint brush in pen form which can so easily be used to design emblems, grotesque figures and giant monograms or names, at a stroke, and then be quickly hidden before the desecrater can be seen. Much school furniture has thus become a mess – and the school walls as well!

Most of us, and certainly our older brethren, were taught by the formal method, in rows, a method now so often denigrated as the almost evil chalk-and-talk. But was it really such a terrible way to carry on? Was there not at least some value in this traditional strategy of working with thirty or more young lively minds, all together, all as one?

Of course, a silent-unless-spoken-to attention was required by the teacher. Any loss of eye contact could be detected immediately – what would the child be about to do, instead of listening to instructions given or responding to the questions with a controlled and disciplined raising-of-the-hand? Can you remember the enthusiasm of classmates leaping up from seats, waving arms and shrieking "Miss!" or "Sir!"

in their excitement to join in the class discussion? Can you remember joining in, looking keen and interested, hoping that you would in fact not be picked, because you did not know the answer!

It is the teacher's job to excite the pupils into enjoying learning and this can be done in group work of this kind, where every pupil is involved, but must be more difficult to maintain when working with only one individual at a time, while the others hopefully get on with their individual work.

Before considering such questions further, it is essential to comment on the paramount need of any teaching strategy. The teacher must always be in charge of the class and be positively directing any activity, no matter what form that activity may take. Every pupil must have half an eye on the teacher at all times, awaiting the next instruction, or wary of the reprimand which it is known will come if attention wanders from the task in hand. The teacher must have eyes everywhere, including the back of the head, to ensure an oversight of each and every pupil's movements. Only then can the unexpected act, harmless, stupid or dangerous, be anticipated and prevented. Then a good harmonious, even friendly, working atmosphere will prevail, enthusiasms be encouraged and learning be enjoyed.

As a student teacher, I was taught to use the chalk-and-talk strategy to advantage. Where possible, any blackboard work was supposed to be completed before the class arrived: as a geographer, sketch maps and outline notes on the main elements of the lesson, for instance, should have been placed on the blackboard before the lesson started.

When you think about it, this aspect of the teacher's work is now so much easier: it can be prepared before hand on a slide and projected onto a screen or even put onto computer software. But this must be more expensive!

The prime objective, as with any lesson, was to have a structure to follow with a clear aim in mind and specific objectives to achieve. The chalk-and-talk was the first section within the structure and intended to concentrate the minds of the youngsters, to direct their thinking, to encourage each to start the task, to involve each in a controlled debate in which the teacher guides the learners through appropriate stages towards meaningful conclusions. The teacher should have ready carefully thought out questions for leading the group forwards to be directed at the class as a whole but with the instruction that, in order to give answers, hands must be raised and the respondent wait to be asked to speak. The responses were controlled: the teacher deliberately calling on a variety of youngsters in the different quarters of the room and also commenting on, and encouraging, any who did not respond. The carefully directed questioning draws answers from everyone in the class, all are brought into the learning situation at the same time. There is no opportunity for any pupil to nod off to sleep!

Answers can be good and very much to the point, satisfactory and suitable for adapting to lead onto the next objective or wildly off the point. The skill of the teacher is expected to be used to convert all answers into positive contributions. In this way, all of the children are drawn into the opening class activity.

An important aspect of the strategy is its encouragement of the child who can give oral answers but may not be particularly good at written work. I remember when I was experimenting with mixed ability teaching and using this method in the traditional fashion, very much against the wishes of the mixed ability teaching enthusiasts. One youngster in particular was bubbling with excitement and it was necessary to avoid calling on his answers too often. It was tempting to do so because he clearly understood what was required and his answers were amongst those most useful for advancing the lesson. The shock came later when written work on the same topic was called in for correcting: the brilliant oral child was illiterate!

The strategy also calls upon all of the youngsters to pool their resources, to bring their variety of talents together, for the benefit of the whole class. It is an aspect of a broad education.

It was never intended that the strategy should be the only one used, neither in the one lesson nor in different lessons. During any one period of learning, the best teacher will use a variety of activities. Consequently, after an introductory chalk-and-talk, or more properly, question-and-answer session, with appropriate chalk-work on the blackboard (using the white board and computer today) a different strategy needs to be introduced. This could be reading passages from the text book, each pupil being asked to read a paragraph out loud, the teacher reading and explaining difficult content or vocabulary; or individuals researching the material from nominated pages quietly to themselves. If the length of lesson allows, this can then be followed by a period of individual written work in response to the previous learning, while the teacher moves around the class to see how each child is progressing and to give help or provide motivation where necessary.

It was the worst of chalk-and-talk, with the teacher giving a boring monotone lecture of long duration, which the critics used in their campaign for something different.

That something-different evolved from the one-school ideology. It was claimed that it was undesirable and unnecessary to divide children by ability between grammar and secondary modern schools at the age of eleven, and then equally undesirable and unnecessary to divide them between different classes in the same school. Clearly, for management reasons, an intake year group of more than thirty people needs to be subdivided but in order to serve the notion of one school, one curriculum, one homogeneous population there developed the concept of mixed ability teaching.

The first comprehensive schools organised their teaching groups according to the assessed abilities and achievements of the children. That is, the classes were streamed: the cleverest in one group, the next cleverest in another group and so on, with the least able in a class of their own. Primary school classes also arranged teaching groups in this way. There was originally no objection to referring to those who were quick to learn as clever.

This did not please the educational and social reformers as the classes were clearly ranked in order of their success in learning. There was a top class, an elite! This class also had a majority of privileged conforming youngsters. Conversely, there was a bottom class, where it was discovered most of the underprivileged children seemed to congregate. Similarly, of course, there are whole schools where there is a majority of one or other of these extremes, and this must not be overlooked.

For many reformers, the prime objective is to abolish this social class division which, they claim, undermines the ideals of the one-school or comprehensive philosophy, is divisive, perpetuating elitism and privilege, and, of course, perpetuating and even exacerbating social class division. Their response has been the development of mixed ability teaching.

Their philosophy demands that all have the same curriculum – no one must be denied the opportunity to learn anything – overlooking the fact that people are infinitely different, with different interests, different talents and, dare one say it, different abilities in those talents.

If all are given the same, according to this notion, they need not be divided according to ability. It can be contrived that each class has people from the whole range of ability and attainment. Such classes are mixed ability classes, the arrangement which became fashionable in most primary schools and to some extent in secondary schools. The most enthusiastic supporters of the scheme had mixed ability groups throughout the school, others felt that a different form of grouping is required for fifteen and sixteen-year-olds. Nevertheless, rigid streaming is now rare, division of senior pupils being according to their abilities and attainments in each subject. It is argued that a young person may be good at one or more disciplines, while weak in others and will therefore be placed in a group of different ability for different subjects. Such groups are referred to as sets.

In the mixed ability class, the teacher is faced with the potential first class honours graduate and remedial reader in the same teaching group (so long as the school has its share of the full range of ability) and has the task of preparing individual work programmes suitable for each, hopefully enthusing and supervising each as he or she works through the programmes at different speeds, and assessing the progress of each. Class teaching, with one common lesson to prepare and common exercises to mark, disappears. The excitement and drive of the teacher-led whole class is lost:

and, to some extent, a powerful tool for creating group cohesiveness is lost as well. The teacher has to have much more detail in the front of his mind all of the time. And I develop my earlier observation: the work of the teacher becomes harder, more complex, more difficult, and more stressful.

In the normal class of thirty, during one day, having five hours of teacher-pupil contact time, each pupil can presumably claim the full individual attention of the teacher for ten minutes! For the rest of the time, spelling it out, four hours and fifty minutes, he or she must get on with the set tasks, or take time from others. And it is the one of average or less than average ability who cannot do this, while even the most able is likely to become bored and then distracted without the encouraging excitement of the class-teacher's intervention.

In the school where the catchment area is a district with a large number of underprivileged families, there can be say six pupils in every group of thirty who need individual attention all of the time!

Class teaching, on the other hand, enables the teacher to supervise more closely, enthuse, reward and reprimand most of the children in the class most of the time. It is more efficient.

Mixed ability teaching is not only inefficient but is a teaching strategy in which I suspect it is impossible to carry out properly what the teacher is reasonably expected to do.

Those who claimed that this was the way forward did of course state that teachers could no longer teach in the way they did. They in fact agued that class teaching was not possible: it had to be replaced by teaching individuals. This sounds excellent, but, as I have argued above, not easy, possibly inefficient and may be impossible, when attempted with groups of some 20 or 30 young people.

The further response of the protagonists was to change the material taught in order to make it more acceptable to the widely different children – or so they thought. In my experience, and inevitably so, the course content had to be diluted.

Some teachers in primary schools may immediately claim that they successfully teach mixed ability groups, so why cannot secondary teachers do the same? But this is a false cry. It may be that, even with their young children, it is not the best way, but as the curriculum is broadened and deepened, it becomes more and more difficult to motivate every individual in a class where there are such diverse interests, abilities and attainments.

No matter: our enthusiastic de-streamers have pressed on regardless. Having modified the content of the syllabi they have set about modifying the means of assessing the attainments of the pupils, even claiming that assessment is unnecessarily divisive – and, incidentally, throwing all possible objective assessment of their pupils' learning or their own teaching to the wind. The situation is akin to reforming the teaching of house builders in the following way. As we will be teaching those talented in bricklaying with those who cannot hold a trowel, we shall avoid using trowels in our teaching. As it is not possible to lay a course of bricks without using a trowel or something similar, we can no longer teach bricklaying so we shall teach brick piling instead. You can imagine the nature of the houses which will be built in the future!

Amongst the enthusiasms of the moment, of which mixed ability teaching is one, variety is too often lost as one well tried method is killed-off in favour of another, which is itself then destined to be over used.

Looking for a moment at the primary infant school, the teaching of reading was once completed by use of the class group strategy. All seated in their desks with the same class book, each would be instructed by the teacher and then asked to read a section out loud in turn. For the competent this would be dull and boring because their progress would be held back. For the slow learners, the exercise would be an embarrassing trial, as they struggled to sound out words which meant little to them, and their off-beat guesses bringing howls or titters of laughter, depending upon the class discipline, from the rest. Clearly, in this mixed ability situation, the teaching method was inappropriate.

Nevertheless, this does not mean that children should never be asked to read out loud in front of their classmates, particularly if it can be contrived that they are then in a group of near equal talent and attainment. It is flexibility which is so significant.

One method of teaching reading is to use a system of graded books, in which the vocabulary and comprehension increase in difficulty through the grades. But critics argue that this has the disadvantage of producing an inter-pupil competition, with the inevitable result that those who progress slowly suffer from an unnecessary sense of failure. Yet, so often youngsters bow to peer group pressure, so why not harness this pressure to urge each to strive more? The matter is one of class management, where the teacher uses strategies to protect the underachiever from any damning sense of failure: a reason for variety in teaching strategies again, seeking the stronger talents in each of the children and encouraging them to project their individual strengths while accepting the reality of their areas of failure without despair.

Is it also likely that children who find reading difficult will suffer less from a feeling of inferiority if they meet others with similar difficulties and this means they need to have reading lessons with those who are like themselves. Indeed, as some children will learn easily and others slowly, should those who struggle with their reading be given special help, using the various modern technical aids which we now possess? Of course, many will exclaim that this is what already happens: the remedial readers are taken out of their normal class for special tuition. But this is not what I mean. As reading is a basic skill, necessary for future learning, I would like to see its tuition given absolute priority in the early years of schooling. An intensive on-going course, using each of the known strategies for teaching the skill, look and say, phonics, graded books, interesting stories and so on, seems to me to be required. Then, at the end of the day, I suspect, some will still not be able to read fluently: but, being identified, different methods of teaching, which do not rely solely on the written word, can be used to encourage these children to learn other knowledge and skills. I anticipate that their teaching group would be small and the teacher all the time interacting with the children to encourage, even excite, them in their work.

I am not convinced that young children wired up to headphones and with eyes glued to computer screens, with stories being read into their ears while they hopefully follow the print, are going to learn very much. It is the enthusiastic encouragement of the real life personality of the teacher which motivates and this is still most efficiently completed in the group teaching situation – where the pupils react to the teacher's questioning, and to each other's responses carefully translated and used by the teachers.

It is also essential that there is a structure to any reading scheme, with books of increasing difficulty which can be used to judge objectively how a youngster is progressing. That these books are the same for everyone makes the teacher's task more manageable. There must be a limit to the number of stories of equal difficulty but with variety of interest which can be, on the one hand, written, and, on the other, efficiently assimilated and handled by the teacher. Some may well attempt to over do the strategy of trying to motivate the children through individual work projects when it is more efficient to use at least some group teaching to do so.

The teaching of reading cannot be glossed over without reference to the famous, or infamous, depending upon where-you-stand, strategies of teaching phonics and by look-and-say. In phonics you learn the sound of letter combinations and hopefully apply these to new situations. In look-and-say you do just that, you learn the spoken interpretation of the printed word. There is sense in both of these methods but somehow, typical of education theory and practice, each in its turn has been applauded and rejected, decrying the half way situation of using both, in order to give variety, or each with different children, depending upon how each youngster seems to respond to the teaching. Certainly both rely on the child's concentration on the task, its perception of the material, its ability to understand and remember the elements and application of the old to new situations. These characteristics of learning will vary in different children and those well endowed will learn easily while those with poor concentration, perception, understanding, memory and translation will learn more slowly.

It is the teacher's job to teach: to ensure that the child concentrates on the task; to anticipate a child's perception of material and to ensure that material is presented in a variety of appropriate ways; to interpret the material; to foster the child's understanding; and to ensure the child learns by applying its memory and practicing what is to be memorised. And that returns us to the discussion on group teaching methods. When the whole class is in eye contact with the teacher then each pupil is more likely to be giving full attention to what is going on. Each and every pupil is constantly assessed by the teacher, who then modifies his or her responses in order to encourage and assist each youngster.

When only one pupil is dealt with by the teacher at any one moment, the others will inevitably concentrate less on the job, will not be given immediate help with the perception and understanding of material, and will not be driven to more urgent practice. Those most likely to succeed will be the most able – as always – while the least able and average pupil will surely be left too long to drift without the motivating support of the teacher.

Furthermore, the teacher, working only with one child, I suggest, will become mind-deadened, by the lack of stimulation received from its responses. But, once again, I am not saying that a teacher should never work with one individual child. There are those youngsters whose personalities are such that they need a constant bombardment in a one-to-one situation in order to be brought to make any progress at all: another reason for assessing an individual's needs and applying teaching strategies which are appropriate to those needs.

It is not that people do not agree that children need to be taught as individuals. It is how it is most efficient to teach individuals where there is disagreement and I have argued that group teaching may well have its advantages in this. Certainly, we cannot afford to have one teacher tutoring each child all of the time, although it is certainly worth considering whether supportive tutoring could be built into the system. With such a facility, it should be possible to rectify the step-by-step failings of the average pupil, but I fear that the least able will need very frequent, if not constant, tutoring facilities.

An alternative to class teaching, individual project work, has been introduced in an attempt to overcome difficulties perceived in teaching mixed ability groups. In theory, each learner has an individual programme to follow at his or her own speed.

The prospect is, if you care to think carefully for a moment or two, quite horrendous: the teacher has thirty different programmes to prepare, oversee, assess and correct. It is inevitable that the efficiency of the teaching will suffer. It is just not possible to give the necessary attention to thirty individuals on a regular basis. It has already been noted elsewhere, but we need to remind ourselves, that in a five hour day each child in a group of thirty can claim the attention of a teacher for ten minutes. For four hours and fifty minutes the youngster must *get along* on its own – or by interacting with its fellows in the class, and here lies another problem.

There are, of course, strategies which can be used within this approach to make life tolerable. The same programme could be used for each child, who then progresses at its individual rate. This immediately makes the teacher more efficient because it is no longer necessary to try to keep up with thirty different exercises: it becomes a matter of overseeing, assessing and correcting the same exercise at thirty different levels. But this does not please those who object to anything which may even seem to facilitate competition.

Assuming that each child has an adequate level of reading skills and understanding, individual work sheets (or computer programmes) can be prepared. While the teacher is giving full attention to any one pupil, the others it is intended become thoroughly engrossed in their own programmes.

And that is all wishful thinking! In reality all of the children will not be able to read and understand the worksheets, no matter how carefully they are prepared or graded. Some will not even want to do so! While the teacher works with one, their minds will wander, their attention caught by much more attractive occupations − or they might drift away into the land of daydreams, or even go to sleep.

The ultimate stage in the development of the structured worksheet is programmed learning and the use of teaching machines and computer programmes. Very carefully defined steps are set out in text or computer programmes, each step requiring a response from the learner. Correct answers are rewarded by the learner being allowed to progress to the next goal. When errors are made, the learner is directed along a revision route, where the required element of learning is presented in a different way. Each stage in a programme is graded according to the abilities and attainments of the user. In psychological terms, correct responses are reinforced, while errors are carefully corrected by guiding the learner along a different simpler route in order to incite responses which can be rewarded.

With such programmes used in teaching machines or computers, the individual can, at least in theory, work at his or her own pace, being supported, corrected, guided and assessed by the apparatus. This is a form of trial and error learning and introduces yet another aspect of controversy in education. How much should a child be told and be expected to accept? How much does it need to know before it can work through an individual project or programme? How much the learner should be told without always being expected to start at zero? Is it really a good idea to have every new human mind re-inventing the wheel?

This is the discovery method of teaching and, once again, has its place in the variety of approaches which the best teachers will wish to apply. But, if it is used all of the time, it will become as boring an approach as any other. In addition, the preparation of structured investigative learning programmes, graded to cater for numerous individual abilities, is critical, requiring a great deal of time. And is this, an impossible task? An infinite number of individual programmes will be required.

The interaction of human pupil with human teacher, in the extreme however, has gone! So long as the programme motivates the learner to continue, learning is expected to progress with a minimum of outside help. And it does seem that some youngsters at least can become completely hooked on computer programmes. Nevertheless, before we become too excited we need to know much more of this. Which programmes are so attractive: purposeful learning programmes or games? Which particular types of young people become so attached to their machines? What do they learn – anything worth learning? Which personalities are most excited by this strategy? Do quiet withdrawn introverts become even more withdrawn, to develop into complete isolates – and insecure in their dealings with others? We need to know.

Certainly a study of programmed learning makes us more aware of the elements required in structured learning. It teaches us to consider how to set goals which are attainable by each learner and how finely graded the steps should be to enable the learner to progress from one goal to the next. Steps can be constructed of increasing difficulty or complexity: from the simple statement of an accepted fact, to complex reasoning from evidence, and the formulation of hypotheses. When applied to individuals, each step being planned and agreed with the learner before progressing to the next step, we have what is known as the negotiated curriculum.

A variation of the project method is to divide the class into small groups, each group being given a task at which to work. If the groups are carefully structured, with able children, average and less able in each group, then they can help each other – so some would have us believe. The reading can be done by the one who reads well, who will comprehend easily and who has most knowledge to call upon to back up the research – and who will be able to form new hypotheses and develop new concepts.

But instead of getting on with the task, which may well cause an initial excitement, he or she is supposed to stop, interpret, explain and support the others in the group. This is teaching social co-operation and tolerance of one's fellows – perhaps.

More likely, the group will be dominated by the most extrovert aggressive personality in the group, who may well not be the one with the most appropriate skills. We may argue therefore that the teacher needs to be aware of the whole personality of each child and construct the groups accordingly: another job to do, another area of understanding which the teacher must develop. I would anticipate that the most excellent teachers have some intuitive skill which allows them to assess their children accurately and quickly, and to adapt their teaching strategies to the optimum advantage. Most may be capable of being taught and helped to develop this facility but some will never understand or master it.

The success of much of what has been described above, for instance, individual project work and the negotiated curriculum, must depend upon the number of learners in each teaching group and the total number of learners with whom the teacher has to work in any one week. The bigger the group and the more groups, and the more personalities with which the teacher has to deal. The more individual work programmes there are to devise, supervise, assess and adapt. The greater the teacher's work load. And still I have doubts about whether this is the way to inspire and excite the learner most of the time. It may well be one approach amongst many, to be used some of the time, and in particular in the one-to-one situation when this is necessary. But it is unlikely that it will be the panacea for all teachers' problems everywhere. And it will certainly not be the perfect teaching strategy for every learner!

A concluding word is perhaps required which considers the timetable implications of some of the strategies which have been suggested. With the use of streamed groups, children remained for most of their time in the same class and in the same classroom. Movement of youngsters was kept at a minimum, and there was little chance of anyone not being missed if they were out of class. The same could apply to the mixed ability class. But where a compromise is sought, where individuals are grouped according to their abilities, attainments and interests in many different subjects, they constantly move to different groups in different classrooms. They have individual timetables, not class timetables. In order to check where each should be during any one period of the week, it becomes necessary to make an individual check, not a class check. The administration for such an arrangement is very considerable. In order to record attendance, a register must be checked in each and every lesson, electronic systems have been devised to help with this and it is a task which must be done, but teachers vary in their perception of this task as a necessary duty. And, certainly, opportunities for those youngsters who may be inclined to skip lessons have immensely increased.

9. Vocational versus Academic Learning

In February 2005 the Government published the White Paper 14 – 19 Education and Skills, with the purpose of addressing the problem of young people rejecting and dropping out of education after the age of 14 years: the observations and suggestions given in this document are considered here (with appropriate references given in brackets after each item).

The falling away of interest among some of the post 14 age group was observed in the non-grammar secondary schools immediately after the implementation of the 1945 Education Act and in the comprehensive schools which developed subsequently. The Newsom report (1964 – see Chapter 12: The Curriculum) tried to offer some solutions to the problem and the Training and Vocational Education Initiative tried once more. None succeeded.

The 2005 White Paper was a further attempt to improve the appreciation of learning through the provision of vocational teaching programmes. Learning in the workplace is emphasised *(9.10)*. There *will be more opportunities*. But the considerable implications of providing this require considerable co-operation from the employees and, although *encouragement* may be given *(7.16 and 7.17) incentives* would help more, particularly for the small employer. It is therefore essential that full and careful consideration is given to the implications of such proposals.

Changes since 1945

The raising of the school leaving age from fourteen to sixteen since 1945 has seen a large number of young people, who would have happily entered employment, forced to remain in a school environment. A first question could therefore be: was it proper to force this position onto young people? At first sight the answer may well be yes! However, an extra moment's thought will remind us of a significant change in the employment prospects of young people as time has progressed.

There has been the loss of low-skill manual jobs and it is not only employment requiring physical strength which has and is being lost. Opportunities in the manufacturing industries, where workers apply relatively straight forward easily learnt repetitive skills, have also declined. It is no longer possible to rely on earning one's livelihood by obtaining employment in a reasonably well paid low-skilled job in a factory. It is essential that this loss of low-learning, low-skilled work is seen as a serious problem insofar as there are those who are able and happy only in this type of employment.

Differences in learning ability

The White Paper recognises differences in learning *(2.17)* and advances vocational education as a motivator for some learners who, at present seem to reject education but the situation is not straightforward. Different learners respond to different teaching methods; learners respond to the same teaching method differently; and further study of the relationship between academic and practical learning should perhaps be considered.

Academic and practical styles of learning can both be vocational and confusion can arise by suggesting the division is between academic and vocational teaching, as most learning requires some academic work: calculation, writing, reading, understanding instructions and so on. The significance lies in the *styles of teaching and the ways in which different people learn*. Just as it said in the 1945 publication, some people find it easy to learn via an abstract or academic style of teaching, while others are more successful when taught through a hands on or practical approach. And most learning involves a mixture of both.

Learning for vocational goals

All learning should have clearly defined vocational goals although it should not be essential that learners aim for these goals. There can be learning for its own sake and, on the one hand, this should not be discouraged, while on the other, all learners of employment age should be expected to aim for qualifications which will enable them to earn a living and promote the national economy.

The greater emphasis to be placed on vocational programmes is designed to attract those who opt out of what they perceive as unattractive traditional academic school based learning *(6.4)*. This should not be allowed to encourage those who are well suited to academic learning to opt for low learning practical programmes simply because of peer pressure, youthful fashion or because qualification may seem to be easier. Both styles of learning are necessary combined with a wide range of qualifications.

Standardised testing and experience of the learning abilities of young people suggest that the problem of the "switched-off" is not solely one of motivating ability by introducing vocational learning strategies. There certainly are able, probably very able, learners who will be motivated more by what they perceive to be courses leading directly to vocational goals rather than via academic study. They are not motivated by study for its own sake (although this attitude may change as they grow older), but will be able to progress and tackle high level vocational studies. There are levels of achievement in both academic and practical learning and people who cannot reach a high level in either.

The vast majority of poorly motivated learners do not fit into the able learner category. They are more likely to be of average and below average learning ability and will be greatly helped by the proposals to strengthen the teaching of functional language, functional mathematics and the use of computer technology: that is, teaching through practical experience in real life situations, using only those aspects of these subjects which have practical applications. Where they see real life vocational applications to what they are expected to learn they will be much more likely to become enthusiastic about their studies. They will be particularly motivated where they can see any qualification leading to real employment – that is, leading into a work place situation in which they can earn money and it may be that the extension of apprenticeship schemes that will be the only route likely to be successful. Only the provision of courses in which there are real prospects of wage-earning employment will motivate the vast majority of young people who are not motivated by the traditional academic approach.

The White Paper 14 -19 Education and Skills reinforces the need for and intention to establish realistic lifestyle workplace courses and equivalent meaningful usable qualifications. This is very important and the stated intention is to specify areas of study in the new Diploma qualification and the need for the student to reach a realistic standard in these areas. At the heart of the proposed qualification is a core of what are described as functional skills in English and maths; and with these primary requirements the courses will provide learning in a chosen subject. The award of the Diploma will also include qualification in appropriate GCSEs or A level subjects.

With regard to national standards in the subjects studied government expects to define the content of courses together with in put from employers.

Similar diplomas should also be well suited to those who enjoy and are successful learning through academic style teaching but at a low to intermediate level. They are perhaps people who will enjoy and be successful in what we can call routine clerical work: thoroughly boring for some but enjoyable to others.

It is essential that we should not lose sight of the fact there are learners who can achieve high levels through academic styles of teaching and there are others who can achieve lower levels, but equally valuable, via the same styles. There are those who can reach high levels of achievement via practical learning and others who will achieve more moderately but can and should be valued for the contribution they will make to our complex society.

The Problem of Generating Equal worth in Academic and Vocational Qualifications

The Tomlinson Report advocated replacing the General School Certificate Examinations with a system of diplomas covering both academic and vocational qualifications. This suggestion was not taken up by the Government and the charge has been laid that the opportunity of generating equal worth for vocational and academic studies has been lost. But the significance lies not in *what you call the system but the way in which it is perceived, used, and valued*. We have struggled with attempts to produce equal worth via sameness for too long: providing the Certificate of Secondary Education for those not able to attain General Certificate of Education passes and then combining these into the GSCE. We have struggled to give all a sense of achievement by pretending to give them the same things: courses, styles of teaching and examinations, when differences are essential. The route forward is to bring people to value different qualifications, generated for different occupations, equally.

What is required is a well organised, clearly defined practical education system, where teaching is done using more practical strategies, as an alternative to the more traditional academic approach but not a complete replacement for it.

A long standing problem has been the tradition, arising from the days of the Industrial Revolution, when factory and workshop employment came to be seen as inferior to office work. It is essential that different types of work be valued equally and industry and commerce have the responsibility of fostering this ideal. Only they can equate wages and salaries for different styles of work. It is essential that practical and academic learning are also valued equally.

Some implications of introducing vocational courses

The obvious implication is that vocational, or practical, teaching requires learners to be involved in a substantial period of structured practical work, requiring a different environment from that traditionally associated with schools where the learners sit at desks or tables in a classroom. Specialist accommodation is required.

It is very likely that the practical approach would motivate many of those "turned off" traditional school-style learning **but** needs to be introduced at the age of 14 years, as it is at this age when the young begin to be attracted to what they perceive as more adult activities – when the turning against the more academic approach to teaching begins to demonstrate itself.

The most sought after adult activity by those not interested in further study is the ability to earn money and to have the freedom and ability to make one's chosen purchases. This is a strong motivating force. Consequently, the feasibility of developing an education system that places older pupils in what they can see to be real life work situations needs to be considered. Such a system would be a development of apprenticeship schemes in which a wage is paid. Day or half day release from the work environment for purposes of study in a college may well be a more successful way to motivate young people than vice versa.

Although some employers already play their part in work placement, many do not and many small businesses may not be able to do so for financial reasons. Any expansion of vocational courses and their assessment will require more placements to be available in industry and commerce and the co-operation of many more employers will be necessary. A change of culture is required to one in which it is the general rule for employers to become a part of the education system insofar as it caters for the post 14 year old. If the initiative is to be taken seriously, government funding (in the form of tax incentives and/or grant aid to employers) will be a necessity.

Provision of vocational learning in more than one institution

It is expected that schools and colleges will work together to provide facilities for vocational courses *(11.14)* but this is not by any means a new or untried exercise and the implications of such arrangements should already be fully appreciated. For instance, the transfer of young people from one institution to another at various times during the education week provides opportunities for inappropriate behaviour. Who has responsibility for these people when between institutions? Each institution involved has to be responsible for behaviour standards, attendance, monitoring progress etc for learners when in their institutions. To help with this, to avoid conflicts and confusion, there needs to be agreed a mutually recognised code of expected behaviour and clearly defined actions which follow misbehaviour. Where more than one institution is working with the same learners there is the additional responsibility of liaison between institutions: particularly significant in compiling any student reports or records.

Vocationally orientated courses for 14-16 year olds

When referring to those who become disillusioned with secondary education, we are talking about a significant proportion of the 14-16 age group as well as those over the statutory school leaving age and the White Paper (9.29) accepts this and proposes a new work-focussed programme for 14- to 16-year-olds. This is where the provision of workshops and plans for school-college schemes of learning needs careful consideration.

Who is this to be for? One group of young people who are not partaking fully of educational opportunities is certainly that where they are not only "switched off" educationally but are antisocial and probably delinquent. These individuals need to require "general skills, attitudes and behaviours so important to employment and progression in learning" *(9.29)* but the implications of getting these young people onto and fully involved in any disciplined activity are enormous and not purely educational.

The White Paper *(Executive Summary note 17 paras. 2, 3 and 4)* referred to people who have serious personal problems and suggests that a suitable course would offer work-based learning, for something like two days each week, providing a study route to a level 1 Diploma qualification which would lead to further training further areas such as apprenticeships. But are the problems relating to the education of these young people fully realised?

For those with serious problems consistency and stability are essential. Movement from one institution to another, implied by the work-based learning for two days per week, is unsettling. It is these young people who will need the closest individual supervision and continuous individual counselling. Only as they make progress through solving their problems, may they eventually come to a position where they can follow the programme suggested.

Another group, in terms of the ideal objective of natural justice quoted in the White Paper, more deserving of help with learning, is that containing well adjusted self-disciplined low-level learners. The programme suggested is more appropriate to those with learning difficulties without personal problems of other kinds. Even so: only two days a week out of five – will this be sufficient to give the desired motivation?

Young Apprenticeships

In September 2004 the government introduced the Young Apprenticeships scheme for 14-year-olds, where the students are expected to combine traditional school work with learning in the work place. This is probably the most successful way forward (in terms of motivation of the disaffected), BUT will it be possible to provide the required number of work placements for more young people?

A longer school/college working day

The intention *(7.11)* to have all 14- to 16-year-olds working towards the Diploma (with workplace content) and the full National Curriculum raises the question: is there enough time in the week? Is a longer working day required? Is a longer working day desirable? After all, the intention is to bring young people into the real world of work and secondary school student-contact teaching hours do not at present match employment hours. If the intention is to prepare young people for integration into the work places of industry and commerce it would surely be advantageous to introduce older students into longer working hours while they are in training.

Personalised learning programmes

The White Paper proposed personalised programmes, including personal development and, presumably, individual counselling and guidance with an adviser. This is expensive because of its tutor-to-learner ratio and the specialist staff required. Personal one-to-one guidance is an essential part of education for all young people and particularly so for those who have difficulties with learning. Certainly the creation of more openings in employment for those with learning difficulties is *(9.25)* is essential BUT this applies to many who, for various reasons, do not thrive on academic learning NOT just those with the most obvious learning disabilities.

Provision of accommodation and teaching for vocational education

The notion of providing vocational or more practical based teaching strategies for those who do not find academic learning attractive is fine and the Government proposals are based on giving them courses which lead to vocational qualifications at 16 and which will be a stepping stone to further post-16 vocational courses and qualifications. The notion is an excellent one but who and how these courses are to be provided requires careful planning. The White Paper outlines some thinking on the provision of resources but how realistic is this?

There certainly is a serious intention *(outlined in the Executive Summary Note 20)* to extend the education system so that it can provide for vocational courses by, for example, increasing the availability of Centres of Vocational Excellence and establish Skills Academies which will be expected to be centres of excellence for the teaching of skills. There is the promise of appropriate accommodation and resources becoming available to provide for vocational education and a clear indication that government would support high performing 11-16 schools with the development of courses for older students.

Government is keen to build on existing strengths and this is obviously a sound policy, but how far does this help in real circumstances? The number of Centres of Vocational Excellence needs to cover all geographical areas. Can such Centres cover the whole country? Is it possible for all learners to have access to them from within easy reach of their homes? In the larger cities, towns and conurbations a variety of provision is more viable than in the sparser populated areas. Choice is therefore more likely.

This argument also applies to specialist schools. By definition, a specialist school should specialize in its nominated discipline, but it may be that a considerable proportion of those in the immediate catchment area do not want this particular specialism. Where do they find what they do want? In large towns, conurbations and cities it is likely that another specialist school will provide what is required within reasonable travelling distance. Reasonable travelling distance is a function not only of simple mileage but also of available transport. At one time (was it 60 years ago?) young people could and would cycle across town to school – now, in spite of recent initiatives to promote cycling among the population, it is probably not safe for them to do so. Accessibility to the education of one's choice therefore becomes a problem.

Transport to school/college and for transfer from one institution to another is already provided for some BUT will surely be required for many more.

It is expected that schools will provide the resources and accommodation for extended vocational education although it is understood that all schools will not be able to cater for all vocational lines *(7.26)*. It is also expected that schools and colleges will need to expand *(11.12)*: a fine idea so long as the need for resources is fully understood and those resources are provided.

There is the expectation that the best institutions should give help to the less successful, BUT it is those schools which are not doing so well which need more resources, such as buildings, real life workshops and commercial premises and the staff to supervise them, not the most successful which are presumably thriving on what they already have. It is essential to recognize that the traditional "thirty to a class" is certainly not possible in realistic work place environments, with costly implications applying to the employment of teaching staff.

It has been accepted that more post-16 places will be required, with the expectation that both schools and colleges will make this provision. But, without more resources they will not be able to. They need additional industrial and commercial-standard space and equipment, and the staff to run them.

There is also an expectation that high performing 11 – 16 schools will provide some of this. Why only high performing schools? It is those schools which perform worst in the academic areas where most vocational provision is required. To deny them resources in favour of those already doing well will see them fail further. Is this the intention? Should they be closed? If they are, it is logical to suppose that the good schools will have to become larger, more impersonal and needful of firm discipline: producing a harsher society with less easy mutual understanding and co-operation.

As a one-time head-teacher of an 11-16 comprehensive school having an intake where a large proportion of the young people had poor language skills, where motivation in academic learning was poor among many and where there were a considerable number of youngsters with personal problems, I always wanted extra resources to improve the learning facilities. I would have liked to introduce more practical, vocational courses. We did try: sending some to the neighbouring technical college for some of their curriculum time and, insofar as limited accommodation and equipment allowed, tried to develop more practical learning possibilities in school.

The Government is also keen to show things can be done and are already happening. It is shown that schools already offer courses in vocational subjects to the 14 – 16 age group and that there are now GCSEs in vocational subjects and circa 2005 that some 90,000 young people were already spending some of their time learning in the more adult environment of colleges rather than schools. Indeed, my school was involved in such a scheme some thirty years ago. It can be argued however that trials and local enthusiasms are one thing: providing for all in need is something different.

Does the provision of vocational education suggest that a sensible development would be the division of school from college at say 14 or 15 years of age, with pupils qualifying by studying for a primary level education certificate in school and then progressing as students or trainees to the more grown up environment of college for further study? The actual physical change from the environment of school to college could be a useful factor in the motivation of the young learner.

The **Great** Education Controversy

10. Assessment: tests, examinations and qualifications

Those who have promoted the philosophy of one school for all have, perhaps inadvertently, while driven by an underlying ideology, helped to create a major dilemma in the field of assessing learning progress, diagnosing learning problems, reporting attainments and in the development of a realistic system of qualifications.

In simple terms, a number of assumptions appear to have proved a hindrance to objectivity. Confusion has arisen over such concepts as: the division of children according to their ability – it is elitist to show some as being more able than others, to encourage elitism is undesirable – and it is socially unjust to send academically able children to grammar schools. There is confusion concerning the definition and value of elitism; a denial that some people are more able than others in a whole spectrum of human activities. Ability has been correlated with social background, individual circumstances of birth and early upbringing and, its identification and application subdued.

These assumptions are, of course, oversimplified, and oversimplification results in the refusal to accept people as being unique individuals with many varied individual strengths and weaknesses, different talents and indeed different personalities. This has too often led to the narrow focussing of attention on academic ability and learning alone, and the eclipsing of other significant forms of human talent and their cultivation.

So long as academic success is overemphasised, only those with academic ability can be seen to succeed. It is this insistence on there being one all important ability encouraged by one teaching strategy which has given rise to difficulties with the establishing of a realistic system for the assessing, grading and reporting of achievement.

If the above assumptions are taken to be sacrosanct, it follows that selection procedures become suspect. It is as though the division of people according to their strengths and weakness is an evil in itself. All tests and examinations which are then used to show up differences, where some must fail to reach given standards, are seen to be undesirable.

This has led to the abolition of the 11 plus examination and the continued pressure for the closure of the remaining schools which select their intake by referring to academic ability. In February 2006, education reforms which the Labour Government was attempting to bring to Parliament had to be watered down due to pressure from the anti-selection lobby. More recently there has been the initiative to forbid schools to select their pupils according to their perceived abilities, and a ban on schools interviewing parents of children as a part of the procedures for school entry. This is disastrous when what is required to enable the full development of human talent, and satisfaction for individuals, is more selection on grounds of a spectrum of abilities, talents and personalities; selection brought about by the use of appropriate tests, interviews and counselling; and selection for entry in to appropriate courses, with appropriate teaching styles, in places tailormade to provide an essential variety of instruction.

The denial of the need to select has also led to the construction of a clumsy all-embracing school-leaving examination in which no one must fail: but with an apparent contradiction seen in the introduction of standardised testing at ages seven, eleven and fourteen, with the extension of the system to those entering school for the first time. Of course, the former is meant to be a *qualification* and the latter a *means of assessing general standards*.

It is time for a re-appraisal of the testing and examining aspect of education, asking the question: why do we need to test and examine at all? Finding a sound objective educational answer to the question, rather than a stereotyped, ideological, misconceived and confusing response, should show the way towards a more universally acceptable, understood and valued system.

Reasons for testing and examining

A moments' reflection suggests that we do indeed need to test, examine and report results. The reasons are quite clear. There is the need to give learners a meaningful knowledge of the results of their studying: demonstrating what they know, whether they understand what they apparently know, and whether they can use what they have learned. It has been shown by psychologists that knowledge of results is all-important for the learner and is significant in the promoting of successful learning. Secondly there is the need to diagnose problems arising in learning, to find weaknesses which need putting right. Diagnostic tests are the tools which help teachers find appropriate strategies for helping individual learners overcome their problems. Thirdly there is the need to provide qualifications: the certificates and diplomas which tell employers and course organisers, as precisely as possible, what people know and what they can do. Fourthly is the need to demonstrate accountability so that parents can have confidence that information provided by schools and colleges presents a correct summary of what they offer and the degree of success which they achieve and indeed, people outside the profession should also have confidence in the performance of the country's educational establishments.

The subjective assessment of learning

Testing has always been an element of class instruction with teachers using their own methods to assess their pupils' learning. For instance, a piece of learning, memorising, could be tested by the teacher asking ten questions, the pupils writing their answers on sheets of paper, and the pupils marking each other's papers when the teacher reads out the answers. The system worked well, generated motivation and gave a knowledge of results.

In the post war years most secondary schools measured progress in terms of a child's position in its class, based upon the marks collected from tests such as those above and internal, teacher set, bi-annual school examinations; only those attending selective schools taking an externally set and marked leaving examination.

The pupils earned 'points' according to the teachers' marking schemes in each of the school subjects. For convenience, the total in each case was contrived to be one hundred and the marks described as percentages. So far, so good!

Problems arising from the use of subjective or informal assessment methods

The advantage of this system is the facility of regularly and frequently giving marks for correct answers or parts of answers, each being awarded for a right response. The pupil can see at a glance how well he or she had done in terms of the highness or lowness of the score, and by reference to the ticks and crosses on the answer paper see immediately which aspects have been, or not been, learned. The strategy provides the valuable sound knowledge of results which has already been emphasised as being so important for the learner.

Inadequacies originate from the lack of objectivity, different standards being applied by different teachers. A mark of 65 per cent in one class can equate to 80 per cent in another. High marks could be achieved say in geography because its teacher liberally gives out points for each one of the simplest facts recalled. Conversely it could be extremely difficult to earn marks in a modern language test because that teacher deducts marks for each simple error, quickly reducing a score to nothing!

Pupils' marks were ranked for each subject enabling them to see where they were in relation to the rest of the class. To be bottom of the class was seen in terms of the pupil having not paid attention, not given enough effort to learning the material, or had not carried out procedures properly. Success or failure was placed clearly at the pupil's door, seen as his or her fault and, more significantly, could be rectified if only he or she set to work more diligently.

The whole system was based on the teachers' ability to gauge nationally expected standards and could therefore be wildly inaccurate, there being no external scale against which the teachers' or the schools' standards could be judged.

The scheme has merit where all of the learners start from a similar baseline, that is, have already reached similar standards of achievement and have been shown to be of similar in learning ability. Where learners start from different baselines, those who find learning difficult will always be at the bottom, no matter how hard they try. This perceived injustice, particularly obvious in classes comprised of all ranges of academic ability, leading to a number of bizarre developments.

On the one hand it was argued by some that pupils should not be compared with each other at all and yet on the other it was seen as essential that an individual should be able to see their position in relation to some kind of criteria. Presumably to reduce the stigma of failure in comparison situations, the reporting of marks actually gained was frowned upon, in some schools replaced by putting raw scores into broad banded grades, and the publication of rank orders abandoned. Giving the grades letters A, B, C, D, E or numbers 1, 2, 3, 4, 5, for example, was seen as more acceptable than marks out of one hundred.

Some of the earliest comprehensive schools grouped pupils so that those of similar ability were placed in one class. That is, they used streaming and quickly developed a rank order of classes rather than individual pupils within one class. It became plainly obvious that there were 'top' and 'bottom' streams and failure was even more clearly defined according to the class one was in. Surely, being in stream three in a three stream school with people of near equal ability, is less demoralising than being in the bottom stream of a school with eight or more streams.

The response from the educational establishment has been to try to disguise this perceived humiliation by disguising the rank of the classes by awarding them odd coded labels; but it was soon very clear which class was top and which was at the bottom, and every rank in between was known by all of the pupils in no time at all. Within each class of similar ability, rank order did not matter too much – but human nature determined that it did matter if you were in a low ability class!

The Normal Distribution Hypothesis

Another development in testing and reporting of results has been the application of the normal distribution hypothesis which states that in any test situation, "test" being defined in the widest terms, that so long as there is a sufficiently large number of candidates, the distribution of scores earned will follow the normal distribution curve. Using a five point grading system, A to E, approximately fifty per cent of the subjects can be expected to obtain scores in the middle C band, twenty-four per cent to obtain scores in bands B and D, and three-and-one-half per cent in bands A and E. If applied over the full range of pupils in one year of an eight form entry comprehensive school, one-hundred-and-twenty would be expected to come within grade C, about fifty-seven in each of grades B and D and three in each of grades A and E.

A number of observations can be made about such a method of grading test or examination results. Firstly, the bands are far too wide. Half of the candidates are going to be labelled average. Half of those will have gained scores above the halfway point and half scores below, but there will be no means of indicating which of these have been the most successful. A considerable number of pupils obtaining scores above the half way position will be judged equal in attainment to those with scores below this point. Secondly, approximately one quarter of the candidates will be labelled either above or below average in bands B and D respectively. Finally, only a handful will be shown to be very good and a handful very poor.

Even if a youngster's subsequent test scores vary by a considerable amount, unless already a borderline case, no change in grade will be recorded. Consequently, most will never be able to climb into a higher grade, and they have no incentive to try to score more marks. The most able, scoring grade A, will be so few that it will be they who are shown to be the odd-ones-out. The majority of the most successful workers will always obtain grade Bs and again will have nothing to urge them to strive harder. Those who find the work difficult will always be grade D, below average, or, in a very few cases, E, poor. There is no means of escape from this trap because, by definition, it has been decided that the tested group will always have its scores distributed according to this pattern. Even if a seven point scale is adopted, the problems remain, although with less severity.

A further problem with internal testing is the validation of the grades against standards outside the school. Any grading system of this type shows a rather inexact and rather vague level of achievement within a class, a year group, or even whole school. It can be arranged that the year group always has its correct number of pupils in the various bands, but what does this actually mean in terms of real attainment? In one school the average could in fact be rather poor, while in another it could be high. A possible cause is that different schools and different year groups in the same school may be comprised of learners of greater or less ability. Another possibility is that the teaching in the different groups is different and may be either good or bad. With the desire to ensure a fair education for all it is necessary to know which case applies and to do this some comparison between the internal distributions and the national picture is required.

It appears that those in favour of such broad grading systems are arguing against the showing up of differences resulting from competition, but they are also arguing against human nature. People are individuals, all different, having different talents and different levels of competence and attainment in a variety of abilities. If society, and indeed an individual within that society, is to thrive, this wealth of human talent has to be encouraged, developed, and used. Therefore, the application of norm referencing, as in the system illustrated here, is inappropriate because it does not emphasise success where success is achieved and does not motivate the learner to strive for higher standards.

In an attempt to reward hard work, not only have grades been given for attainment, but also for the perceived effort. The claim in this case is that the hard worker can be rewarded with a grade A, although only reaching a low attainment. Unfortunately, human nature is such that individuals quickly convince themselves that there is no point in working hard when you can reach the same level by applying rather less time and energy to the task! This is perhaps particularly pertinent in the learning of school work as youngsters can find so many more attractive occupations on which to spend their time.

There is also an unreality in this concept: it is good to know a learner is hard working but a hard worker who has learnt little is of less value than one who has learnt a great deal, the ideal being, of course, the one who has a high level of achievement and works hard.

It is easily understood that the school teacher's major task is to encourage the learner and that a scheme which more or less pre determines that the learner will always obtain poor grades does nothing to assist in this matter. The key of course lies in the reason for the comparisons.

Standardised tests

Having considered the disadvantages of norm referencing, when applied in individual schools, it is important to note that there is a situation in which this system does have value. If applied to tests given to very large numbers of candidates, from a large number of schools, areas of the country and social groups, the results do properly conform to a distribution of scores for a normal population. When the tests are afterwards given to other smaller groups, the individual scores will show where each stands in relation to the national distribution. There is value in this. Such tests are referred to as standardised tests.

A problem with the application of such tests is the knowing of precisely what element of learning, knowledge or skill is being measured. Many have been developed around the concept of reasoning ability, how well people can recognise and comprehend relationships between variables. Again, there is some value in knowing how well a person can think in these terms – not least because the ability does seem to correlate with the ability to understand new material. But there are other factors in learning: an obvious one must be the ability to memorise data. If you easily memorise data and have the ability to reason, it is likely that you will be able to learn new material more easily than someone without these facilities.

The content of such standardised tests can be controlled. It can be formulated around the elements of reading, spelling, more advanced mathematics, or of language skills, or concepts in science, or geography – and so on. They can be used to find out how an individual compares with the national picture in any single area of learning. But it must be remembered that most will be average, by definition.

Where this system has been used in the assessment of arithmetic and reading standards, there have emerged the concepts of arithmetic and reading ages. Simply set the learners the appropriate test, read off their actual test scores and see how these compare with the national picture. If the score matches that for age 12 years, the candidate has an arithmetic age or reading age of 12 years although its chronological age may be below or above this level, in which case the he or she is seen to be advanced or backward for their age.

Standardised tests are also useful for selecting those who are doing well and who stand a good chance of doing well in the future – so long as they are not used as a one-off-and-for-ever fixed grading system on a narrow range of abilities. People change as they go through life and children change most dramatically. Furthermore, the work of the psychologist, Piaget, showed that the ability to reason develops throughout childhood and at different rates in different children. If this is the case, those who develop the power to reason efficiently earliest may quite rightly be labelled the most intelligent in their early lives, but what about those who develop later? There are also other changes which occur with maturity: greater emotional stability; a more settled, or for that matter, a less settled, social environment: all influencing the ability of a person to think and learn.

National Standardised Attainment Tests STATS

In recent years there has been much argument about the programme of national testing of children using the Standard Attainment Tests at the ages of seven, eleven and fourteen, with the extension of the system to those entering school for the first time. The reason for these tests is to measure how an individual and how schools compare with the national picture; and this is a necessary facility. The wrongness of such a scheme lies in *how the results are used.* It is for to the administrators to use the system in a reasonable way.

What has been done has proved to be unreasonable. A big fuss is made about the importance of the tests and of preparation for them, undoubtedly causing stress among the most conscientious but struggling learners. This is not a purpose of the testing situation. Surely it is not beyond the powers of teachers and administrators to treat testing as a normal part of the routine day. Frequent tests should be a part of routine, each exercise, or group of exercises being assessed to check the effectiveness of both the teaching and the learning. Longer tests or examinations have always been routine in secondary schools, and so they should be, and standardised tests should be a part of this routine.

As far as the individuals and their parents are concerned the results of these tests should be confidential between them and the school, results being sent home via the pupil report system (in the traditional paper and envelope fashion or by today's electronic mail) with face-to-face meetings between teachers and parents to discuss progress and necessary follow up action.

In addition to this aspect of the programme is the desire to know that a school is serving its pupils well – that the overall results of the school are up to the expected standards. But who should know? The current fashion is to say that parents must know and in order for them to know the school's results must be published – the league table method. But parents do not need to know *in this way*. What parents need is to have confidence in the work of the school and to be in a position to trust the system that their children's schools are doing a good job. The emphasis must be on trust.

Whether the school is doing well is a matter for the inspectorate to assess. The inspectors need to know the position of each school within its jurisdiction in the national scheme of things. It is for them to immediately spot shortcomings and to have the authority to take appropriate action for putting matters right. This is nothing to do with the press or the media (although they would like it to be involved because news is their business).

With the publication of league tables has come the public castigation of schools with the consequent damaging of the morale of both pupils and staff. It has not resulted in the successful input of resources to help the schools reach higher standards.

It is claimed that the testing burden has become too great, causing stress among the children and that teaching has become dominated by the time taken up teaching to the requirements of the tests: this is surely due to the social climate that has been allowed to grow up around the system and not the system itself.

School leaving examinations

It was reported in chapter 3 that the introduction of secondary school examinations as we understand them started with the School Certificate Examination in 1917, when only grammar school pupils remained at school to the age of sixteen. All others left to continue training, as opposed to education, in the work place, and may have attended night school in order to earn other recognised qualifications from such bodies as the City and Guilds.

The certification of standards reached by most learners comprised of a collection of school reports and a leaving testimonial. With the striving for equality of educational opportunity came the introduction of a school leaving examination for all.

The General Certificate of Education

In 1944 the School Certificate was replaced by the General Certificate of Education, GCE or "O" level, where it was possible to gain a qualification in one subject only, instead of having to pass five subjects selected from three compulsory groups under the old regulations. The secondary modern schools adopted the examination for those of their youngsters who could gain some benefit from such an academic course of study.

On the question of the lowering of standards it is obvious that it is easier to gain a collection passes in a variety of freely chosen subjects than it is to pass a strictly defined five. In the former you simply avoid those you do not like or those you cannot do. In the latter you have pass all of the subjects in the stated categories whether you are good at them or not.

The Certificate of Secondary Education

In 1965 the new format Certificate of Secondary Education, CSE, was introduced, with five grades: grade 1 was to correspond to an "O" level pass (without admitting that there were different levels of "O" level pass, and without stating which was expected to correspond with the CSE 1. In reality, as there was no subdivision of grade 1 CSE, it came to be equated with the lowest "O" level pass. Grade 4 CSE was defined as the standard reached by an average pupil, while grades 2 and 3 were rather vaguely described as standards between 1 and 4. Grade 5 was awarded in cases where it was judged that it had not been inappropriate for the candidate to have taken the examination.

No one failed: an attempt to deny the concept of failure in the misguided belief that a failure in an examination labelled one an irreparable total failure for life. A strange concept, for those who have failed once, may struggle again and eventually achieve success. Furthermore, failure in one area is not failure in all and, risking repetition different people have strengths in different areas: failure in one should lead to the struggle for success elsewhere. Those who did in fact fail to produce an appropriate standard of work in the CSE, yet were somehow entered for the examination, ended up with the odd grade U for unclassified.

Surely a school leaving examination only has value if it demonstrates what the candidate knows and what he or she can do. To define a reasonable level of expected standards is sensible and it follows that the candidates either reach the standards or not. A system which provides a certificate to show how badly a youngster has done is of no value in employment and is demoralising for the youngster.

A further lowering of standards can be explained by the confusion resulting from the content of courses which could be taken in *Three Modes*: Mode I, Mode II and Mode III.

Mode I was the traditional format for school leaving examinations: an examination board set a syllabus, the school taught to it, the examination board set and marked the examination paper. That is, the examination was an external examination, external to the school. In Mode II the school set the syllabus, that is the teachers set the scheme of work to be taught; an examination board moderated and accepted or rejected the scheme, if accepted, set and marked the examination papers. In Mode III the school established the syllabus, set and marked the examination papers.

Within such a system there could be a myriad of different groups of subject material established under various titles and only a thorough perusal of the individual syllabus in each case gave the reader of a certificate an indication of what should have been taught and learned.

As subject syllabi become so numerous and varied, an average standard, labelled grade 4, is difficult to describe in terms of real criteria. Furthermore, the story which was put about in the early days of the examination, before the statutory leaving age became sixteen, is worth repeating. The scene was a school corridor where a teacher had stopped one of his pupils (we will call her Julie) to enquire whether she would be staying on to complete the CSE examination.

"What do I want to do that for?" she enquired.

"To obtain some school leaving qualifications," the teacher responded.

"What grades do you think I could get?" she asked.

"Well Julie, I think that you could manage grade 4 in most of your subjects."

"What does grade 4 mean, sir?"

"It means that you are a good, average girl," the teacher replied with confidence.

But the girl began to laugh.

"Why do I have to take examinations and be given certificates to show that I am a good, average girl? I know that already!" And she walked away laughing loudly at what she saw as an absurdity.

Because the level reached by any candidate taking the examination relied on the concept of an average standard, the problems associated with validation by comparison with the theoretical normal distribution curve, applied to the CSE grading system, involving the problems previously seen to exist with any system based upon grade bands. Once again, most could expect to get, and would get, irrespective of effort, an average grade – and this is not an acceptable system of qualification. Qualifications should not be the same for everybody. Different qualifications are required for different occupations. Qualifications must clearly show what a person knows and what he or she can do.

The assessment of a general level of education

There is an exception to the rule that different people should have different qualifications: it is the need to show that all young people have been educated; to show that they can read and write, measure and calculate, work with the technology of the 21st century; and have a reasonable amount of knowledge relating to the world in which they live, found in such subjects as art, history, geography, music, science and so on. With this notion there develops the need for a common curriculum with a general qualification: a qualification which could be achieved by different students at different ages and at different grades, but the lowest grade having real meaning. That is to say the lowest grade measures a positive level of attainment.

Such a primary level of qualification would be remarkably similar to that in use during the pre-CSE era and of value to those not going on into further education – now everyone is expected to remain in education until they are at least 16 years of age.

Weaknesses in the present examination system

Nevertheless, returning to what occurred rather than what could occur in the future, with the raising of the school leaving age and with the encouragement from teachers; a large number of youngsters have indeed joined in the exercise of scrambling for the best grades they can achieve in a variety of academic areas. But the question remains: what is the sense in suffering the restrictions and trials of a complex examination system in order to show that you can obtain an average grade on a conglomeration of ill-defined variables?

Schools played the game to their advantage. As raw examination scores were subjected to the normal distribution hypothesis, if more pupils could be encouraged to enter the examination, more would obtain better grades and the number of pupils gaining five "O" levels or grade 1 CSEs could be increased – and that looked good for individual schools in the list of published examination results.

It was inevitable that schools with pupils gaining a large number of "O" level "passes" would be judged as good schools, better than those with few such passes - particularly with the publication of school results, emphasising the differences. Tradition determined that the Grammar Schools, with their high percentage of pupils gaining good examination grades, going on to gain what were perceived as the best rewarded positions in employment, must be the schools providing the best education. The next step was for secondary modern and comprehensive schools to try to copy them.

Disaster lies in this direction: the abilities and attainments of the pupils in the schools before they started the examination courses were not considered - and what abilities are being talked about anyway? Largely, of course, traditional academic abilities!

There is also a tendency to claim that differences are nothing to do with individual inherited differences – denying that people have such a great variety of individual strengths and weaknesses by birthright and early nurturing – and attempts to blame the failure totally onto social and environmental factors. As so much is laid at the door of social background, some people may be tempted to say that we had better not have any examinations at all!

In spite of all of this the examination system began and continued to grow. As trying to administer two different examinations in all-in-one schools caused problems; a growing number of borderline cases being entered for both "O" level and CSE, the examination timetables overlapping and the whole thing an undesirable burden; the common to all General Certificate of Secondary Education Examination was eventually introduced to replace the two separate examinations. This was a further move in the direction of one system of education for all.

Accompanied by the publication and close scrutiny of the number of pupils gaining average and above average examination grades in a school – league tables, and the consequent realisation that some schools were apparently far better than others, comes the manipulation of students' entries, their choice of subjects and the actual content of syllabi in order to maximise the number of good grades obtained by the schools.

There has developed an annual scramble by the individual students for examination pass grades at "O" and "A" level which has led to an emotional and unrealistic striving for apparent higher and ever higher standards in those examinations: a kind of wishful thinking in which everyone will somehow earn more and better grades each year. Yet, on the one hand Government tries to show how standards have gone up year after year, while on the other employers and universities complain about how incompetent their applicants for jobs and places on courses actually are. And even the Government shows some indication of uncertainty as in the 14 – 19 White Paper it admitted that there are weaknesses in the system *(for instance in Chapter 8 where it is proposed to strengthen GCSEs and A levels)*.

It has already been emphasised that the school leaving age has been raised from 14 years in 1945, to 16 years now, with the expectation that more and more young people should remain in education until at least 19 years of age. The corresponding educational provision however has failed to cater for the wide range of abilities, personalities and aspirations of the young people who are involved. Education in schools has largely followed the academic style, failing to cater for those who cannot or do not wish to take part in such learning and for those who do not wish to be in a school or college environment, no matter what is taught or how it is taught.

For the most part, young people in secondary education have been encouraged to follow traditional academic-style courses consisting largely of academic style subjects and taught using academic styles of teaching – with various initiatives being developed to make the subject matter interesting! These courses have resulted in greatly increased numbers of students taking an increased number of academic style examinations in a wide variety of subjects. In order to bring more young people to succeed in this system the original academic examinations have been variously extended, contents modified and standards confused. The end product is *(The Tomlinson Report, page 84 note 222)* that there are millions of examination entries each year, many of which merely indicate that the student has followed a course in general education with various degrees of success.

The *standards* reached are unclear. The system does not provide a suitable qualification for employment, or a qualification for entry into further education, or a diagnosis of weaknesses which could be addressed. It is a white elephant – a huge unnecessary and largely useless burden on young people, teachers and those who examine.

The demands of the growing examination system

There are also other developments which have arisen from the phenomenal growth in the school leaving examination field which need serious consideration. There is the sitting of mock or trial examinations for all young people, once at least and possibly twice in a school/college year. These examinations involve teachers in setting papers, marking scripts, and invigilation duties. They cannot take on these responsibilities and teach at the same time.

Even a quick look at the extensive examination timetables of the school leaving examinations for the 1960s cannot fail to demonstrate the demands on teacher and teaching time. The start in late April or early May means that normal teaching ceases for much of the summer term: in turn meaning that course instruction in the last two years of the 11- to 16-year education programme lasts only for one year and two terms.

An examination system requires invigilators to supervise the candidates in the examination halls and teachers had to take on this task, taking them away from classroom teaching. Furthermore, the system is complicated, disrupting the normal lesson timetable because different members of classes take different examinations at different times. A teacher may be unavailable to teach because he or she is invigilating and, when free from this duty, a large proportion of his or her class is absent taking papers in a different subject. It may seem to be a good idea for classes to continue for purposes of revision but either the teacher or some of the pupils are not available to take part. If remnants of classes are combined, some learners will not have their original teacher, a factor that may be seen as insignificant, but in reality can confuse the learners.

The conclusion has been for lessons to end for the candidates when the examinations start, excluding pupils from normal school from May onwards. As the results of examinations are not published until August the young people are placed in a limbo-like situation for something like three months. The conscientious and able spend their time privately revising for their examinations, finding a vacation job to earn them much sought after cash and possibly taking a structured holiday. Many however do not revise, even temporary employment is scarce and young people are left with time on their hands – life seems to be one long rather aimless session of perceived pleasure and this is not a good foundation for subsequent disciplined learning or for the routine of the work place.

As the CSE examination introduced a greater reliance on internal assessment by teachers, a high proportion of marks being awarded for projects completed, in theory, through the private study of the young people. This was another aspect of the new examination which created a huge time consuming burden on teachers: each individual project had to be assessed by them and their assessments moderated by other teachers external to the school.

Projects in academic subjects have proved to be of doubtful value in determining what a young person can do or has learnt. In the practical subjects the craftsmanship in the making of wooden or metal artefacts; the producing of items of clothing or the cooking of culinary dishes; and the talent of the artist in the crafting of pots, design, painting and photography, can be measured – and the work known to be that of the candidate.

Many of the academic projects proved to be no more than a conglomeration of materials copied from elsewhere – and possibly the result of assistance by well meaning parents, not entirely the work of the candidate. A further impingement on teaching time was the decision to involve teachers in the constructing of the syllabi and the construction of the examination papers, that is, in deciding what shall be taught. A whole host of staff were suddenly required to be out of school attending subject panel meetings.

In addition, the notion that teachers should decide what to teach and what is to be examined is flawed. Too many individuals and groups suddenly produced their own ideas on what a subject discipline should contain. No longer was it possible to know from a nationally produced syllabus what was being taught. Consequently, any grade in any examination on any subject so compiled became meaningless – unless the user of the results was prepared to personally study a vast mass of individual work programmes, an unrealistic situation.

Subject content

There is no point in arguing the case for this or that mode of assessment until *the content of what is to be assessed is made perfectly clear and is of value to the learner in terms of qualification for employment or further learning.* This is recognised and emphasised in Chapter 2 of the Tomlinson Report, page 19 note 1, where the 'diploma framework' being recommended is the development by Tomlinson for a new examination system, but the message should apply just as well to the system in existence. It is essential that this realism is understood to apply to all courses, whether academic or practical, and requires the careful defining of course and subject content. Too many courses evolved from Mode III CSE programmes, created out of the desire to provide certificates for all, or due to a failure to recognise the value of true subject knowledge and skills, have become socially acceptable but valueless in terms of qualification for anything.

The wrongness of "none must fail"

There are dangers in the concept of none must fail and in the desire to provide a qualification for everyone. It has already been noted that, in an attempt to provide some qualification for all, the curriculum has been broadened. The new initiative in vocational education is a further example of the introduction of more subjects to be studied and assessed; and this is fine so long as the subjects contain worthwhile knowledge and skills. There may be a temptation to introduce trivial content, and this has to be guarded against, new areas of study being properly validated to ensure that they do indeed contain realistic useful knowledge and skills, and this must be done by nationally recognized and accredited institutions.

Proposals to "strengthen" "O" and "A" level examinations

The proposals made in 2005 did recognise the need for courses and subjects to have real meaning and value, useful knowledge and skills: it is essential that this need is answered. Proposals to strengthen 16 plus qualifications have been outlined: for instance, there has been the suggestion for the creation of a General (GCSE) diploma to provide a separate qualification for those gaining 5 A* to C GCSE subjects but to include English and maths in order to give encouragement to both the pupils and schools to reach higher standards in these subjects *(6.16)*, which is reminiscent of the original "O" level, and should be welcomed as a positive step taken to add to the value of the GCSE qualification.

Labour-market recognised qualifications for 14- to 19-year-olds were proposed in the White Paper *(Chapter 6)*: a welcome and necessary step with the reservation that academically able students are not encouraged to opt for workplace orientated vocational courses at 14, 16 or 18, when it is they who should be working towards academic based vocational courses in the universities.

The Tomlinson Report recommended a complete change in the qualifications system in which GCSEs and A levels would be abolished and replaced by one single diploma. Some see the continuation of GCSEs and A levels side by side with new diplomas as a failure to bridge the academic-vocational divide. They see a name change as essential, but there is another view, that success will lie in the realistic value of each qualification. Thinking continues to be dogged by the political misconception that all must have the same while experience demonstrates human nature displaying many unique differences.

Once again there is an underlying current of perceived social equality in this which is so unreal. Do we really need a system of diplomas which *appears* to give similarity when we know the content of the system must cater for wide spread differences? Why do we all have to have diplomas or all have to have degrees? Why can we not call a qualification in high intellectual learning, which must in the end have some vocational application, a degree; and a qualification in highly skilled practical learning a diploma? Each will have grades of achievement from average to high and some will fail in the sphere they have tried. The problem is one of perception and what is needed is a more equal recognition of the different talents people have to offer, which, in turn requires the provision within the economic system of employment areas which use and value all of these talents.

The Assessment Burden

It is recognised that the examination and testing system in our schools has become a burden on pupils and teachers alike and is recognised by the government in the White Paper 14 -19 Education and Skills *(10.9)*. There is the implication that government wants to ease this burden.

Teacher-led assessment

Teacher-led assessment, internal assessment for purposes of providing qualifications, increases the burden on *teaching staff* who need to be left to teach not examine. There are two separate tasks here.

The National Workforce Agreement

A new staffing structure has been applied to present day schools and colleges but does it fully recognise and take account of all of the non-teaching staff needed to run the examination system? Does it accept that there should be *teachers* who specialise in classroom teaching while others specialise in administrative duties, including those *teachers* setting, supervising and marking examinations, and setting and assessing practical test situations? Is it a good idea to have those who do the teaching also do the assessing? We already have specialist teachers who act as examiners. Do they need to be internal to the teaching institution? Is it sensible to have those who teach having responsibility for granting, or not, the qualification for those they have taught? Is this an appropriate route for nationally recognised qualifications?

The growth in assessment has come with the recognition of the value of testing in the diagnosis of learning difficulties, the need for objective measures in the pursuance of accountability and with the vast expansion of the 16-19 examinations system. There is a conflict between the desire to continue with these admirable objectives and the cost involved. Cost includes the loss of valuable teaching time and the increase in the teachers' work load, as well as the more obvious expenditure on testing materials. There is also the pressure placed upon the learners – mainly a personal problem. There are those who take testing and examinations in their stride (without a care in the world), there are the majority who display a healthy and relatively harmless conscientious approach to the situation, and there is a minority which is overburdened to the extent of becoming unwell.

Possible ways of easing the burden of testing

The need for diagnostic testing and testing for accountability should be accepted as a necessary part of any education system but the area should be carefully studied with a view to:

a) Ensuring that testing (for knowledge of results, diagnosis and accountability) is seen as a routine aspect of learning, and not as something special and demanding of the unusual expenditure of nervous energy. A lessening of the public pressure to do well in league tables would help with this and could be achieved by abandoning the publishing of league tables while retaining the need to make results available to parents and professionals.

b) Ensuring that teaching time is not unduly lost by national testing. It may be worthwhile considering lengthening the teaching day. Many 14 to 19 institutions seem to finish formal classroom teaching before 3-30 in the afternoon, and this is not good preparation for transfer into the work place or further education.

c) Recognising that increased testing requires supervision from teaching staff, even if the setting of tests and the marking is carried out by agencies outside the teaching institution.

d) Recognising that counseling of those tested is necessary and that teaching staff are needed to do this, a system expensive in terms of workforce time. Once again, stating what should be so obvious: teachers cannot teach and take on the duties of counselors at the same time. To use teachers for counseling takes them away from teaching and the logical conclusion is that the workforce needs to increase, with costing implications.

Possible ways of easing the burden of examining

Through the careful re-appraisal of GCSE and A level examinations and the defining of new diplomas, ensuring course work is only used when it is essential to do so, sharpening content and making qualifications of real value, some easing of the examining burden is possible. Nevertheless, the raising of the school leaving age, the expectation that all will remain in education or training for longer and all will earn some form of qualification will change, and has already vastly changed the examination system from what it once was into an even greater mammoth activity. Therefore resources need to be brought in line with the present day expectations.

All aspects of examining need to be divorced from the teaching tasks. Staff cannot invigilate, moderate, complete internal assessment and themselves be examiners and, at the same time, teach efficiently. The tasks of teaching and running examinations need to be separated.

Eliminating the break in learning at the age of sixteen

If different teachers examine and invigilate from those who teach then teaching can continue during the examination period and afterwards: it should not be necessary for pupils and students to be denied revision classes or subsequently, more advanced instruction. The habit of breaking the learning pattern at 16 could and should be changed, with young people expecting to go on to further learning and/or work experience before the summer break.

Condensing the Curriculum

The White Paper *(4.18)* referred to proposals to introduce a two-year Key-stage 3 programme where the avoidance of the duplication of subject matter and better planning could sharpen the curriculum. The avoiding of duplication is an attractive idea, but in practice not so saving of time, without loss of efficient teaching, as may at first be thought and may also lead to confusion. Knowledge and skills are "packaged" and each package an understood unit of learning. The traditional "packaging", namely subjects, have proved to be an efficient grouping system and should not lightly be abandoned, although the notion that material can be taught through modules is already used in some learning situations.

The use of ICT in internal (teacher) assessment

The use of ICT in the assessment process is claimed to ease the burden of marking and recording results: For instance: it is suggested that the introduction of an online assessment system and electronic marking will help But this type of testing still needs invigilators, either taking staff from teaching duties or employing extra people.

The recording and reporting of the results of assessments

School Reports
In the post war years pupils were issued with twice yearly reports showing marks earned in both routine and examination work, brief remarks made by the teachers relating to the work done in each subject, an observation made by the class (registration) teacher, attendance and punctuality.

In addition the teachers' remarks would contain references to effort made, conduct and involvement in extra-curricular activities.

A collection of reports over a number of years would demonstrate a young person's attainments and progress: the final year's reports being, together with a testimonial, a kind of certificate of qualification which could be shown to prospective employers.

This twice-yearly exercise, where a report for each child in the school had to be circulated to each of his or her teachers so that the required entries could be made and afterwards to the head-teacher for an official signature, was a considerable exercise. A set of reports would need to be in the hands of each of some ten teachers for a significant span of time in order for them to be completed. The teachers would have this task to complete on top of their normal routine teaching of classes, meaning that they may have to do the job out of school hours, possibly at home. There would be opportunity for delay in cases where a well intentioned member of staff would hold on to a set for several days. But this was the system and the system was made to work.

In the grammar schools the report system was backed up by the results obtained in the external examinations, and with the further development of secondary modern and comprehensive schools, became the accepted method for reporting progress to parents.

A Student/Pupil Profile

In recent years the continuous recording of the more detailed achievements of pupils in the various elements of the curriculum, including the extra-curricular, throughout the whole period of education has come to be seen as a means of rewarding achievement. Such a system is known as a student or pupil profile. In basic terms it is what they were given before but with much more detail given on each of the included items and the whole collection given a formality, so that the young person ends up with a folder which contains everything recorded about his or her progress through a school or college.

Trials and seminars examining the case for such records have been taking place for many years and the experience gained by those involved in the introduction of these types of record in local schemes should not be overlooked.

If what is to be included is standardised, a nationally recognised format can be applied to the reporting of each young person's progress through school and the question arises: should the profile consequently *replace* traditional school reports? If not, work will be duplicated. If the profile replaces the traditional school report, yearly or twice yearly entries, and even entries at any time in the year, still need to be made in the profile. Who will be responsible for this? With so much more detail being required, the task becomes greater than with the old system.

There has been considerable debate about what should be included in a pupil's profile, the alternative title 'record of achievement' emphasising the notion that only positive aspects of the young person's progress should be recorded.

The growth in the litigation culture has also influenced what should and how it should be written. No longer can the teacher report that a pupil is lazy, for example, without backing up the statement with real events to prove it!

As well as personal student achievements it has also been suggested that test and examination results for the school as whole, the local authority and country be included in the profile. Perhaps this is the answer to the problem of reporting information confidentially to parents without actually publishing it in the press and media. But is this really a necessary inclusion in a personal document?

A very significant question is one of ownership. Is the profile the property of the learner? If so, will it be kept at home? If so, many will become lost and damaged. If profiles are not kept at home, how is pupil/student/parent access to them to be arranged? Again, a response is that information will be available online. There are already institutions where such a scheme is in use.

Not all parents/pupils/students have access to online facilities and it is those from the less advantaged homes that will most likely be in this position.

How is such a document to be presented to a prospective employer or college? Email?

Traditional paper and post methods are still required to reach these people: are these methods to be continued for all, and if so, tasks are duplicated, the workload increased.

Electronic recording of personal data raises questions of confidentiality, restricted access and data protection; furthermore electronic systems are known to fail, making the provision of a back up system essential.

The electronic system may well be *perceived* as labour saving but there remains the work associated with entering the data. Who is going to do this?

Will profiles really be more efficient in this, the school/college, setting? They are expensive. Will an employer or college really want to look at what appears to be a bulky all inclusive document?

The Tomlinson report visualised the electronic transcript or profile as a "gateway" to a more detailed portfolio giving, for example, component scores, examples of the person's work, an extended project and a personal statement. Is this another example of European standardisation, the Europass? Standardisation has the advantage of being broadly recognisable and understood but the disadvantages of having to leave things out because they do not apply to all or of becoming so all inclusive and bulky that no one has the time to consider their contents. Is such a massive and clumsy document practical?

If the system is adopted, what, in particular, would be contained in a "personal statement". Are only positive things to be included? Who is to decide what are positive and what are negative items? Are inclusions only to be recorded after consultation with the pupil/student and parents?

Who will be responsible for the profile in the school or college? Who will be concerned with bringing all the components together and ensuring that all appropriate documents are put in place and that confidentiality is safeguarded? Who will the pupil/student/parent go to when they want access to the profile? If they are not able obtain access online? Who will they go to for face-to-face consultation or advice arising from the reporting? All of this places a burden on institution staff.

11. The Curriculum

The simple notion that the comprehensive system will give equal educational opportunities to all children is very quickly seen to be not so simple after all. We have already noted some of the differences between schools which have developed in response to the call for comprehensive reorganisation and some of the problems which have arisen – problems which have evolved as educationalists have struggled to interpret and put into practice the philosophy of comprehensive schooling. Yet we have barely looked at the surface features of that philosophy.

It is claimed that the primary ideals are based upon egalitarianism, denying competition and anything which may result in elitism, privilege or divisiveness. Choice is seen as advantageous only to the most articulate and most determined, who are somehow always equated with the middle and upper classes. Yet this trait is surely as much related to personality as it is to class and is demonstrated to its maximum amongst politicians, aggressive television interviewers and commandeering salespeople – it is they surely who have and use the "gift of the gab", irrespective of any class factor!

So, whether we have seen the salvation of civilisation in this theoretical philosophy or not, what has actually happened to the curriculum, the content of what is taught as a result of this movement towards the all-in-one school?

The development of the curriculum

It can be argued that the traditional secondary school curriculum is that of the grammar school, a curriculum evolved from the academic approach to learning and developed as the route to university entrance, and consequently dominated by the requirements of those institutions, requirements which it may be assumed are right for those who possess minds which thrive on this type of activity. As there is a need in our society for academic thinkers, it is proper that such a curriculum and study-route should be provided.

In the 1940s, pupils attending grammar schools sat the General School Examination at the age of sixteen, or earlier if they were thought to be ready. In order to be granted the certificate it was necessary to qualify at the pass level in five subjects chosen from three groups: English; history and geography; foreign languages, ancient and modern; mathematics and sciences. There was consequently both a basic requirement and some choice. It was not essential to study such things as art, music, physical education, games, domestic science, woodwork or metalwork, although these were nevertheless usually found in the total curriculum, most being taken by all pupils in the lower school with choice and some resulting specialisation amongst older pupils. On the other hand, religious education was compulsory.

As well as providing the route to sixth-form studies and university entrance, this qualification developed credibility as a valid certificate for entry into employment at sixteen. Prospective employers accepted its standards as evidence that candidates had the abilities and basic knowledge which were required for entry into their various occupations. Indeed, when established in 1917, it was anticipated that it would replace the many existing examinations then being used by employers and it is interesting to discover that employers have long required young people to have certificated evidence of their attainments.

As these occupations were invariably seen to offer better conditions of employment, greater prestige and higher financial rewards, grammar school style education was recognised as being valuable and consequently desirable. It was desired as a route to the better class of employment – not as one route amongst many for one particular type of person developing their unique skills for specific purposes. And consequently, those who gained the qualification came to be seen as an elite.

At the risk of overstating the case; it is wrong to argue that this curriculum is the cause of the elitism, when it is its misuse as an inappropriate qualification, people's erroneous interpretation of its value, and the lack of available alternative qualifications which are the true causes of the problem.

The majority of young people left school without taking any such external public examinations and, armed with only school reports and, possibly a testimonial, as evidence of their attainments and what can loosely be called their character, more or less everyone was then able to seek and obtain employment.

Another very significant point, however, is that the leavers did not necessarily stop learning when they left school. They continued to receive training on the job, one apprentice amongst several qualified workers, away from the world of children and school, learning skills easily recognised as relevant to their money-earning lives.

The alternative curriculum to that of the grammar school is demonstrated by that of the Eastbourne Boys' and Girls' Schools, Darlington, which opened in purpose-built accommodation in 1936. At the time they were examples of the most modern provision for the education of children not attending the secondary grammar schools and leaving when they became 14 years of age.

The Curriculum

An indication of how the curriculum was devised and applied is illustrated in the notes given in the Darlington Education Authority's Regulations for 1938.

Both the curriculum and the timetable, compiled by the school, had to be approved by the Education Committee, and no alterations were to be made which could involve additional expenditure without the approval of the Committee.

The teaching of secular subjects had to take up at least two hours in the morning and two in the afternoon and had to take place immediately after the closing of the registers. (The registers at that time being completed in pen and ink.)

Surprisingly perhaps, in view of the present day healthy school concept, a copy of the Hygiene of Food and Drink syllabus issued by the Board of Education had to be held in each senior school and the subject had to form a part of the curriculum.

And, interestingly, practice in the taking of intelligence tests was prohibited in school.

The regulations indicate the priorities visualised by the Committee. There is an understanding that the curriculum is generally accepted, but must be approved by the Education Authority – and its specific concern is that developments shall not involve expenditure without its permission.

The only other directive at the time was that there shall be an act of worship and Bible instruction each morning. The regulations stated that the door of the classroom should be closed at 9 o'clock, the register be taken and prayers offered. Following prayers the doors were to be re-opened and latecomers let in, and then there was Bible instruction. A list from which prayers considered to be appropriate was provided with the regulations in the Handbook.

In practice Prayers and Bible Instruction evolved to become the daily school assembly, an act of worship.

The Education Act of 1870 is quoted as authority for these regulations and it was also stated that 'no attempt be made to attach children to any particular denomination'. There was provision, quoted from the Education Act of 1921, for children to be withdrawn from religious instruction and morning service at the request of parents. Children withdrawn were expected to be given instruction in secular subjects during the period of withdrawal and, where practicable, in a separate room.

The rest of the early curriculum was lacking in complexity: it was uncluttered, covering relatively few and well defined subjects which were taken by everyone. Nevertheless the pupils received an extremely broad and rich education because of the wide range of activities which supplemented the academic studies.

The twice yearly examinations consisting of the writing of a composition, and tests in English, English Literature and Arithmetic, suggest a concentration on the basic skills of language and calculation.

The subjects, as listed on the twice yearly individual reports sent home to parents, were clearly defined and their content generally understood, being based upon the content derived from established University, Business and Trade organisations.

Subjects in the curriculum as shown on the Eastbourne Schools report forms for the period 1945 - 1955		
Arithmetic	Literature	Biology
Algebra	Music	Domestic Science
Geometry	Geography	Woodwork
Reading & Drama	History	Metalwork
Composition	Art	Physical Education
English Language	Needlecraft	

As indicated by the entry in the girls' school log book dated 2nd September 1947, the basic subjects were taught in the junior part of the school by the same teacher: in the core of the school, defined as the junior two-and-a-half years of the school English and maths were to be taken by the class teacher whenever possible. The class teacher being the form teacher, the teacher in charge of the class for the registration, prayers and Bible study, having charge of the same group for a significant proportion of the week. Such a policy reduced movement of classes about the building, increased the close supervision of the pupils, and produced a calmer more stable environment than is often found in the larger schools of today.

Most pupils studied Arithmetic, with frequent tests in mental calculation, the reciting and memorising of the multiplication tables being particularly significant at this time. The more inclusive mathematics was reserved for the more able senior pupils but, with the raising of the school leaving age and the realisation that not all able youngsters attended the grammar schools, a more demanding syllabus was introduced to include algebra and geometry as separate disciplines.

As early as the Autumn term 1946 it is remarked that Mathematics would be taught to the A & B (top) streams throughout the school This is apparently a change from merely teaching Arithmetic, showing that the pupils were placed in classes in strict order of their perceived ability, and that top streams were given a more extended curriculum than the lower groups.

Nevertheless, in the pre-war Senior and post-war Secondary Modern Schools practical subjects were a major part of the curriculum, Housecraft and Needlework for girls, Woodwork and Metalwork for boys, Housecraft, later known as Domestic Science, in the girls' department, being given one complete day each week *(one-fifth of the timetable)* whenever staffing allowed. Boys were not expected to take part in these perceived domestic activities and the girls were not expected to take courses in wood and metalwork.

Even the layout of the building emphasised both the importance attached to these practical subjects and the gender differences.

The Domestic Science rooms at the Eastbourne School were placed in a separate wing of the building, outside the main blocks of classrooms, and the purpose built flat played a significant part in the teaching programme, the girls taking it in turns to care for it and to prepare meals for invited staff, giving them not only experience of cooking and serving, but also the prestige of being able to provide for their elders.

In needlework, after passing the test of making a satisfactory apron and cap for use when cooking, girls graduated to knitting, embroidery and the making of other garments for themselves.

One of the teachers, Miss Dorothy Manfield, working at the school from September 1950 till her retirement in July 1983, recalled that 'the pupils learnt how to run a home – how to make a coal burning fire in the open grate *(there was no central heating at the time)*, how to make beds *(using sheets, blankets and eider downs)*, how to prepare food *(no ready-made meals were sold in the shops)*.' Senior girls progressed to making lunch for invited members of staff and tea trays were sent to the head-teacher's room twice daily, often with extra ones prepared for visitors.

The syllabus included the care and use of equipment, including sinks and waste bins; safety in the home; and choice of foods, their nutritional value and cooking methods – in the 1950s, including the use of dried egg powder in place of fresh eggs. The girls were taught how to budget and be economical when shopping.

A Child Care Course for senior girls was held in the flat and taken by a visiting nurse.

Similarly, for the boys, there was a workshop block constructed outside the main building where wood and metal work were taught by industry-orientated male staff having specific City and Guilds qualifications in these practical subjects. While the girls' practical teaching was home orientated, the boys' was work skills orientated, taking pupils outside the purely academic style environment of typical classrooms.

There was recognition that the language and reading skills of some pupils were below the acceptable standard. In Mid March 1947, Mr Armstrong, the Educational Psychologist from the Child Guidance Clinic began a testing schedule of backward readers with the intention of identifying those who would benefit from remedial reading lessons.

After testing it was agreed that 25 girls should benefit from attending a remedial class and, in spite of there being difficulties with staffing the programme, it was considered that this class was of such importance that it was agreed the class should commence for two periods per day.

There were frequent follow up visits by the Educational Psychologist but the success or otherwise of the work was not reported in any detail. The head-teacher does later report that progress was being made when she regrets that she cannot staff the desirable two classes.

The problem was a sizeable one as in September 1947 it was estimated that more than 40 girls should be in the remedial class but staffing did not allow for the organisation of two groups. It was concluded that the priority should be to teach 25 girls from the new entrants with the inclusion of some older girls. From this evidence it can be seen that at least 25 girls out of the intake of about 100 from primary schools were poor readers, one quarter of the intake. The failure to reach perceived acceptable standards in basic literary skills is certainly not new!

An entry in the Boys' School log for 11 February 1947 also refers to the Educational Psychologist visiting the school with reference to the 'Remedial Classes', showing that there were similar needs in both departments and that there was more than one class involved.

This is a problem that never seemed to be resolved. In spite of efforts made over many years some children still entered the secondary schools unable to read to an efficient standard.

The growth of a senior school curriculum

The 1944 Education Act required that pupils remained in school until the end of the term during which they reached 15 years of age, making necessary the provision of an extra year of school education in all secondary schools, previously only a requirement in the grammar schools.

The girls department was already experimenting with examination courses for the academically more able of the pupils, following the pattern of the Grammar Schools, and developing an orientation towards employment. This is evident in October 1947 when a visiting teacher was appointed to teach the Shorthand Section of the Business Knowledge Section of the School Leaving Certificate. There were to be two sessions of three hours on each on Wednesday and Friday morning and two one hour-twenty-five minute sessions on Wednesday and Friday afternoons. The significance of this course is its vocational orientation.

An optional element in the curriculum of the Girls' School

In many ways, the Girls' school appeared to have a progressive outlook towards education, for instance at the beginning of September 1947 the head-teacher introduced, as an experiment, an optional period for the last three-quarters of an hour on a Friday afternoon when pupils could choose from a number of activities: the choir, crafts, discussion, physical education, drama, and other unspecified activities. However, the practicalities of running the optional classes seem to have put constraints on what could be done in some of the subject areas.

The broader curriculum

Extra curricular activities in both the boys' and girls' schools significantly broadened what at first sight appeared to be a relatively narrow curriculum. One event at the boys' school which took place immediately following the end of the summer term was the annual camp, illustrated by the extract from the school log book given below.

Eastbourne Boys' School Annual Camp
Log book entry for 22.7.49

An advance party of the School Camp in charge of Mr W.A Brown, Mr J Waddleton, Mr E Smith, Mr J K Farrage and Mr G Brockway left at 10.00 a.m. by motorbus for Reeth. 30 boys were in the party.
Friday 4.15 p.m. School closed for the Midsummer Holidays. A party of 137 pupils in charge of the headmaster and 16 Assistant masters left school at 5 p.m. **for a week's camp at Reeth, Yorks.** Three guest masters (Mr J.J.Clarke, Mr J Redpath and Mr D Lockhart) and four guest boy campers also attended. The Camp was held 22 July to 29 July 1949 and the charge per head was One Pound Ten Shillings.

Both schools organised annual outings on the Ascension Day holiday, that in the boys' department taking on the characteristics of a major expedition.

Two examples of Ascension Day Excursions
made by the pupils of the Eastbourne Boys' secondary modern School

30.5.57
School closed. The Annual Ascension Day Excursion was held and 371 boys in 9 motor coaches and staff travelled to Holwick by motor and then walked via Juniper wood, High Force, Blea Beck, Cronkley Fell, Cronkley crags, Falcon clints, Cauldron Snout, Widdy Bank Fell, Cow Green to Langdon Beck where the whole party had tea returning for home at 6.15 p.m. The weather was delightful.

> **7.5.59**
> Ascension Day. Schools Annual Exursion took place and 364 boys in 10 motor coaches and in charge of 20 staff travelled to Upper Teesdale. The coaches were left at Langdon Beck and the party walked to the Tees, joining near Cronkley Crags and proceeded up stream via Falcon Clints to Cauldron Snout, Birkdale, Widdy Bank Fell to Cow Green where we rejoined the Motor coaches. After tea at the Langdon Beck Hotel we returned home – the outing was very successful

Ascension Day was not the major outing day at the Girls' School although small groups did take the opportunity of making visits on this holiday. For example, in 1952, a party of girls and staff visited Durham and this was repeated on several other occasions. By 1961 those girls working for the Duke of Edinburgh's Award, nearly fifty each year, completed the Expedition Section, visiting Marrick Priory and walking to Reeth.

> **Further examples of Ascension Day excursions made by the Eastbourne Girls' School**
>
> **10.5.56**
> A party of 2nd year pupils visited Finchale Priory and Durham Cathedral.
> **30.5.57**
> One party visited Durham cathedral and Museum, another, Raby Castle and Auckland Castle.
> **15.5.58**
> School journeys to the Tees, Piercebridge and Gainford; and a party of 58 visited Raby Castle and Staindrop Church, Escombe church, the river Wear and Bishop Auckland.

The equivalent of the annual boys' camp was the girls' annual visit to the abbeys after which the School Houses were named: Fountains, Rievaulx, Bylands, Whitby, Easby and Egglestone. The first journey took place on the 26th of April 1948, the outings becoming a major event in the school year. The girls were expected to wear the school uniform on these occasions and an educational programme vigorously followed. When abbey staff were not available to act as guides the teachers were expected to be prepared to take on the task.

Visits were rotated in such a way that each girl would have the opportunity to visit each of the abbeys during her time in the school.

Financial assistance of one shilling per girl was given by the Education Authority, the girls contributed four shillings each and the School Fund was used to cover additional expenditure.

The importance attached to these excursions is illustrated by the annual entries made by the head-teacher in the log, for example, frequently reporting the excursions to be most successful, helped by ideal weather and thorough preparation.

The figures in the adjacent table tell a story of a very popular extra-curricular activity extremely well supported by both the staff and pupils.

Girls' School Annual Excursion to the Abbeys				
Year	No on Roll	No of Girls taking part	No of Staff taking part	No of guests taking part
1948	549	400 plus	22	
1949	671	303	16	
1950	653	348	15	
1951	648	428	20	
1952	595	331	17	
1953	512	347	17	
1954	517	349	16	
1955	520	373	16	
1956	525	388	16	
1957	522	397	18	
1958	578	422	18	2 students
1959	591	458	19	
1960	658	522	22	
1961	676	559	28	
1962	647	499	24	2 students

Field work and out of school visits

Field work and out of school visits had been a part of the curriculum during the war years and were subsequently developed further. For instance, on Saturday 13 September 1947 a visit to Gainford Hall was organised by the Girls' Geography Staff, and with the kind permission of Mr Harrison, for the purpose of making a Farm Study.

In the following November one half of a lower school 2nd year top stream visited Peases Mill in the centre of Darlington *(now demolished)*.

The use of youth hostels played a large part in these activities, for instance, in 1947, 22 girls from the Lower IV year and two staff left for a week-long education visit into Upper Teesdale, staying at Langdon Beck Youth Hostel. Visits to other hostels became regular events.

It is also clear that there was a Junior Field Club at the Girls' school which is mentioned in the entry of 8th April 1949 when a party of pupils under the leadership of Miss Hunnam and Miss O M Nichols left school at 3 p.m. for Barnard Castle, where they stayed at the youth hostel until the Saturday evening. The importance of there being teachers willing and enthusiastic enough to organise such activities cannot be ignored.

Earls Orchard

The Darlington Education Authority's house known as 'Earls Orchard', situated on the outskirts of Richmond, expected to accommodate groups of between 30 and 40 members of Darlington Youth Organisations at weekends and during holidays, and senior school pupils for short periods during term time, was regularly used by Eastbourne boys and girls. A scheme had been established by the Authority whereby each of its schools was allocated particular blocks of days, Monday to Friday, for their visits.

Speech music and drama

The classroom curriculum in speech, music and drama was supplemented by internal House competitions and concerts given to audiences of invited guests. The Boys' School also produced an annual pantomime at the end of the Autumn term.

Such activities were a part of the broad field of educational opportunity offered by the schools of the time.

Before 1944, we need to remind ourselves, there was no division into primary and secondary schooling for the majority – logically, their curriculum continued unbroken, progressing according to age and attainment, through classes called standards, from five to fourteen years of age. It was possible for a youngster who found school work easy and consequently who showed evidence of successful learning to be promoted into a class above the norm for his or her age. Conversely, those who failed to show they had learned what was taught could be kept back in a lower class and be made to repeat the course.

With the development of the ideal that slow learners should not be shown up in this way, the arrangements changed, children being promoted according to their ages irrespective of their attainments. The obvious consequence of this was that children with different attainments would be located in the same classes: unless, that is, there was a sufficient number of classes in each age group for them to be divided into a number of groups according to their apparent abilities or attainments.

The timetables for the traditional schools of the 1940s and '50s were both simple and fixed: once the class groups were constructed, allowing for some movement of individual pupils up and down through standards or streams, they were fixed for ever. Almost all subjects were taught by the same class teacher and the children remained in the same one classroom for practically all of their lessons. There was a significant stability in this arrangement.

When the senior schools became secondary modern and the leaving age was raised to fifteen, two divergent schools of thought developed. There were those who thought that the curriculum should be free from the domination of external examination requirements and actually tried to avoid entering their pupils for any examinations. There was a vague notion that such schools would work out for themselves the best types of education suitable for the variety of young people attending them. There was even the view that the object of education should be to somehow cultivate fully developed individual personalities without considering the academic development of the child at all – and, in some cases, without attempting to produce good employees or even good citizens: a kind of idealised development of self centred individuals without considering the requirements necessary for an individual to thrive in a real society.

Other schools, supported by the demand from the parents of children who had marginally failed to gain entrance to the grammar schools, were encouraged to establish certificate courses for the "brightest" of their children. And this, at least in some ways, was a good thing. Late developers, or those who genuinely failed to pass the eleven-plus examination, and yet had a substantial amount of academic ability, were given the second chance they deserved.

In 1951 the General Certificate of Education (GCE) replaced the School Certificate, introducing the single subject qualification: it was then no longer necessary to pass the five subjects, including one from each of three groups, in order to gain an external examination qualification. This opened up the system to more candidates, particularly amongst those in the upper streams of the secondary modern schools. The examinations industry began to expand and thrive! And, you might say, the standard of the examination system began to fall.

A disadvantage was possibly that some young people were forced by the school, parental pressure or both to attempt an academic exercise for which they were not really suited. As far as the school was concerned, of course, the more pupils gaining the more "O" levels the better its reputation.

Nevertheless, in some modern schools there developed a system of different courses for different pupils. There were the academic courses already considered. Technical courses for those shown to have considerable ability but without being academic by nature, as it were. Vocational courses for those who found traditional school learning difficult. And other courses merely designed to give the most troublesome something to keep them occupied until the day they could legally leave. The days of the older disruptive pupil and truant were beginning to appear!

In all fairness, however, it has already been pointed out that schools had developed woodwork, metalwork and domestic science classes before the war, and the objective in these schemes was indeed seen as preparation for adulthood.

An advantage which it was argued the secondary modern school offered was its provision of opportunities for their senior pupils to take the lead in activities which, if they had been placed in grammar schools, they would have been denied because the more able would have taken up the limited number of available leadership places. Through their "O" level successes and the social training of their senior pupils, many secondary modern schools served their clients very well and prospered.

When they were amalgamated with the grammar schools to form comprehensive units, the social advantages for these young people disappeared. They could be submerged by people more able in the traditional academic skills, their own different strengths possible unrecognised, consequently feel defeated and give up trying. However, the more one thinks about this aspect of education, the more it must be realised that it is the whole personality, not merely the academic aspect, which should be considered. There are a whole collection of traits which need developing: for instance, it may be claimed that the extravert who is not an academic high flyer needs to be encouraged to make full use of this strength in a socially advantageous way. A rich reservoir of human abilities derives from a great variety of personality traits and the unique educational environment which is desirable for the best development of each individual needs very careful consideration indeed.

A more serious influential and damaging problem, soon to become apparent, turned out to be peer group pressure. Where the upper part of a school is dominated by large numbers of school drop-outs there develops a social climate in which it is not acceptable amongst the peer group to be seen successful in either academic or social activities – that is, it is not possible to be seen to conform to those standards which have previously been so highly valued.

The early comprehensive schools did indeed seek to expand the number of areas in which the variety of young people could succeed. The significance of "O" levels continued but in addition specific courses were developed for fourth and fifth year pupils with different talents and these led to external examinations provided by the Royal Society of Arts and City and Guilds organisations.

The youngsters who would become drop-outs from the system had not yet gained very much influence. In eleven-to-eighteen schools they were likely to be outnumbered by the sixth formers, or in schools without sixth forms, by a majority of conforming fifth year pupils – it must be remembered that those not wishing or not able to take examination courses could still leave in their fourth year. There was an escape from a system which, if they were compelled to remain in, it would cause frustration and rebellion.

However, as early as 1959, there were rumblings from those outside the education system about the inappropriateness of the school curriculum. They began to argue that decisions relating to what should be taught should not remain the sole responsibility of the professional educators. Just who these professionals were supposed to be was perhaps unclear, although it was too often implied that they were the teachers. Yet, in general, the majority of teachers have always taught those things which other experts, academics, teacher trainers, local education advisers and inspectors, and Her Majesty's Inspectors, have promoted as being proper and appropriate.

During the first half of the 1960s there were several events which were to substantially influence the development of the curriculum. There was the establishment of the Schools Council, the introduction of the Certificate of Secondary Education and the publication of the Newsome Report. In view of the continued criticism of the education system into the 1980s, these developments presumably did not answer the criticisms coming from those outside the profession. It may be considered that these developments actually aggravated the situation.

In February 1962, David Eccles, then Minister of Education, established the Curriculum Steering Group, bringing into the public domain the question of what the state education system should teach. The immediate response from teachers' leaders, their trade unions, and the local education authorities was to object to what they saw as an intrusion into their areas of responsibilities – an objection wrongly interpreted as a complaint made by the teachers themselves. In reality, the policy of objection was determined and advanced by those far removed from the classroom, holding positions as administrators in trade unions or local authorities and influenced more by political than by professional matters.

The story continues with the appointment in July 1962 of Edward Boyle as Minister of Education and his initiative to create a new body to be responsible for the curriculum and a national system of school leaver examinations. This body evolved, in 1963, to become the Schools Council constituted from representatives of the local education authorities, teachers, employers and higher education. Consequently it suffered from a similar disadvantage to that advanced above, the problem of "political" or ideological enthusiasts dominating the scene, rather than the dedicated classroom teachers who were reluctant to give up precious pupil-contact time to become involved in aspects of administration.

Nevertheless, the mood of the moment, generated by the Council, was that diversity should be encouraged, schools should continue to determine the curriculum best suited to the needs of their particular pupils, and the Council would disseminate examples of good practice.

A further influential occurrence in 1963 was the publication of the Newsome Report, "Half Our Future", the findings of the Central Advisory Council for Education (England) which considered the education of young people aged between thirteen and sixteen of average or below average ability. The terms of reference assumed that pupils in this age group would be continuing full-time courses in schools or establishments of further education and that education should be meant to include extra-curricula activities.

The first recommendation was that the school leaving age should be raised immediately to sixteen, a recommendation which was eventually enacted in 1973. As it happened I was appointed to a headship from January that year and, as I was leaving my previous post, one of my pupils took the trouble to inform me of his opinion that those consequently forced by law to stay in school would be set to cause trouble. Although the trouble which he claimed to be imminent was far less than he described, there is no doubt that there was resentment from many who would have preferred to have entered the world of work as soon as possible. This resentment continues today in the form of disruption and indiscipline and it can be stated with confidence that the system has not developed in ways to satisfy the needs of the potential drop-outs - although strategies are being considered and tried out, and there is a considerable initiative in this direction in the Tomlinson Report "14-19 Curriculum and Qualifications Reform" published in 2001 and carried forward in the subsequent White Paper.

In 1963 the Newsome Report called for research to be carried out into teaching techniques designed to help those with abilities thought to be artificially depressed by environmental and linguistic handicaps. This emphasis distracted attention from the possibility that some may have depressed abilities for other more deeply set individual reasons, and consequently diverted those responsible for finding solutions from looking in appropriate directions. For instance, it was unfashionable to seek reasons for the inability to learn in terms of genetic factors: to suggest that a youngster may be born with certain disabilities became taboo – unless, of course, you were referring to the most obvious and undeniable incapacities.

However, it was recommended that all schools should provide a choice of courses in their fourth and fifth years and that these should include some related to occupational interests. Indeed, this was the pattern which I had seen in operation in the London County Council comprehensive schools during the 1950s, but, however you looked at it, it was still school and not work as far as some young people were concerned. Furthermore, there was also a call for improved facilities for practical and technical work.

Newsome also called for a broader curriculum, seen in terms of courses catering for the personal and social development of the pupils. For instance, it was suggested that schools should give adolescent boys and girls positive guidance on the subject of sexual behaviour, including the biological, moral, social and personal aspects. It may be claimed that an entirely new area of curriculum development was defined, but it was not, in spite of its intentions, necessarily recognised by the young people as particularly useful.

It was recommended that the whole programme in the fourth and fifth years should be an initiation into the adult world and the world of leisure. And the question must surely be posed: is this an impossible task for a school which is by definition not of the adult world?

Specifically, schools were encouraged to build links with the youth employment service, further education, the youth service and adult organisations. These areas, formerly largely left to the youngsters and their parents to explore for themselves, were to be brought in to the world of school. Two thoughts immediately come to mind. How could schools cope with all of this additional responsibility? And, in any case, is this the converse of what the youngsters want? Do they want the world outside brought in, or would they be more receptive if those matters were clearly based out of school?

It was recommended that all youngsters should be given opportunity for some residential experience.

The report was opposed to the fine grading of pupils and students by ability and argued that in the final school years groups should largely be based upon choice. The feeling amongst many at the time was that giving choice to young adults would mean that they would be better motivated to learn. To be realistic, choice must be such that each stands a chance of achieving some success. There is no point in permitting unrealistic choices to be made which place people on courses for which they are not equipped. Guidance is essential for beneficial placements, whether these are academic or practical, and all courses must be seen to have equivalent value, leading to qualifications which provide entry to employment situations.

In reality it has become evident, some young people do not want to choose anything other than the most direct exit from the school situation and, so far at least, no courses have been devised in which these young people see value.

A further recommendation was that every effort should be made to emphasise the status of the older pupils and I well remember, as a deputy head, providing a makeshift common room for the fifth years: a good idea but not very realistic. Before the school leaving age was raised, some forty-five per cent of all fifteen-year-olds stayed on for a further year. In a school with an eight-form intake, two-hundred-and-forty people, that meant making provision for over one-hundred physically large young people. After 1973 provision for two-hundred-and-forty would be required: a large number of people to make feel grown up and trusted! And that is without considering just what the provisions should entail. Should there be food and drink making facilities; games facilities; private study areas; areas for sitting and talking? Should all of this be in a non-classroom social atmosphere? And is it satisfactory to say that the provision should come within the framework of *school* rules and regulations, being seen as a part of the child's world and not that of the adult?

There was no real attempt to transform teaching from its school-for-children environmental format into something more obviously designed for young adults. There remained some kind of unstated blind belief that a poorly defined traditional something called education, combined with the above curriculum developments, was enough in itself. The more you had of it, the better it was for you.

It was also advised that schools should provide all pupils with some form of leaving certificate, although it was not intended that they should encourage those to enter external examinations which were not appropriate. And, as we have already seen, courses were not provided which led to meaningful qualifications for all.

The teacher shortage is not new, there was one in 1962 when it was also reported that those in the service were changing their posts far too frequently. And some eighty-per cent of buildings were deemed inadequate. The service has been under resourced from the time of the revolutionary introduction of secondary education for all, and throughout the whole of the subsequent period of constant change, a period of almost fifty years.

So, with the raising of the school leaving age twice between 1944 and 1973, from fourteen to sixteen, training, which previously took place in the adult work place, has been converted into education, with all of its airy-fairy ideals, taking place in the children's world of school.

In the recommendations in the Newsome Report can be seen many of the facets of the secondary school curriculum of the sixties: the development of option courses, careers education, education for life programmes, social service projects and so on – another enthusiastic boost to idealism but, possibly, without recognition of and paying sufficient attention to the realities of life – although the intention to do so was there.

Newsome's idea that not all young people should be entered for external public examinations, however, was to be rejected and, at first sight, this was not a bad thing as it may be claimed that qualifications, evidence of learning or training and competence in the application of skills, should be sought by all. Our modern society, today more than ever before, functions through the application of specialist skills, no matter how insignificant any one skill may at first appear, and all must surely be seen to be properly qualified.

The educational establishment, realising that a number of pupils still had nothing to work for in terms of leaving qualifications, and anticipating a further rise in the school leaving age to sixteen, sought an examination which, they imagined, could be taken to advantage by most, if not all of those likely to be unsuited to "O" level.

As early as 1960, the Beloe Report had recommended that a new examination should be established for those able pupils for whom "O" level was not suitable and this concept eventually crystallised into the Certificate of Secondary Education (CSE), approved in 1963 and operational by 1965.

It can be argued that subsequent developments took a wrong or confused path. A number of problems evolved from good intentions; for instance, in order to facilitate the most useful development of courses capable of satisfying the great variety of individual pupil needs, the examination was established with three modes, that is three different ways of establishing and assessing courses (as described in Chapter 10).

As the school leaving age was raised so teachers were faced with a need to provide a school leaving qualification for the majority of young people but were governed in their thinking by a number of contradictory motivations.

There was the well worn concept of equal opportunity for all, which inevitably became entwined with the oversimplified ideals of egalitarianism. There were those who genuinely believed that competition is wrong and that examinations of any kind lead to elitism, privilege and divisiveness.

At the same time, teachers know that all children are different in their attainments, abilities and personalities, no matter how much anyone may try to pretend that all could be equal if only the sociologists could sort out environmental inadequacies.

They were torn apart in their objectives. On the one hand they did not wish to show-up children against each other, providing grounds for jealousies and injustices. On the other, they wished to provide appropriate educational challenges for the great variety of young people they knew to exist and to provide them all with realistic individual goals which eventually would provide them with meaningful qualifications. That is, qualifications which could be used to gain employment.

Not least amongst all of this was the knowledge that young people were going to be required to remain at school until the age of sixteen and that they had to be motivated to learn, to feel that there was a real purpose in education for them.

Consequently, the original objective of the CSE, which was to provide a qualifying examination for those in the second twenty per cent of the ability range, was stretched to involve almost all.

It must not be forgotten that the prime task of teachers is that of teaching – that is what they are trained to do. It should be their responsibility to determine workable teaching methods through which they can teach the knowledge and skills which they themselves have learned during their initial training. They are not necessarily in a position to determine the content-definition of subject disciplines, an area of responsibility which it may be suggested should be largely left to other staff in the university departments of education. That is not to say that teachers should be denied an opportunity for input into this world of subject definition but this should be a voluntary additional area of responsibility quite separate from their teaching. Perhaps there should be teachers who specialise in teaching, while others specialise in syllabus and curriculum development. Certainly, those who want to concentrate solely on the teaching should be able to do so without any fear of loss of status or remuneration. There are different areas of responsibility within the teaching profession.

Unfortunately teachers have for a long time been receiving conflicting signals from those who have held responsibility for subject definitions and content. Not least amongst these has been advice or suggestions which their experience tells them is inadequate. In turn, the leading specialists in the subject disciplines seem unable to agree amongst themselves and there are enthusiasts who seem to have decided to move into controversial areas.

To make the situation even more difficult for some teachers, such conflicting advice has often been promoted by their colleagues, local authority advisers and the government inspectors with great enthusiasm, each according to their own particular prejudices. Sound objective advice backed up by realistic evidence has been hard to come by and teachers have been placed in the classic frustration-causing situation of being drawn in opposing directions at the same time: another factor in the lowering of their morale. They have, in spite of their apparent authority, variously not been able to control the examinations system, seen colleagues promote schemes which they themselves see as simply wrong, or worked to no avail to promote that which they feel is right.

So what has happened? Some have followed the enthusiasms of the day, developing unrealistic courses and assessment techniques: others have tried to rationalise current educational fashions with reality; and some have retained a rigid traditionalism. The result has been a delightful hotchpotch.

Side by side with the development of strategies designed to bring the youngsters to understand what they are learning, rather than merely learn parrot fashion, there has been a dilution of content found in the traditional "O" level syllabi. This has, at least in part, resulted from the fact that everyone is not able to comprehend the reasoning behind everything, and the failure to accept that to have some factual knowledge, without understanding how more able minds have proved its truth, is better than to have no knowledge at all.

Just as there has been the dilution of traditional subject content, so there has also been the introduction of new subjects into the curriculum: some obviously meaningful and practical, others the weird and dubious concoctions of a single individual's, or minority group's, enthusiastic but misdirected thinking.

For instance, historians and geographers will recognise the title Social Studies, but they will not know the content of the subject's syllabus unless they examine it. In some cases they will find attempts to integrate historical and geographical knowledge, concepts and skills into one discipline. In others they will find nothing of their subject disciplines but, instead, content more properly called sociology, or even a collection of material compiled to suite the unique objectives of the compilers. No two of these syllabi will be the same, some will be meaningful, some confusing and some trivial.

Another attempt at subject integration is seen in Environmental Studies but again, sometimes the discipline is based upon a diluted combination of history and geography, sometimes on geography and biology, sometimes all three, and at other times something entirely different.

Difficulties experienced with trying to teach all children a second language led to the invention of such subjects as French Studies, German Studies and Language Studies, in which there was a large proportion of cultural topics in place of real language. Such courses were usually designed in an attempt to provide something, easier than "O" level or, in educational language, something more appropriate to the needs of the non-academic pupil. But an underlying ideology was, and still remains, the blind belief that everyone must have the same curriculum. If geography is good for one, then all must have it. If knowledge of foreign languages is essential to produce linguists, then everyone must study something called language, even if the content only remotely relates to the learning of a foreign tongue.

In a different category was the Humanities Project, devised by Stenhouse, in which the whole concept of teaching was modified from one of imparting recognised factual material to that where the teacher takes on the role of the chairman of class debates on topics which are intended to have personal relevance to the pupils in their everyday adolescent lives.

Another aspect of all of this has been the attempt to encourage young people to understand, to reason, and to develop opinions, rather than blindly accept a digest of factual material. The extreme form of this apparently sensible strategy seems to deny the existence of any factual knowledge, the children being encouraged to debate topics without any understanding of the factors involved. I suppose the rambling, random, untrained mind might stumble across something useful but being untrained it will not be able to recognise its usefulness! And, of course, those who have that unmentionable high intelligence will stand a better chance than those who lack this valuable facility and who, incidentally, need more real teaching.

Furthermore, reasoning ability develops at different ages and for different reasons in different individuals. In general, the younger the child, the more simple its reasoning, resulting from, in part, its lack of information to reason with, but some older youngsters may find reasoning very difficult. And furthermore, how is anyone supposed to reason sensibly without knowledge of the accepted primary facts relating to the subject under discussion? There can be no proper development of worthwhile opinions and arguments without a basic understanding of underlying knowledge. Those who deny this presumably think that the subject matter of a syllabus can be conjured up from thin air!

Even in mathematics teaching there has been the attempt to replace the traditional learning of techniques which could be applied to the solving of problems by, it is claimed, a more enjoyable, broad field of understanding. The result seems to be that where people used to be able to solve arithmetical and other problems necessary in life, many now cannot do so because they are taught a broader mathematics syllabus.

Similarly, in English language syllabi, an emphasis on spelling and grammar has been replaced by one on creativity – believing that this improves the motivation to learn.

All of this has resulted in a multiplication of syllabi, a dubious development of syllabus content and confusion of understanding. The only way for anyone to determine what is being taught to any particular class under these circumstances is to study the details of the one-amongst-many syllabus and to observe the ways in which the content is being taught and assessed: an impractical solution to say the least. Consequently, with the development of the Certificate of Secondary Education alongside the General Certificate of Education, "O" level, an understandable unity was exchanged for an incomprehensible conglomeration.

Also there were schools which promoted the notion that their young people should only be entered for CSE: that is, "O" level subjects would not be part of the curriculum of their schools.

Standards changed and possibly deteriorated. In any case, with the further development of comprehensive schools, both "O" level and CSE were being taught in the same establishments and the differences between syllabi proving difficult. This was particularly the case where a candidate was considered of marginal "O" level ability. Should he or she study "O" level or CSE syllabi? As the contents were not identical, it was not a simple matter to change from one to the other. Differences were so great that an outsider could justifiably question the validity of a subject definition – for instance, a school geography syllabus complied by one would be unrecognisable to another! There was no longer any consensus of what secondary school geography should entail – and similarly in a hundred-and-one other subject disciplines.

The government reaction to all of this has been seen in its disbanding of the

Schools Council, the establishment of the General Certificate of Secondary Education, including the intense revision of subject syllabi, the introduction of the National Curriculum and national standardised testing at the key stages of seven, eleven, fourteen and sixteen.

There is now in place a government initiated and directed system determining what shall be taught, linked with a national testing system which indicates standards each child should have reached in every element of the curriculum at certain stages in its life. In addition a mass of statistics is published each year to indicate how well schools and colleges have used the system, exposing schools with a high proportion of struggling learners as failing that system.

The Government web site *Directgov/parents* says the National Curriculum is a framework used to ensure teaching and learning is balanced and consistent, it states which *subjects are to be taught*, the *content* of each subject and *standards* that young people of different ages are expected to reach. For each subject there is a programme of study which *defines the subject content* in terms of the knowledge, skills and understanding the children are *expected* to develop. Parents are informed that schools are free to teach according to the needs of their pupils, but are also told that many schools use schemes of work prepared by the Qualifications and Curriculum Development Agency (QCDA). This body is a government established organisation given the task of developing the curriculum, assessment strategies and qualifications; and is governed by a Board of 13 and managed by an Executive of 6 members.

All 13 Board members are eminent and very experienced people in their respective fields: many are or have been in managerial posts, for instance in education, Children's Services and industry; there are others who have specialised in, for example, medicine, accountancy, and banking; and those associated with defining establishing qualifications.

The professional expertise of the Executive therefore varies between accountancy, the retail trade, public relations, curriculum content and examining.

Asking what is needed for the development of a sound school curriculum and appropriate qualifications, it could be said that the requirement is for professional bodies in the various fields of knowledge to define and keep up to date the content of their subjects, translate this material into appropriate learning for young people and establish assessment procedures for the granting of qualifications. In addition, a co-ordinating body of educational specialists is required to bring together and maintain the appropriateness of the various inputs to form a common school curriculum and system of qualification for all plus additional individual specialisms appropriate to the older learners.

Is this what we have?

The National Curriculum

> **Subjects given as compulsory in the National Curriculum for 5 to 11 year olds**
>
> English
> Maths
> Science
> Design and technology
> Information and Communication Technology (ICT)
> History
> Geography
> Art and design
> Music
> Physical education

Religious education is also, as it has long been, compulsory, with the proviso that parents can withdraw their children from these classes. In addition schools are *advised* to teach **personal, social and health education (PSHE)** and **citizenship** and **at least one foreign language.**

> **Subjects given as compulsory in the National Curriculum for 11 to 14 year olds**
>
> English
> Maths
> Science
> Design and technology
> Information and Communication Technology (ICT)
> History
> Geography
> Modern foreign languages
> Art and design
> Music
> Citizenship
> Physical education
>
> **In addition schools have to provide:**

> **Careers education and guidance (during year 9)**
> **Sex and Relationship Education (SRE)**
> **Religious education**

A primary or stage 1 curriculum

If there is to be a common curriculum, what is required are syllabi designed to promote the imparting of a generally useful knowledge and usable skills NOT a deep intellectual study of each discipline. It is therefore for each subject specialist to define those elements of the subject which will be of value to the population at large and will usefully provide the learner with basic skills and knowledge.

In the 2005 White Paper Education and Skills the core curriculum for 14 to 16 year olds *(5.4 and 5.5)* included basic skills, knowledge, the most significant being functional English and maths with ICT, and knowledge and skills thought to be required for citizenship, employment and additional learning.

In answer to the repeated concerns shown by employers and others the government explained its intention to strengthen the teaching of the basic subjects referring in particular to *functional English and maths*. This sounds good: the teaching of practical, everyday usable language, basic mathematical knowledge, and skills – functional English and maths, indeed being defined as the English and maths required for use in every day life.

There is a necessary word of caution in this: firstly, the content of *functional English and maths* needs to be clear and secondly, in reality will all young people have the ability to reach GCSE grade C standards? Problems like those seen in the Eastbourne Secondary Modern Schools, where there was perceived to be a need for a large group of pupils to be given remedial teaching, has apparently not been rectified after some fifty years of innovation in the delivery of education.

The Secondary National Strategy

In item 5.7 of the White Paper there was a clear intention to answer the question in terms of the provision of adequate teaching resources and strategies but the implication is that all pupils will reach the required standards when the teaching is put right – but will they? Concentrated individual tuition certainly helps those who find group teaching strategies to be inadequate or who have missed out on significant steps in the learning process, but, in addition have the ability to succeed.

It is fashionable to assume *all can* if only their social and educational circumstances are put right. Failure to succeed is seen as the result of underprivileged upbringing and poor teaching, and, as a partial cause, this cannot be denied – environment makes a difference. The gap in the argument is to omit the significance of natural ability and the consequence of this is to alienate the proportion of young people who *can not*.

A basic stage 1 curriculum for all up to 14 years of age

The curricula of the Secondary Modern and Grammar Schools were relatively uncomplicated and yet rich in content, particularly when the extra-curricula elements were included. With the introduction of the Certificate of Secondary Education, with its encouragement of teachers to draw up their own course syllabi; and other innovations revolving around differently perceived approaches to teaching, the system has grown without a sufficiently clear structure into a burdensome complex which barely fits into the school day.

It was time to re-examine what teachers are expected to teach and how they are supposed to teach it.

A traditional curriculum based on primary skills and basic general knowledge, not unlike that of the traditional schools, delivered with intensity to young people up to the age of 14, may be the answer. Necessary primary skills are still those associated with reading, writing and arithmetic: in today's or Tomlinson's language, the functional aspects of mathematics, literacy and communication, to which must be added functional information technology.

Functional mathematics must surely start with the basics of calculation: measurement, addition, subtraction, multiplication and division; growing into the principles of geometry – each presented as practical, usable skills.

Functional literacy is the use and comprehension of language and its components usefully illustrated in the activities of the Eastbourne Girls' Secondary Modern School. On the biannual report forms were the headings Reading and Drama, Writing and Composition, Language (grammar) and Literature. These headings include the skill of writing, the structure of language, the reading and understanding of language, written and spoken communication (drama), the writing of moderately long scripts (in story and report form) and the understanding and appreciation of outstanding authors.

Functional information technology hardly needs mentioning as young people seem to be almost intuitively expert in its use but it is on the basic educational and work purposes that a school syllabus will focus attention.

To this may be added functional general knowledge: the development of science, early and later discoveries, the ways in which everyday things work, scientific methods of investigation.

The physical aspects of geography with geology; and world studies including human geography: world resources, agriculture, industry, conservation, people of the world and their cultures.

The study of history which provides incite into the development of national cultures, the ways in which systems of government have evolved, and some knowledge of the people and their actions involved in the development of civilisations; the basis of the making of music and the appreciation of the works of outstanding composers; the tools of the artist and the appreciation of the work of outstanding artists; and the basic aspects of physical fitness, participation in team games and athletic sports.

To all of this there has been added the inclusion of a foreign language and here there is a problem: which one shall be studied - and for what purpose? The functional purpose of language is to enable people to communicate with each other and, perhaps for some who have problems with their native tongue, wrestling with another is not a good idea.

Remember all of this is a basic primary curriculum into which depth and breadth can be added when the young person demonstrates the mastering of the basics and the ability to progress further.

Particular progress, involving pupil choice and depth of study would come in the post 14 stage, i.e. stage 2, involving students' ambitions, orientation towards individual careers and the gaining of specific qualifications.

Other aspects of any general education curriculum

It has been recognised for almost as long as education has existed that a full programme of learning includes more than basic skills and academic subjects. In schools attention has been given to behaviour and welfare, adopting different strategies and priorities over the years. Many teachers have considered it to be a part of their professional duties to take part in out of school activities, where children and young people have been encouraged to take part in clubs and school journeys: and, although participation of staff suffered with the rise of militant action in the 1970s, many teachers are once again very active in this area of education.

The attention given to the pupil welfare side of the curriculum has been seen in the growth of the House System, which has included the appointment of staff with special responsibility for pupil's behaviour and well being, and has come about to answer the pupil-problems arising in the comprehensive schools, where largeness has caused a break down of the more easily generated interpersonal relationships of the smaller schools generally existing before the comprehensive movement came into being.

The Tomlinson Report *(page 37)* referred to "wider activities" undertaken "outside formal learning time"; in other words the extra-curricular activities noted to have been a significant part of the Eastbourne Secondary Schools' curriculum both before and after the 1939-45 War and which certainly included many of the areas mentioned in the report (the arts; sports and recreation; science). Additions in Tomlinson, bringing the list into the 21st century included technology, family responsibilities, community service; and part-time employment (all of which were made available to the pupils in Eastbourne Comprehensive upper School from 1968 until its closure in 2007.

The Report recognised the participation of young people in a whole range of award schemes, such at the Duke of Edinburgh's Award, which the Eastbourne Schools enthusiastically embraced – as did many other schools.

Taking on the organisation and supervision of such activities have always accepted by large numbers of teachers as a part of their extra and voluntary work and have taken place outside class time with volunteer groups of students. With the great surge of government involvement in the control of the curriculum there is the expectation that all (staff and pupils) will take part and the whole content become formalised. Either extra staff will be required to do the work or existing staff be required to work longer hours (and extra pay will be expected and demanded by the teachers' trade unions). The enthusiasm of the volunteer will be in danger of being stifled by the ethos of paid work.

The idea was advanced *(Tomlinson page 37 note 83)* that these wider activities could become a compulsory part of a qualification system but if encouragement becomes coercion or partaking becomes compulsory this would be an undesirable interference in the life of the individual, a restriction on the individuals' freedom, a narrowing of free choice; and a very good reason for many to reject them.

Many of the traditional extra-curricular activities take place outside the school or college regime and this is a significant reason why people take part. They want a change, even an escape, from the daily routine and ethos of school.

Conversely, there may be a reason for compulsion in some form of national service in a society where young people have time on their hands and a significant proportion fill this time with unruly antisocial behaviour. Having a variety of elements from which individuals could choose their activity according to their temperament, abilities and aspirations, could be of advantage to both the individual and society. Participation should be *expected* and only involve *compulsion* where individuals fail to take part *and* come into conflict with society because of their delinquent behaviour.

Recent ideas proposed as a part of the wider curriculum

Personal, and Social Education
Recent developments in educational thinking place significance on the involvement of schools in the teaching of matters which may be regarded as personal to the pupil

and family. There is a desire to improve behaviour, create positive attitudes and promote the illusive social justice. But the involvement of the educational system in at least some of these areas may be seen as controversial, being seen as too great an interference of the state in matters personal to the individual - and cause presentation problems for the educator.

It is an area of education which takes us into the realms of wider personal development and involves the consideration of the nature *(the temperament and personality)* of the individual learner. This is significant at an *individual* level: in personal guidance, counselling, behaviour modification, and so on.

One aspect focuses on requirements for employability and refers to personal skills such as the capacity to communicate, present oneself, work in teams, and understand diversity of opinion. These items are themselves complex. For instance communication can be spoken or written but both are a function of the communicator's skill in the use of language *and* his or her personality. The teacher can teach the structure, meaning, and use of language by both practical and academic methods and current initiatives are advancing the importance of doing so. This is the more or less traditional and impersonal teaching of knowledge. It is right to stress the importance of knowledge and the rights and wrongs of using language, defining, and distinguishing between good and bad usages.

When communication as a function of personality is considered, education moves into a different field of a play. It is that of personal qualities which in turn have their roots in the individual's personal make up. Educators can teach, in an objective fashion, such things as:

    a. understanding how groups work;
    b. learning that people play different roles within group situations;
    c. that views need to be expressed and challenged;
    d. that compromise and mediation play important parts in resolving conflicts;
and e. that the ideas and needs of others should to be considered.

BUT, it is not sensible to suggest that all should be thrust into undertaking each of different roles within any group and individuals should not be penalised for failing in this respect. For instance, some people have the personality attributes which make them natural leaders others do not – each should be valued for their contributions made from their different positions within the group.

Strategies for developing good democratic leadership styles can be taught. The need for co-operation, negotiation and compromise can be taught. The willingness to follow the principles involved is a personal attribute.

Values can be demonstrated but it is the individual who decides whether they are accepted and acted upon. Where values are adopted which are antisocial, the reasons for education move beyond the normal realms of the classroom or workshop.

How to organise one's life and work can be suggested but it will be the nature of the individual that decides how far this characteristic will be applied. Some people are neat, tidy and organised; others are not.

The showing of initiative is dependent upon confidence. Young people can be helped to become more confident. Some need teaching that they are over confident and that over confidence can bring danger to them, inconvenience to others and lead people to make faulty decisions.

Such things as being aware of the needs of others, owing responsibilities to others, the family, the community (and one's country?) can be pointed out. It is the will of the individual that decides whether such things have real meaning. The business is a matter of cultivating attitudes over a long period of time.

Children and young people (and indeed adults too) can be told how to behave; be taught strategies for dealing with aggression, how to combat bullying, how to be more confident in different situations etc., BUT they must want to co-operate, to follow the advice. They will know what is required of them but they may not choose to conform.

This area of behaviour is concerned with the psychology of the will and is a neglected area: it is concerned with changing attitudes and established attitudes are difficult to change. They are formed over time through the absorption of observed examples.

The inclusion of teaching social skills in education may well be a waste of time and money. There are those who come into education with all of these skills, developed by the interaction of their individual natures with their upbringing. They may benefit from further instruction and from structured learning situations in schools and colleges but *do they really need to spend time doing this?* In addition, they will inevitably place less importance on studies which they do not see as directly leading to their desired qualifications.

Others need this kind of help but *are not likely to recognise the significance to themselves of such programmes.* If they do not see the significance they will merely be disaffected.

This is also a difficult area in which to try to define curriculum and assessment criteria because instead of dealing with generally accepted knowledge and skills it involves personal behaviour and qualities.

The reporting of positive personal qualities used to be seen in the remarks on conduct, attitude to work and so in traditional school reports and leavers testimonials, but in today's litigation climate anything not be shown to be perfectly objective and backed by proof proposes serious risks for the author.

This area of any anticipated educational programme would perhaps be better understood, and a more workable notion, if described and explained in terms *developing a positive school/college ethos*, in which positive attributes are encouraged through the constant approval of positive attitudes and disapproval of the negative. It can be argued, for instance, that teachers teach more by what they do than by what they say.

Religious education

Schools have been obliged to start the day with an act of worship and to teach religious education according to the Christian faith and this was a fairly straightforward exercise when there was an acceptance among the majority of the population of the National Religion. With the promotion of a multicultural society the situation has changed but the clear explanation of change has not been adequately translated into practice: education has been placed in a state of uncertainty.

Religious education, inclusive of world religions, can be an academic exercise. It, however, is not seen as an academic exercise by the many different faiths which are now followed in multicultural Britain.

Traditionally the UK has had a common state religion, Christianity, based on the teaching of the Church of England, with relatively easily tolerated diversions. The festivals associated with this faith have been long accepted and celebrated by the vast majority. This is no longer the case and, with the establishment of other religions within the UK, children and young people of other faiths have been brought into the state education system.

This division causes problems: it causes division where we should have integration. Is it therefore time to separate the personal aspects of religion (faith and beliefs) from the objective academic study of world religions and from nationally accepted standards of behaviour?

In other words, traditional religious education in state schools becomes the academic study of world religions; the faith and beliefs aspect of one's personal religion is seen as the province of the family and their church, synagogue, mosque or temple; and the ethical aspect of religion becomes the nationally agreed practice of national behaviour.

It may be that the majority of the people want to keep Christianity as the national religion, but to define this as the religion practiced in our schools leads to opting out by those of other faiths, which leads to disintegration rather than integration.

This, in turn, leads to the acceptance of faith-based schools and detracts from the integration of young people from many backgrounds.

A multi-cultural agreed code of ethics

Whatever route is taken, we need a mutually agreed code of ethics to which young people of all faiths can be expected to adhere. A part of this will surely include the teaching of such things as the consequences of one's actions for oneself and others.

Physical and health education

Schools show concern for the physical development and health of their pupils: physical education is an accepted part of the curriculum and in addition the school medical service has carried out regular medical and dental examinations – the visiting school nurse has inspected the cleanliness of heads, at the same time being able to detect other problems (health and social) as each child presents itself.

The question arises: How far should the teacher and schools be expected or required to be involved in this aspect of peoples' lives?

12. What is the purpose of education?

What is the purpose of education? What is it for? In particular, what is the purpose of a state education system? Referring to Sarah Atkins and her sister growing up in Great Yarmouth in the second half of the 19th century, their parents paid sixpence per week for them to go to school so that they would be able to find positions in service, serving others, but in a better class of service, where they would be treated well. For them, education was to provide them with a means of earning their keep and improving their quality of life – but within the bounds of their position in society at the time.

So what did their schooling include: the elements of reading, writing and arithmetic; how to behave themselves, how to present themselves, how to eat and exercise properly, how to keep clean? The teachers would have given priority to the first of these, the intellectual skills, but insisting on good and proper behaviour, largely a matter of obeying the instructions of your betters, remembering the requirements of displaying good manners; and paying some attention to cleanliness.

The parents of the Atkins sisters would certainly have seen the intellectual instruction as the teachers' job and other matters as a family responsibility. They would, to the best of their ability, send their children to school clean, adequately clothed and knowing right from wrong. (They were a church going family, the father a railway porter, and living in a small rented terrace house.) However, human nature being what it is and families being what they are, the latter standards would, by the time the children went to school, present the school with various problems and a need for the teachers to play some part in the teaching of things which may be regarded as more personal matters and giving rise to the basic principle, in the operation of a state education system, relating to how far schools and teachers should become involved in the welfare aspects of the lives of the children and young people in their care.

There has always been a two-fold aspect to education: teaching knowledge and skills, with the correcting of general conduct or behaviour; and, up to a point, overseeing the health, physical development and well being of the young.

For social reformers, health, physical well being and social improvement, seen to be correlated with social class and deprivation, have become more and more significant aspects of education. A search for an illusive *social justice* has caused the significance of how and to what degree it is a school's responsibility to become involved in social and personal matters relating to children to be re-examined.

The health, physical development and wellbeing of children and young people

A look at the events and activities taking place at the newly opened Eastbourne Schools in Darlington during the late 1930s, during World War II and in the immediate post war years, demonstrates how the health, physical development and well being of the pupils were seen and dealt with.

Before and during the war concern was shown about the health and fitness of the nation, in the schools physical education in the form of lively exercise encouraged children and young people to get out into the fresh air and take part in team games. In doors gymnasiums were equipped with ropes, beams and horses for climbing, balancing and leaping: lessons included programmes of exercises; bending, stretching, astride jumping and the dreaded press ups. Such regimes were not unlike the basic training given to the military, for boys at least, although girls were subjected to the more ladylike gymnastic dance routines: all of this was at a time when diets were restricted by what a family could afford and what war time (and post war) rationing would permit.

Health checks were made by the schools' medical service, doctors performing routine medicals; the school dentists inspected teeth; and there were the regular visits by Nitty Nora looking for head lice. Teachers observed and reported health and care problems to the head-teacher who informed the medical authorities.

Cleanliness

Although recent scares (in 2007/8), such as the spread of MRSA in our hospitals and the threat of swine flu (2009), have caused us to focus our minds on the question of personal cleanliness, we can claim to be a cleaner nation than in the 1930s – at least in many respects. Occupations are cleaner, the smoky grime of belching chimneys largely eliminated, and houses fitted out with modern sanitary and washing facilities. In the 1930s it was more difficult to keep clean and easier to get dirty: many men worked in heavy industry and women cleaned the home by hand. It is with this scenario in mind that the need for the following instruction, issued by the School Medical Officer, Mr G A Dawson, in September 1936, can be understood. The head-teacher was authorised to examine any child (and clothing) who was suspected of being dirty or filthy, with the proviso that any such examination of girls should be carried about by a woman teacher.

Hair inspections were made regularly, special visits sometimes made in relation to the health of a select minority of girls and in July 1943 the head-teacher called in the clinic nurse to complete a cleanliness inspection of the whole school. There was obviously some concern about the health and cleanliness of some of the pupils.

Physical fitness

As early as 1935 the Central Council for Recreative Physical Training had been set up to promote the pursuance of physical fitness through keep fit classes, a campaign which gained great support with thousands of young men and women wanting to take part and creating a great demand for gymnasia. Modern schools, of which the Eastbourne Schools were an example, were provided with gymnasia, hard surfaced play or recreation areas and playing fields.

In 1937 there was a further drive to make the population healthier and fitter, extending the provision of gymnasia, playing fields, swimming baths and camp sites; and creating a national college of physical training.

On 10th March 1939 the Eastbourne Schools closed 'on the occasion of the National Fitness display held in the Baths Hall. A class of boys in charge of Mr Moss and a girl's class in charge of Miss Storer took part in the display'.

During the early years of the war the Local Authority's Physical Education Adviser, Miss M Potts, frequently visited the Schools, and in February 1940 arranged for Teachers' Physical Education Classes to be held in the school gymnasium. In April she returned to discuss a programme of Physical Education Lectures and later again with Miss E W Scott a member of the CCRPT staff, to discuss arrangements for a Preliminary Course for Women and Junior Leaders in Physical Education.

On 16th September 1940 Miss E W Scott took a Physical Education class for all girls eligible to leave at the end of January in 1941. Classes began at 7:30 in the evening.

Colleges of education were soon training specialists in the subject and Eastbourne saw students from Darlington Training College coming to the School to practice this element of their courses.

On the 22nd April 1940 Mr G Richards, an organiser from the Central Council of Recreative Physical Training, gave a talk to all 3rd year boys at 4 pm. on 'Physical fitness after leaving School'.

On Wednesday 24th April, Thursday 25th, Wednesday 1st May and Thursday 2nd May Courses for Junior and Senior Leaders were held in the Boys' School Hall.

The CCRPT also promoted the physical fitness campaign by showing films in schools. In March 1941 the girls were shown films on Physical Education and, in May, on Tennis Swimming and Physical Training.

It can be seen how the school curriculum and its allied extra-curricula activities reflected this search for physical fitness. Very early in the development of the Eastbourne Schools physical education, games, camping and excursions into the countryside were encouraged.

Health

There are health scares and campaigns today: immunisation for the elderly against influenza, numerous injections given to children and with the suggestion that more are necessary.

With the food shortages of war time conditions, there was no fear of there being an obesity problem but there is evidence from the Girls' School log of other more obviously life-threatening diseases.

Infectious diseases were treated seriously, pupils being excluded, not only if they were infected but also if they had been in contact with others who had contracted one of the illnesses.

At the start of the September term 1939 Miss W Storer was absent from duty suffering from Diphtheria, a very infectious disease in which a membrane forms in the air passages of the throat threatening death by suffocation and poisoning the body system: clearly a very serious medical problem in places such as schools where people are in close proximity to each other.

On the 19th December 1940 the headmistress, Miss Fenby, left school 1.45 pm. to report to the Education Office that one girl had been removed to the isolation hospital on Monday evening of the 16th November and another girl of the same class had been taken at 1 p.m. on the 12th of the following month. (It is easy to imagine an anxious Miss Fenby almost running out of the school, to catch the trolley bus perhaps, in her hurry to report this event as it is clear from her log entry of 9th October 1941 that only then was a telephone installed in the head-teacher's room.)

Darlington County Borough Education Committee Regulations for 1938 explain this apparently rapid exit of the head-teacher where they refer to infectious diseases. Head-teachers were instructed to inform the Chief Education Officer immediately of cases of infectious diseases reported to them by parents or guardians, including those where the child was not necessarily ill but lived in the same house as someone who was infected. The list of infectious diseases included Smallpox, Diphtheria, Croup, Erysipelas, Scarlet Fever, Tuberculosis, Infantile Paralysis, Measles, German measles, Whooping cough, Chickenpox, Scabies, ringworm and Influenza.

The seriousness of the matter is illustrated by the visit to the school on the same day made by the School Medical Officer, Dr Brown, who examined the throats of girls in classes 3.1 and 1.1, returning to re-examine them on the following day.

He came to the school in January 1941 to complete the routine medical examinations of pupils but first, yet again, re-examined the throats of the same girls (for symptoms of diphtheria) and returned the following day to carry out a further examination.

In March 1941 Dr Dawson, the Medical Officer Health visited the School with reference to the cases of reported diphtheria and arranged for a programme of immunisation. This was followed by Dr Brown once again visiting the school to begin the immunisation of 207 girls. A second injection was given a month later.

Tragically, on 7th April 1941, an Eastbourne girl died in the Municipal Hospital after being a patient there for 7 weeks suffering from the disease, and on 29th September 1942 it was reported that a second girl from Class 1.1, had died from the same complaint.

Earlier, in February of the same year, the school was informed that a pupil had died of pneumonia, and in July 1945 there was the death of pupil after an operation, emphasising the fact that ill health was, at a time preceding the discovery and use of antibiotics in treatment, a serious and significant problem.

The familiar regular dental inspections, routine and leavers medical examinations of today were already taking place, and the examination of girls' throats continued. Health education was promoted, for instance, in January 1942, at the request of His Majesty's Inspectors of Schools, certain classes in the school listened to "Health Talks" broadcast by the BBC each morning between 11 and 11.15 a.m. for a period of fourteen days.

There was also concern over the nation's diet, this being a period of food shortages and rationing. In March 1942 the Assistant Schools' Medical Officer of Health began a nutrition survey involving 50 girls who were taking school dinners and 50 girls who were not, with a follow up a year later. A similar survey was made of all First Year girls in 1943.

So it seems that education, schools and colleges, have been and should be involved in the fostering of the physical development of young people and have some responsibility for their welfare, but this responsibility should not be taken too far. For example, during the 1939 – 45 war years, as the country was working under the emergency conditions associated with the extreme needs of the time, the scheme for the provision of school meals at lunch time was introduced, but it has subsequently become an expected service, welcomed by parents because so many of them, both mothers and fathers, are in full time employment during the day and value having their children looked after during their working hours.

There was a voluntary involvement of teachers in the supervision of children at lunch time; indeed, many used the longer lunch break of previous decades to organise club activities, an aspect of their job which many teachers valued. In later years the expected supervision came to be seen as an imposition and this resulted in a withdrawal from all lunch time activities. With non-teacher assistants being employed to cover the supervisory duties there was a change of behaviour among the young people, the school-teacher orientated discipline, evolved from regular pupil-teacher contact, was no longer there.

There is a dilemma here: supervising children having a meal may be seen more as a welfare activity than an educational one and, although having a significant place in the training of young people, is rejected as a part of their responsibilities by some teachers.

At the time of writing (September 2009) there is a further initiative on the part of government to give a *free* midday meal to *all* children, with trials taking place in several regions.

The situation may be seen as the thin end of the wedge which is driving teachers in the direction of becoming welfare or social worker orientated at the expense of their true function: the providing of instruction in knowledge and skills.

The introduction of comprehensive education may be in part to blame for the further development of the welfare aspect of the teacher's task. As grammar, secondary modern and all the other varieties of schools were combined educational establishments became larger and more impersonal. A need was identified, a need to take action to ensure that no child was lost in the larger unit. Tutors and Heads of Houses were introduced, formalising a system of care, but the actual people in these new positions were the teachers themselves – some teachers were given special responsibility for the welfare (up to a point) and discipline of pupils and students, a pastoral role, and they were given special status and remuneration. Their duties included meeting parents in order to solve problems of behaviour, to discuss learning difficulties and to bring welfare matters into focus.

Such situations as a child not conforming to expected behaviour and learning standards came to be seen more clearly as a function of the family situation, and the situation at home being used as a reason, possibly an excuse, for the non-conformity, whereas previously, no matter where the child came from, the responsibility was placed on its shoulders. And this was possibly not a bad thing – a divorce of the child from a dysfunctional family, the treating of the child as an individual in its own right.

Nevertheless, the impingement of welfare matters into the world of education has multiplied. Considering more recent government thinking, as indicated in the White Paper Higher Standards Better Schools for All for example, there does seem to be an intention to give a greater priority to the welfare aspect of education. Even the present title for what was once clearly The Ministry of Education, now The Department for Children, Schools and Families, illustrates a suggested turn away from the understanding that the purpose of education is to teach knowledge and skills.

Chapter 6 of the White Paper is entitled Supporting Children and Parents, and as a general statement most people would probably agree this is an understood aspect of education, a task for schools and their teachers. The Paper states that schools will be enabled to support the health and well being of children and young people – so far so good, but it goes on to say schools will be *expected* to develop childcare and other services to give children and parents more opportunities and support *outside normal school hours* and this sounds like social work.

Furthermore there is reference to ensuring schools identify children who may be at risk from abuse or neglect and take positive steps to ensure something is done. In one sense schools have always observed and reported children who they have felt are at risk but it must be stressed that this must merely be a requirement to pass identified problems to other appropriate professionals. The teachers' responsibility ends there: but there is the strange suggestion schools are expected to make sure children are kept safe at home! There is also the implication that schools should help to improve children's health and be concerned with the food they eat, actions echoing the initiatives of the war years, and being seen as in part reasonable but unreasonable if taken too far. Education has been concerned with physical education and the teaching, for instance, of cookery (originally only for girls) for many years.

Together with all of this the government sees schools being open from 8 am till 6 pm in order to support pupils' learning and involve parents in school activities. Does this really mean the provision of *childcare facilities* before and after school? If so this is *a welfare matter* and teachers' should not be expected to be involved. The staffing and accommodation required needs to be carefully considered. Schools have school rooms where pupils' work and facilities provided for their courses are of first importance. Immediately outsiders, those other than the teachers in charge of their rooms, are allowed onto the premises the problems associated with multiple-supervision have to be addressed. In the matter of childcare facilities, separate buildings on the school site may be what is envisaged, separate units serviced by welfare and medical staff, not the responsibility of the teaching department of the school.

A final thought on all of this, the bringing of parents in to school, the involvement of schools in family counselling, parenting classes and so on: at one time it was considered that the pupils preferred their school lives to be quite separate from their home lives.

Raising standards

Governments have been introducing change after change until the education system has become submerged in new initiatives, often giving rise to uncertainty and controversy. The paramount objectives are often stated as the raising of standards and the reduction of social inequalities; but has the legislation, in reality, addressed the problems facing education today?

In the 14 – 19 White Paper three objectives were advanced: the first is the raising of achievements in the basic subjects, the second is the providing of a "sound education", and the last is the creation of an enthusiasm for learning. Have recent actions achieved these objectives?

There is the strong desire to *ensure* more pupils reach National Curriculum level 5 in English, maths, science and ICT; and that all young people are helped to do well in their studies. A General GCSE Diploma was introduced with the expectation that more teenagers will achieve grades A*- C including English and maths. There is also the intention of awarding a grade C or higher in English and maths only when the appropriate level has been achieved in the functional elements of the subjects but where the student only masters the functional element only, a separate qualification will be awarded to show success at this level.

All of these objectives are concerned with raising standards of achievement in the traditional basic subjects, to which relatively recently ICT has been added. Undoubtedly, some improvement is possible and it is pleasing that different levels of achievement, including the higher levels, will be recognised, but can all young people realistically be expected to achieve a meaningful qualification in these subjects? Furthermore, is the content of this sound basic knowledge a sensible requirement for young people growing up in a modern world, clear and generally agreed? Consider the discussions in the chapters on the curriculum, examinations and qualifications. Is the content of the "functional" elements of knowledge realistic, properly defined and understood? Has sufficient thought been given to the possibility that some can achieve only a small amount and that this should be recognised but not in such a way as to devalue high levels of success – reminding us of the need to value differences more equally and to ensure there is employment for all?

Recent governments have *attempted to define standards in certain skills and subject knowledge which they say children should reach at particular ages.* They have *designed standardised tests to assess whether or not children have reached these standards:* resulting in the expression of surprise, controversy and accusations when the defined standards at each stage have not been reached by the designated number of young people! Once again, is this giving families what they want for their children or concentrating too much energy on the failing minority?

Consideration of individual needs

There is the intention of catering for individual needs but is the problem of individuality, considered in chapter 4 of this publication, fully understood and realistic procedures put into place to develop the full potential of all, while also giving necessary consideration to the nature and cost of the provision?

Young people and full-time education

Proposals have been put forward for raising the participation rate in education and training of those over sixteen: there is a strong desire to keep young people in full-time education when many would probably rather be in employment, but at a time when employment prospects for the young and inexperienced are poor. The way forward is seen to be through vocational education but it is important to avoid making 14-19 education like school and to give participants on vocational courses the real prospect of gaining meaningful employment. These objectives are dependent on motivation and this question needs to be examined carefully. What is it that will bring people into education?

Young people want to be independent, to pursue their own interests and to do so they know they need money. A basic motivator therefore is the opportunity for them to earn a wage and this is also a sound educational objective: to encourage young people to earn their own keep, and if they so wish, to make provision for marriage and family life, is a sensible purpose of an education system. Unfortunately, *education does not provide employment*, it merely provides the knowledge and skills which can be applied in the work place if the work is there and it is pretty obvious that this is not the case: particularly so in the present circumstances (the recession circa 2009) but there is a more general problem: too great an emphasis is placed upon the notion that all can achieve if only the social and educational conditions are right. This is not so. There is a whole spectrum of personalities and talents among the young: some are highly motivated and richly talented, others are not so. Where there is this spectrum of human nature there needs to be a *corresponding spectrum of employment*. As wide a range of styles of work is required as it is possible to provide. We do not make enough things, preferring to buy products from abroad where the labour force is as skilled as our own but less expensive to employ. Thus we deny a proportion of our own workforce the opportunity to apply their abilities where they can and where they wish.

Another facet of this argument is that of national security: we do not have sufficient control over those things which we need to keep ourselves secure. Much of our energy supply is bought in, insecure and denying our population a work opportunity. Much of our food is bought in; much of our clothing, furnishings and fittings are bought in, much of our transport is bought in; all with the same consequences. We do not cultivate enough of our own research; the applications of the results of that research are not sufficiently encouraged - with the same results.

Is this what parents, children and young people want from the education system?

Education of the infant

The new parent is most likely to see early education as training: training in the basics of growing up; using the potty, feeding oneself, learning to walk, learning to talk, and so on. They will also quite quickly include training in acceptable forms of behaviour and they will put emphasis on mixing with other children of their same age that is, socialising. Most will consciously or otherwise instil in their children a morality, what they see as right or wrong: some will be doing so via religious education in the faith of their choice.

Experience shows us that not all parents are either willing or able to carry out the early training of their infants: we witness serious examples of abuse and neglect and government reaction has been to involve the education system in the righting of these wrongs through the imposition of responsibilities onto teachers and the using of school premises as day care centres. There is a tendency to make provision for the needy available to all with the consequence that it is easy for parents to abdicate their responsibilities: the state will fill the gap!

Where intervention in family matters has proved to be *essential for a minority* the measures introduced *impinge upon the lives of the majority*, for instance, some finding the provision of day care for their children convenient, an easy way to enable them to go out to work, earn more money and apparently raise the standard of living of their families. The converse of the *apparent* advantage is that children are taken out of their family environment for much the working week and this may not be either desirable or what parents really want.

Education of the young child

A little later, once the baby becomes a child, most parents recognise a need to read, write and calculate (and today to use a computer): those parents who can, and have the motivation to do so, begin to teach their children the basic elements of these skills but others cannot do this or choose not to do so. The question then arises: should the state act to balance this apparent inequality? It does, of course, through the compulsory state education system, but once again, is the system becoming too involved in trying to correct the failings of a minority at the expense of what is needed for the majority?

A good education

Most caring parents (and the majority do care) would, if asked, say that they want a *good education* for their children: but what do they mean by a *good education*? If, at the age of 16 or 18, their children have become well adjusted successful adults successfully earning their own keep, they will no doubt claim that the education their children received was indeed good. If people are not well adjusted and successful adults, they may not only say that the education they received was poor but, in this time of everything being someone else's responsibility, attempt to sue someone for damages!

Education and behaviour

So, is education *a system for producing well adjusted and successful adults?* Are builders, civil engineers, electricians, electrical engineers, heating engineers, sales staff, bus drivers, office staff, dustmen, traffic wardens, brain surgeons etc successful, well-adjusted adults as a result of this thing we call education? Perhaps we should seek definitions of what we mean by the terms *well-adjusted and successful!*

A part of education is the *bringing of people to understand and conform to the rules governing civilisation.* Today there is more free time than ever before for the individual to do what he or she wants to do. Teaching young people to use this time to their best advantage is a significant factor in fighting antisocial behaviour.

Has our education system, inadvertently perhaps, brought about a situation which has discouraged the notion that individuals should be responsible for their own lives, too great an emphasis being placed on individual rights rather than responsibilities and placing the cause of failings on factors external to the self? So, education is concerned with encouraging children and young people to take responsibility for their own lives, providing them with the knowledge and skills to do so: given that every young person has potential, learners need to be clear that personal effort is required for any development to succeed, and also taking into account the fact that the younger the child the more essential is the positive involvement of the teacher.

Education and the economy

The dual objectives of educating the individual and of serving the economy need consideration: the individual citizen can only be served well if the economy allows this.

Should education *produce builders, electricians, heating engineers, sales staff, bus drivers, office staff, dustmen, traffic wardens, doctors, nurses, chemists and so on in numbers sufficient to supply market requirements?* Indeed is it right to insist that education must include the means by which a nation provides itself with the people variously qualified to maintain and develop itself?

Careful and full consideration needs to be given to each of these objectives without overlooking the fact that there are also other educational objectives. There could easily develop an over emphasis on the vocational aspects of learning and how far should the education system be fashioned around the needs of employers? What else is education for? It is essential to ensure that all of the objectives are identified and given full consideration.

Is there too great an emphasis on *preparation for work, with the skills that employers need* and perhaps too little on the *preparation for life* in general?

Is there a danger that the quest to motivate through vocational education could narrow educational objectives?

Education and the national culture

Should education be concerned with the *passing on from generation to generation a national culture?* Should education *describe and explain different national cultures?*

Should education be the means of cultivating a tolerance and understanding of the customs of people of different cultures other than one's own? Should education be concerned with *passing on from one generation to another the knowledge of the world's religions? Should the traditional religion of the nation be given priority in the state education system?*

It is more than half a century, rapidly approaching three-quarters of a century, since the end of World War II, and the people that had the vision of creating a new land fit for the returning warriors, their families and their descendants, are no longer with us: decade after decade the nation has changed, first with newcomers arriving from the former lands of the British Empire, coming to enjoy the culture in place, a culture largely based on the Christian ethic; then more came from the Commonwealth and other lands, and they became more confident in the matter of maintaining the characteristics of their own culture and religious background. The United Kingdom had become, so we are told, a multicultural society: and so we have, in so far as we have people following various cultures living within our land; but have we become a united country with its people following the various cultures in harmony with each other? Are our cultures integrated into a cohesive whole and what part, if any, should a state education system be playing in this matter?

Here lies a basic problem. There is and has been long term evidence that people of various cultures and beliefs can live together in friendship and harmony – but often, driven by the more extreme adherents to beliefs, they do not. How can education bring about the former?

What is the purpose of education?

Starting from the position of wishing to cultivate a society in which people live in peace and harmony with one another all groups start with the ethics and customs established in their families during their early upbringing. None start with a clean sheet and here lies the first of the dilemmas which face society's leaders: should a nation start from the position of retaining its traditional culture, including its religion, as an over riding principle? The United Kingdom's history places it firmly in the culture of the Christian teachings, through the Churches of England, Scotland, Roman Catholic and others; although there has often been conflict between them, the Catholic versus Protestant 'Troubles' being an example. Where there are differences of belief there are reasons for conflict and it is in this matter that it is necessary to determine how education can be organized to bring about harmony.

Among young people there is always the chance of conflict, even in an apparently uniform culture; the causes of conflict being found in the requirements for maintaining acceptable behaviour. Where there are cultural differences these can be used by the young to manipulate the system for their own ends. In addition, some parents support their children; even encourage them, in their deviations from what is required.

A first principle therefore seems to be the necessary reaching of agreement across cultures in the matter of expected behaviour: a principle which at first sight seems obvious to all and easy to achieve. However, a simple consideration of dress quickly complicates the issue. There is conflict enough in the matter of school uniforms but with the introduction of religious requirements the matter becomes more complex.

I recollect the occasion when the teacher of physical education came to me with the problem relating to a girl carrying a sizeable knife on her person, claiming this to be a necessary aspect of her religion. The act was of course one of bravado and challenge to authority rather than one of piousness, and was resolved by counseling the child and her parents with the involment of a leader of the appropriate religious community. A previously agreed written code of behaviour would possibly have made the situation less confrontational.

Consider the child who, in accordance with its parents' wishes, wears a necklace displaying a cross in order to confirm its faith, when the school has a rule that jewellery must not be worn by pupils. Again, the pre-determined compromise written into a multicultural code could make the situation clear from the outset and give clear guidance on how challenges to the written rule may be resolved.

Now let us go a step further and consider the child who insists on coming to school in the hooded jacket, or other face-concealing garments for personal reasons. To see the faces of one another is a means of judging mood, happiness, dismay, and so on: it is the means by which, in part at least, we recognize each other and adjust our responses to others, surely an essential aspect of the teaching-learning situation.

Is it possible to reach a comprise on the rules set for all of our children, no matter what culture or religious background they come from – or does the solution to required differences lie in the setting up of different state schools to cater for different customs? If so, with this must come tolerance of the views of others and compromise in order to promote an integrated society.

13. New schools and colleges

In recent years a variety of initiatives have resulted in the establishment of different types of schools for different purposes, a complete reversal of the one school for all notion of the comprehensive system – or so it may seem. In reality the primary notion *there shall be no selection of pupils by schools, with one school for all* continues to dog progress: it is a part of the hallucinatory education system in which we find ourselves. Ideology has produced a deep-seated belief that in order to create social justice, selection must be avoided, one school system, the comprehensive, must be retained with a common national curriculum and common system of qualifications, all producing an illusion of success – a self-perpetuating myth.

Those introducing the new initiatives recognise the folly of the one school for all but are frustrated by its proponents' entrenched principles and unbending opposition.

One situation easily recognised by all interested in education is the failing school, often a neighbourhood school inheriting the social problems of its adult population, and one attempt to raise the standards of the children and young people affected is the introduction of the Academy project – and not without controversy.

The Academy's programme was initiated by the Labour Government during Tony Blair's premiership to raise the standard of education for children and young people in deprived areas, where secondary schools were seen to fail. They are publicly funded, money coming from government and sponsors; are independent of local authority control (but are expected to work in partnership with the local authorities); have independent governing bodies and have some freedom from the control of the national curriculum.

Very significantly, they have been generously funded.

The sponsors are expected to challenge the established methods of running schools and set up an endowment fund with the intention that the proceeds are spent on schemes which hopefully will improve the educational provision in their areas. They appoint the majority of governors, the total relatively small, but the local authority has one seat, two if it is a co-sponsor. The governing body has responsibility, with the head-teacher or principal, for managing the academy.

Academies are not entirely free to go their own way as they are expected to abide by such government directives as the School Admissions Code, certain National Curriculum subjects such as English, mathematics, science and ICT, and guidance on the matter of excluding pupils.

It is expected that each academy will be unique, each developing its own ethos helped by their independence and sponsors. There is the additional expectation that they will play a large part in the regeneration of their communities, sharing both facilities and expertise with others. The latter echoes the Extended School policy of the government discussed later.

So, it seems that Academies are semi-independent schools but clearly restricted by the requirements of governments who largely control the purse strings.

Controversy has arisen due to their independence and perceived uniqueness but opponents have the dilemma of balancing the requirements of their ideology with the clear objective of raising the standards of provision for the under privileged.

Sponsors may come from a variety of sources, for example industry, commerce, other educational establishments, and religious bodies: further controversy is consequently generated through the fear of sponsors having undue and biased influence over the development of the schools.

Up to the present time, some academies appear to have thrived while others, much to the excitement of the critics, have failed.

The Darlington Church of England Academy

In 2005 the Darlington Education Authority announced that it had been making plans to combine the Eastbourne School, taking pupils from the eastern side of the town, with the Hurworth School, located in a semi-rural area and taking young people from that area plus a considerable supplement from Eastbourne's immediate environment. Both were 11 to 16 age-group schools feeding the Queen Elizabeth Sixth Form College and Darlington Technical College of Further Education, both located close to the centre of the town, the latter, in 2008, moving into new purpose built premises.

The people of Hurworth had always been known to value their local secondary school and to oppose any suggestion that it be closed. By 2005 the school had developed into a very successful Mathematics and Computing Specialist School with good GCSE results (the Specialist School being another type of school introduced by government in a bid to raise standards).

The Eastbourne School was a successful mixed comprehensive school formed from the amalgamation of the Eastbourne Girls and Eastbourne Boys secondary modern schools in 1968, one of six 11 to 16 secondary schools in the town. By 2007, after experiencing various problems and having some six head-teachers in as many years, it was decided that it should be closed and that an Academy be opened in its place.

The sponsors of this new venture are the Durham Diocese of the Church of England and business entrepreneurs David and Anne Crossland: the school is a faith school and this immediately brought criticism: there are those who claim there is no justification for faith schools and that such schools are divisive.

In the previous chapter the question was put: how can a state education system help to bring about a multicultural society in which there is harmony, where the multiple cultures form a cohesive whole? So, are faith schools divisive? Surely, the answer lies with the people who operate and attend such schools.

In the prospectus for the Church of England Academy in Darlington the school prints its mission statement in which it says it is a Christian learning environment set at the heart of its community, promoting respect and expecting high standards. Although they emphasise they have a strong Christian ethos, the school is inclusive, welcoming children of all faiths and those with no faith. They describe their curriculum as broad and balanced and is offered to students of all abilities. As may be expected having representatives from the business world as their sponsors the school's specialism is Business and Enterprise through which they endeavour to teach young people the skills and attitudes which equip them for employment or further study. The staff are dedicated to helping the students reach their full potential, and any visitor will notice that this means the whole staff from chaplain to receptionist.

In September 2009 the school moved into new purpose built premises on a neighbouring site not far from the old building, consequently serving the same catchment area but re-named St Aidan's Church of England Academy.

In conversations with the Principal, visitors can be in no doubt that the sponsors recognised a need in the Eastbourne area, where the older school had failed, and wanted to do something to improve the lot of the young people in that area: that, their prime reason for taking the opportunity to become involved in the setting up of an academy. Surely no one can argue against this ideal.

It should be noted that by today's standards the school, with only 700 students, is relatively small and it will be interesting to see if this answers the criticism that larger units cause schools to become impersonal, losing the advantages of the closer community where people have a far better chance of knowing each other – a particularly significant factor in the fostering of good professional staff-pupil relationships.

The difference between the ethos of faith schools and those seen as secular is by definition the matter of faith, in this case the Christian faith, and many people in the world obtain great comfort, peace of mind and strength through the belief in their faith and this should not be denied to them. Our question, of course, is related to the matter of whether or not a school in a state education system should be involved in the promotion of its faith, and this is a complex matter.

There is, the prospectus tells us, a daily act of worship. There is of course nothing new in this – school assemblies are a long established aspect of schools in this country.

In the 1938 edition of the Darlington County Borough Education Committee Regulations the time for Prayers, Religious Instruction and Roll Call was laid down.

Although times of opening school changed from time to time, it was accepted that the day began with an act of worship. The schools were state schools, followed the requirements of the various Education Acts and the teachings and festivals of the Christian Church.

There was however *no attempt to be made to attach children to any particular denomination* and provision was expected to be made for children withdrawn from religious teaching and observance to follow *separate instruction in secular subjects, where practicable in a separate room.*

An appropriate syllabus for religious instruction, *The Cambridgeshire Syllabus of Religious Teaching for Schools*, and appropriate Bibles, Hymn Books and listed Prayers were given in the regulations, which also stated that the Education Committee relied upon teachers to give religious instruction in the spirit of reverence, recognising the responsibility placed upon them in the matter of laying the foundations for the moral and religious lives of their pupils.

St Aidan's Church of England Academy is therefore not doing anything new – what is new is that the country has become multi-cultural, with people following different faiths or no faith at all.

As the principles upon which our democratic society is based include freedom of thought, freedom of speech and, with necessary reservations, freedom of action, there should presumably be the freedom for parents to send their children to faith schools, and that, therefore faith schools should exist within the state system – schools for all faiths, if required.

With this we are brought back to the question of producing a multi-cultural cohesive society and not a fragmented one.

Faith schools within the state education system have the obligation to accept any who wish to attend them and not to impose their religious beliefs on their students. It remains that they will have the ethos founded on their faith and in many cases it is the behavioural aspects of the ethos which many parents find attractive. Non-practicing Catholics certainly attend catholic schools for this reason, as do non practicing church goers attend St Aidan's Academy. In the end it is one's family tradition and one's acceptance or not, with developing independence, of these traditions which determine a person's faith. The matter is not whether there should be faith schools or not but how they should be regulated in such a way as to promote the understanding of multiculturalism and the cohesion of its sub-sections, and the necessary imposition of compromise where it is the only way to bring people together. Where compromise is not acceptable it is presumably because one culture cannot adapt its own traditions and practices to fit in with the requirements of multiculturalism.

A confusion of initiatives

In Darlington, as well as St Aidan's Academy, there are six other secondary schools: Branksome School and Science College, Carmel Roman Catholic Technology College, the Education Village (including Beaumont School Technology and Vocational College, Haughton Community School and Arts College, and Springfield Primary School), Hummersknott School and Language College, Hurworth Maths and Computing College, and Longfield School Sports College. The 'College' aspect of the title defines the particular specialism followed by the school.

Specialist schools

The Specialist Schools programme is another government initiative aimed at raising standards, in this case through the development of a particular specialist area within the curriculum, helping, it is claimed, to give the school a 'distinctive identity'. For example, the St Aidan's Academy's 'identity' is business and enterprise, supported by its sponsors' experience as entrepreneurs in the business world.

There are ten given areas from which schools are encouraged to choose and develop a specialism: arts, business and enterprise, engineering, humanities, languages, mathematics and computing, music, science, sports and technology. There is also the facility for a school to adopt two specialist areas.

The scheme appears to be admirable enough, with its objective of giving schools a chance to move forward and develop a unique ethos, but are there difficulties and confusions beyond the ideal? There is also the burden of the school having to raise some money for the project themselves in order to be considered for specialist status.

Parents expect their children to progress to secondary schools at the age of 11 plus, or later where middle schools are established, and invariably will choose the school situated in their neighbourhood. Indeed, government policy is for schools to be involved with their neighbourhoods. Conversely, parents are confronted with the notion that their children, when they are still relatively young, need to be guided into making a choice of a specialist school, choosing from several which serve the 11-16 age group, only one of which can possibly be local. Therein arises a conflicting situation: children want to go to their local school but do not want to follow its specialism, and, consequently, the specialist teaching part of the curriculum may well be undersubscribed. It is also easily argued that 11 plus is far too young an age for most children to opt for specialist areas of learning.

Parents may be further confused by other descriptions of status awarded to the schools in their area: for instance, Longfield School in Darlington is described as having become a Healthy school and International School in 2008; and a Teaching and Learning centre accredited for providing Continuous Professional Development.

The layperson may be forgiven for assuming that all schools and colleges should without exception be 'healthy' and may wonder at the 'international' aspect of the local one-time comprehensive. And surely by definition all schools are 'Teaching and Learning Centres', but the Government's intention is that expensive school buildings should be used beyond the traditional 9 till 4 school hours.

The Darlington Education Village

The Darlington Education Village opened at the start of the summer term 2006 with 1400 young people on roll. At the heart of the initiative was the intake of 300 children and young people with special needs from the Beaumont Hill Technology College; 200 came from the Springfield Primary School and 900 from the Haughton 11 to 16 Mixed Comprehensive School. Haughton already had the status of a specialist arts school.

The thinking behind this experimental project is to bring together handicapped and non-handicapped, children and young people, in a single educational establishment, but each with its own specialist rooms and recreational areas, in order to foster a greater mutual understanding of each other and co-operation, with a growth in support for the less fortunate.

Previously, in the year 2000, Beaumont Special School joined with the Abbey Hill Special School, Stockton, to bid for specialist status as a Technology College and this was successful, with the school becoming a high performing school in its specialism.

In 2005 the school gained the additional status of Applied Learning (formerly known as Vocational Learning) which provided additional funding and resources to enable it to develop a wider range of courses for its 14- to 19-year-olds and initiatives to encourage them to examine and plan for their future employment.

Haughton Comprehensive School became a Community and Specialist Arts College and joined with the special school and local primary school in what is known as a Hard Federation in new purpose built premises.

The buildings are situated around a central green and open inwards, helping to produce a secure environment There are only two floors connected by external gradual sloping walkways. The absence of high rise blocks of some 1960s schools adds to the concept of the village, rather than town or city.

The imposing main entrance has a glass-fronted lobby with a business-like reception area. Transport, cars and buses, can drive into the grounds to car parks and disembarking points around a circular green, as required. The approach is claimed to be both functional and friendly although its appearance may be awesome when first seen by the young 11-year-olds.

With the buildings set out around a central focal point the planners have provided each of the three schools with its own special area while producing a unity and allowing for the joint use of specialist areas. An external 'ring fence' keeps out intruders and deters those, who for one reason or another, would wander off site when it is inappropriate to do so. Light bright spacious corridors connect the separate working areas, although the required movement of a large number of young people in the secondary age group, from one specialist area to another, will undoubtedly need careful planning involving appropriate but upheld rules for the most peaceful results.

Dining areas are open spaces merging with the corridors rather than enclosed rooms, making supervision more difficult: it cannot be assumed that young people will behave like perfectly mannered and considerate adults. The movement of food on heated trolleys from the central kitchen to several dispersed dining areas is not ideal, although it is difficult to see how the supply and staffing of three separate kitchens could be justified.

With the need for vocational education for some young people, as opposed to the traditional more academically orientated curriculum, it is essential to consider how far the specialist accommodation provision answers this need. It can be questioned how far the 'learning lines', defined in the government White Paper 14 -19 and listed below, are catered for.

1. Health and social care	1. Health and social care
2. Public services	2. Public services
3. Land based and environmental	3. Land based and environmental
4. Engineering	4. Engineering
5. Manufacturing	5. Manufacturing
6. Construction and the built environment	6. Construction and the built environment
7. Information and communication technology.	7. Information and communication technology.

Training Schools

Another quality of the Beaumont Hill school is that it qualified as 'high performing' (as assessed by the Specialist Schools and Academies Trust) and consequently applied for and was granted, in 2008, the status as a Training School for Special Educational Needs teaching.

Training Schools, of which there are some 230 up and running, apply the concept that the art of teaching is best learned on the job and provide a variety of teacher training activities. They use examples of good practice: methods, styles of teaching and resources that have been proved to bring good results. They arrange opportunities for teachers to observe the teaching of other experienced and well thought of teachers. Through the use of teacher mentors and trainers, a variety of paths for training as a teacher are promoted, including training while employed. They also take part in classroom based research, demonstrating that, although much is learnt on the job, there are also theoretical aspects to the work that need to be studied.

All of the government instigated projects referred to bring money with them, a great motivator in encouraging schools to take part in the various schemes. Cash initiates a school's motivation, the requirements of the project then generate staff enthusiasm and involvement; giving the school new purpose and direction.

Extended schools

The Extended School scheme is designed to bring school premises into use beyond the normal hours of classroom teaching in order to provide a range of services for children, their families and the local community. It is another example of the government encouraging a specific type of development through the means of advancing money for that purpose. It is expected that all schools will be Extended Schools by 2010.

On the website Directgov, for parents (30th September 2009), the question *'What is an extended school?'* is answered in terms of what they are expected to provide. For instance the services provided are *designed to help you balance work and family commitments, support your children with their studies and give them a broader range of experiences and interests.*

In the first instance the emphasis is placed on social factors and it becomes very clear that government intention is to involve schools in social as opposed to purely educational matters. Secondly the intention moves back into the field of learning and traditional extra-curricular activities, a further development of what is already happening. It is in these areas where the involvement of teachers was voluntary but with the new imposed formality comes obligation. On the one hand it is useful to have the same staff supervising premises and facilities both during the day and beyond, but it is clearly not possible to have teachers working full time during both day and evening sessions. When groups other than day school staff have access to what was traditionally the school's premises, things can go missing and damage done: the question of responsibility is divided. The Extended School therefore becomes an entirely new organisation with staffing implications. Who is in overall charge of the school? Clearly the principal, the deputies and other senior managers cannot be on duty all of the time so it becomes necessary to devise a new structure in which some school staff work partly during the traditional school hours and partly during the extended opening times: and this must be achieved without detracting from the very significant consistent professional pupil-teacher relationships necessary in the day school. That teachers should know the pupils and pupils know their teachers is a very important aspect of a good school discipline. (An interesting observation was made by a teacher at a teacher's union conference in the 1930s: in order to teach Johnny Latin the teacher must not only know Latin but also know Johnny.) With the introduction of part-time staff the maintaining of a cohesive community becomes more difficult, affecting the upholding of a positive ethos.

Another aspect of extra-curricular involvement is that of pupils wishing to be involved in away-from-school activities, preferring the different participant-instructor relationship to that associated with the classroom. Such activities could be and indeed are held on school premises, returning to the need to control dual use of school resources.

In the matter of *supporting children with their studies*, schools surely have always done this, during day-time class contact time and to some extent beyond those hours: to extend formal learning into the evening may be seen as an imposition too far. Are children to be expected to turn up for extra classes in the evening? It may be that the government has variety in mind, providing a whole range of evening activities for young people, but is it a good idea to have a state-imposed system to answer such a need?

It is clear that another aspect of the extended school is the use of its facilities for adult learning outside day-time hours, but there are colleges of further education designed for this purpose.

The welfare element of the scheme is illustrated by the suggestion that schools should provide access to child care facilities, promote such things as healthy eating and give advice on managing personal finances. Examples of child care facilities given are breakfast and after school clubs, child minding and day nurseries: and this may be interpreted as the state encouraging parents to abdicate their responsibilities, a state of mind evolving from the understanding that a minority of parents do not properly realise these responsibilities. There is talk of the breakdown of family life and its undesirable consequences: yet, surely, too much state provision can easily exacerbate this situation.

For instance, when primary schools become what is described as fully extended they are required, not merely expected, to provide child care and a range of other activities from 8.00 am to 6 pm, five days a week, 48 weeks of the year: if this is not encouraging parents to abdicate responsibility for their children for a large part of the working week, what is it? A young child placed in such care should apparently only be asleep when with its parents!

Foundation, Trust and Voluntary-aided Schools

The Academy initiative has placed the running of some schools in the hands of the head-teacher/principal and governors who are largely appointed by the sponsors and largely independent of the local education authorities. Other schools which have similarly independent governing bodies are Foundation, Trust and Voluntarily-aided schools.

In Foundation schools the governing body the buildings and land on which the premises are built are owned by the governing body or charitable foundation. Trust schools were introduced by the government in 2007 when governing bodies, with parental backing were given the authority to seek trust status, forming a charitable trust with a partner outside the education services, not unlike the academy situation, and with a similar governing body.

Voluntarily-aided schools have their premises and land owned by a charitable organisation, and have governing bodies similarly constituted and with similar authority to those of Foundation and Trust Schools.

Schools established by parents

The notion of schools being independent of local authorities is further advanced by the suggestion that parents who are dissatisfied with their local school should be allowed to form their own, a scheme successfully introduced in Sweden, where the system is funded by the government making available to the parent group the same amount of money as that per pupil in a state establishment.

Business apprenticeship centres

Some very significant factors involved in the motivating of potential learners in the 14 to 19 age range are the desire of the young people to be accepted into an adult environment, their need for employment and the strong desire to gain independence through the possession of their own money. The suggestion of vocational education has been advanced as a possible route to some these.

Fourteen 'learning lines' for vocational education have been advanced in the 14 to 19 White Paper and ten areas suggested for the development of specialisms from which to develop specialist schools.

The principle of involving sponsors in the establishment of schools has been approved.

Considering the change of curriculum at 14 years of age, at the time of the possible introduction of a first level examination qualification for young people and their subsequent advance into post 14 learning centres, should *school* finish at this age and *college* commence?

Should school and college be in quite separate premises?

Specialist schools could be replaced by specialist colleges, thus eliminating the necessary choosing of a particular specialist school at the age of 11 plus and moving choice to the older age of 14 when young people are becoming more able to travel outside their immediate neighbourhoods.

Specialist colleges could be established in a number of related specialist areas chosen from a list of possibilities generated from the integration of the existing 'learning lines' and specialist areas.

Each college could be affiliated to a sponsored Business Apprenticeship Centre. Such a centre would be a commercial venture providing a realistic service or producing a marketable product.

Each centre, managed by a Chairman and Board, as in the business world, would have at its core a staff fully qualified to run such an establishment. Young apprentices from the attached college would have the opportunity to work in the centre and be paid a wage while they learn about the various aspects of the business venture through on the job experience.

The White Paper: Your Child, Your Schools, Our Future

In the summer of 2009 yet another White Paper *Your Child, Your Schools, Our Future: Building a 21st Century Schools System* was published developing further the government's thinking. The proposed legislation included a Pupil Guarantee, a Parents Guarantee, Home-School Agreements, and a new School Report Card.

The Pupil Guarantee, we are told, is to ensure:

1. pupils get a broad and balanced curriculum and high qualifications;
2. every secondary pupil has a personal tutor;
3. all pupils get 5 hours of PE and sport every week and access to cultural activities;

4. gifted and talented pupils get written confirmation;
5. all pupils with additional needs will get extra help;
6. all pupils in Years 3 to 6 falling behind in English or maths get one-to-one or small group tuition;
and
7. all pupils deemed to be below the expected standard at the start of their secondary school years will be offered one-to-one or small group tuition.

It somehow seems unnecessary that a government needs to legislate to ensure such a provision but is a further example of the state dictating what should be happening in what should be a professionally determined institution.

Of course, it is not possible to guarantee that young people will get high qualifications, it is only possible to provide the opportunity for them to do so: the stated guarantee is a further example of the misconception that so long as the resources are provided all will achieve at a high level. It is said that all young people need skills and qualifications to succeed, have potential and can do well with the right help and support. What is not said is that not all are either able or wish to do so. A major fault in our society is that it does not provide the *opportunities in employment suitable for the whole range of abilities and aspirations of its entire population*.

The notion that every secondary school pupil should have a designated tutor is perhaps unnecessary and expensive. What is the purpose of this proposal? Is this person to be a personal counsellor? Is such a provision really necessary? Schools have always placed children in reasonably sized groups in charge of one teacher and, given time, the teacher can counsel *each child when necessary*. Certainly, for any success, there needs to be a mutual respect between teacher and pupil: how is this relationship to be fostered? In any case the majority of youngsters will wish to be left to get on with their lives without any thought of needing counselling. Is this initiative yet another intrusion into people's lives where it is not required – an imposition upon all because a few have a need – a replacement of the parent by the state because a minority of parents do not take their responsibilities seriously?

There is a requirement that pupils be given five hours of PE and sport in each week – and access to cultural activities. If there is a timetable of 7 sessions of 35 minutes per day for 5 days, five hours will take up nearly one-quarter of the week: does this leave sufficient time for subject teaching? If as subjects of primary importance, English, mathematics and ICT (Information and Communication Technology) are given another quarter of the week's total time, there will be some 10 hours left for the rest of the curriculum: science, a second language, history, geography, design and technology, art and design, music and citizenship – 1 hour 15 minutes per subject. And the extra cultural activities, civics, or teaching about violence in families, if they are indeed extra, have not been included. So, are we entering the realm of the extended school with an element of expectation that all will be involved, whether they like it or not?

The Parents' Guarantee is meant to ensure:

1. regular online information concerning their child's progress, behaviour and attendance;
2. access to their child's personal tutor;
3. fair school admissions as defined by the government in the Admissions Code;
3. parents' views are listened to;
4. local authorities will have to respond to these views;
5. all parents accept the school's rules, signing the Home-School Agreement each year;
6. parents have the right to complain if the home-School Agreement is not enforced.

This piece of legislation will formalise what has previously been a voluntary expectation and it regrettable that such action has become necessary, reminding us of the general expectation that the posing of a legal question produces a legal answer. There is compulsion where previously there had been trust.

The Home-School Agreement

It may be expected that all parents want their children to attend a well run, controlled and safe school, yet clearly today there are children and young people in schools who either do not understand the need for rules of conduct or who choose to ignore what they know to be right. The question is: why?

Our culture has encouraged the abdication of family responsibility, its expectations of reasonable behaviour and even an understanding of what is right and wrong. A boundless freedom has been encouraged until there is now wonder at the fact that a significant number of children do seriously disrupt schools, students think that enjoyment comes from swallowing enough alcohol to eliminate the controlling influence of conscience and inhibition, and there is growing concern at the extent of dangerous violence. Those who, without sufficient thought, encouraged the introduction of legislation to bring about this freedom have now brought us to the position of having to introduce more legislation to control the development of uncivilised behaviour which, in reality denies others their freedom.

Parents now have to sign a Home-School Agreement which commits them legally to ensuring that their children abide by the rules of the school.

Because teachers have had their authority eroded it has become necessary to legislate in an attempt to correct this loss. Trust has been lost. Once again, the need to turn to legislation brings legal requirements and restrictions where before there was an informal but accepted way of doing things. This is an unfortunate and undesirable development.

Executive Head-teachers

Another change in the culture of our schools is found in the reinforcing of the concept that some head-teachers are better at their job than others: a notion of super heads has evolved with the appointment of Executive Heads who can run more than one school. The head-teacher then becomes, as the title suggests, a business manager, not the leader of a team of dedicated teachers. He or she must, by definition, be constantly moving from one school to another – never in the right place when he or she is needed.

If, as it is quite reasonable to expect, some heads are better than others (after all, all cannot be perfect) a better solution would be not to have Executive Heads but, instead Executive Advisors who can be appointed to schools where help is required in order to work along side the head-teacher for a specified period of time: advising and showing how things may be improved. As far as the school is concerned such a person would be in position to assist the head-teacher, who would continue to be seen as the leading figure. This approach allows for a more user-friendly ethos to be maintained in institutions where a family-like atmosphere is more appropriate to the educating of impressionable young people. Young people respond better to instructions given where mutual respect exists between the school staff and themselves, which is only possible where the teaching staff is unchanging and not over large.

Accredited Schools Groups

Developing the notion that grouping schools is a good thing, in other words making teaching units bigger, with floating staff and visiting super heads, the Government has introduced the Accredited School Group where high performing educational establishments will be given authority to run chains of schools, colleges, and universities.

Accountability

With the idea that schools cannot be relied upon to do their job properly governments have introduced the concept of accountability, linked with various systems to ensure teachers and schools are indeed accountable.

The School Report Card

The most recent of the accountability systems is the introduction of the Report Card with pilot schemes introduced in September 2009. It is intended to provide information on:

1. how the school is improving standards;
2. how well it is helping those pupils who have fallen behind to catch up, and stretching the more able;
3. discipline, attendance, sport, healthy eating and partnership working; and
4. what parents and pupils think of the school.

There is also a clear intention that this information shall be widely published with each school being given a summary grade. League tables for schools are confirmed.

If there are to be league tables it is obvious that schools will be placed in rank order and that some must by definition be at the bottom of the list; which, in turn generates competition between schools and the search for the means (any means) of ensuring that your establishment is not among those seeming to fail.

So, is this exercise really what is needed?

So long as a school is satisfying its customers, the parents and young people, by giving them what they need, who needs to know *how* it is improving standards? Why does *everyone* need to know how a school is helping the least and most able: or discipline and attendance? What is supposed to be reported on the school's participation in sport? Who on earth wants to know what schools, educational establishments, are doing about healthy eating – other than giving sensible advice in appropriate lessons and at appropriate times? Why should *everybody* be informed about progress made by any partnerships in which the school may be engaged?

The aspects of all of this which are relevant to those who wish to know can be found in the school's prospectus and in appropriate press releases issued by the schools. It must also be remembered that the media are only interested in the exceptional, stories, good or bad, which catch the attention of their readers, no matter how it is presented to them.

Any state system of this kind amounts to the over involvement of government in what should be a democratically constructed professional service. It is demanding of time and energy which would be better spent on getting on with the job of educating the pupils.

14. A new professionalism

Some preliminary thoughts:
The basis for the organisation of society in the United Kingdom may reasonably be supposed to follow the concept of a liberal democracy in which members are, at least in theory, free to control their own lives and have the ability to influence decisions relating to the running of their community.

It is a concept evolved through history from the principles established for the governing of the Greek City State where it is generally accepted that all members of that society had similar interests, attitudes and knowledge relating to the administration of their nation's affairs.

Stating the obvious, such an ideal situation is far from the reality found in the complex densely settled communities in which we live today, with their ever increasing and infinitely varied populations.

Where there are such large numbers of people and such great differences between individuals, where there are numerous sub-groups with different cultures, it may be argued that there will not be a common view on very much at all.

In an attempt to overcome this problem there has developed the system of decision making based upon majority voting. Each participant has a vote and a simple majority determines the decision. But who is satisfied, especially if the voting is something like fifty-one per cent in favour with forty-nine per cent against? In any case, who does the voting? Although some may argue that everyone should vote on everything, such a situation is hardly practical. Do we all, in our complex society, understand the issues behind every decision that needs to be made? Clearly not! In any case, do we all have the time to vote on all of the matters which affect us? Surely not, as we are too busy working in those areas of society for which we have some responsibility and where we have duties to perform for which we are paid. If we do not understand or do not have the time, is it reasonable for us to leave the decision making to those who do? If the answer to this question is yes, then we must be able to trust those to whom we delegate this authority to act with honour.

As everyone cannot reasonably be expected to vote on everything, our democracy has come to rely upon the decision making of experts and representatives who are invested with the authority to reach reasonable conclusions on behalf of everyone. The experts are appointed by reason of their qualifications, their specialised knowledge and their experience of working in their particular discipline. We expect them to keep up to date and to advance the most objective evidence to support their arguments. In theory at least, we can have them removed from office if they are proved incompetent, although it may be claimed that too many remain in post for life. These are the professionals.

The representatives are elected by popular vote at reasonable intervals. They are the politicians, high powered party members, possibly driven by deep seated ideals, salaried careerists, or part-time volunteers. They have varying degrees of expertise in some fields but can hardly be experts in every matter about which they are expected to make decisions. Consequently they rely on information, opinion and fact, provided by numerous other people who are expert, by reason of their specialised training, in specific disciplines. It is the relationship between the experts and the politicians which is of such great significance and the balance of authority vested in each a crucial factor in the efficient but just organisation of society.

Teachers, like other groups of workers, use various representatives to look after their interests while themselves operating as experts in their specialist fields (in their subject disciplines, teaching skills, and their particular knowledge of people as students).

It will serve us well, however, to remember that our society has, amongst its members, those who have no specialist knowledge, or knowledge which society regards as useful, who feel they have little control over their lives and who do not feel in any way genuinely represented by those supposedly elected to make decisions for them either locally or nationally, and who see those with otherwise generally accepted useful knowledge merely as irrelevant, or even hostile authority figures.

One theory which recognises this inadequacy of member representation in our democracy assumes that we operate a system in which elite groups compete with each other over the right to govern. The winning elite is then left to initiate policies and make decisions, while the losers form an opposition.

Any elite, in this sense, for those not politically active, may seem to be too far removed from their lives and quite unable to comprehend their needs and wishes, let *al*one make decisions in their favour.

For those with extreme views, governments, works managements, and no doubt teachers too, are identified, among others, as elite groups operating according to their own priorities. Consequently, they claim that decisions made by such elites cannot be binding upon those who are not members of the elite. Teachers are seen as an elitist middle class determined to impose their own values on a majority of students who hold different, but equally valid, if not more valid, values.

The ultimate outcome of this line of reasoning is to break down existing conventions, previously agreed rules and cultural norms, without putting any other workable socialising system in their place. People who do not like any decision can, and do, refuse to abide by the rules reasonably drawn up for the good of all: even though these rules which can be modified, if it is sensible to do so, through the processes of argument and compromise. We witness the results of this philosophy in so much of today's uncertainty.

The implications for those in the education service are profound. Teachers, it may be claimed, have no expertise and consequently no authority. They do not hold any body of knowledge which they can pass on to their students, whether their students are innocent young children, rebellious adolescents or mature adults. They do not hold expertise in teaching methods, they have no right to expect students to behave in any particular way and certainly have no authority to expect any specific standards of dress. Indeed, the teacher may at best be, according to the jargon, some kind of independent chairman or facilitator, and at worst have no function at all! Those who choose teaching as their vocation need to ask themselves whether they believe in this line of reasoning or alternatively believe that they do indeed offer a more positive professional service based upon values which are worthy of preservation.

Participatory democracy

A less extreme and consequently a possibly more attractive system for managing society arises from the concept of a participatory democracy, an initiative of the 1970s, which requires representative member participation at all levels of decision making. For instance, according to this theory, members of a neighbourhood need a committee to debate and decide matters relating to the running of their neighbourhood. In the workplace the employees require a committee through which they can argue their case in matters relating to the running of the works. In schools and colleges teachers also, in this ideal participatory democracy, need to have their committees which will discuss all matters which effect them, reach decisions relating to these matters and take responsibility for these decisions. But parents and students also have their place in the education service and they also, applying the same principles, must be given the means of deciding their destiny. Indeed, legislation has subsequently given representatives of these groups places on governing bodies and governing bodies have been empowered to run the educational establishments.

This philosophy denies, or at least reduces, the significance of experts and expertise. The opinions of everyone have to be heard and each view be given equal value, irrespective of the level of training and experience of those concerned. The teacher appears to be given a greater say in the running of the educational establishment in which he or she works, but is denied the authority which he or she previously enjoyed as a respected professional. Society comes to rely more upon the consensus of opinion derived from the non-expert, or so it may at first appear. It may further be argued that it is the pressure group which comes to dominate the decision making because it is frequently only those who wish to be politically active who stand for office. Although the system recognises them as the representatives of their respective groups, in reality there is always the danger that they can and often do follow their own agenda, or an agenda derived from the objectives of some other external group to which they belong.

So it may be asked: is this the best way to run our education system? Are those affected by the decisions really able to objectively debate all of the issues, make choices and take responsibility for the decisions which they subsequently make? Have they the necessary knowledge and experience? Have they time available to become involved or are they too busy taking full responsibility for the work they are paid to do? Are they, should they, be fully occupied in the lesson preparation, marking, assessment and counselling of their students? If they are giving time to other matters, although these matters do influence their working lives, are they giving less attention to those they should be teaching?

Participatory democracy and education

Colin Wringe in his book Democracy, Schooling and Political Education (George Allen and Unwin, 1984), says that our educational establishments are authoritarian and hierarchical and not democratic.

If, in order to be considered democratic, institutions need to be organised and run by those who work in them, each with opinions carrying equal weight in the making of all decisions, then this determines by simple definition that schools are certainly not democratic. But should they be? Does not participatory democracy work most efficiently for all concerned when integrated with the concept of authority vested in experts? The simple notion of participatory democracy on its own either assumes all participants have equal knowledge and understanding of the numerously different aspects of what is required for the successful running of their school, or assumes that it does not matter whether or not they do have that knowledge and understanding. The first is impossible, all cannot know everything. The second is unsound, a little knowledge is a dangerous thing. What, in fact, each member of the school staff has is specific knowledge of different aspects of what is required to ensure the smooth running of a complex institution.

Taking as an example one group of specialist workers, the maintenance staff: they should, if properly qualified, know what is required in order to ensure that the buildings, with their furniture and fittings, are kept in a proper state and always fit for use. Yet even within this team each member will have different knowledge and experience from each other. So, should each have equal status? Does the team need a leader in order to function efficiently? If so, does the leader need the authority to decide who does what, when and how, and the authority to discipline any who fall short in the carrying out of their responsibilities? Could it be an efficient state of affairs if all team members were expected to debate together every matter arising in the course of their duties and together reach a conclusion on what should be done before any action was taken? The reality is of course that we all work within established frameworks and only feel the need to express a point of view when the framework is to be modified in some way.

Teachers should, if properly trained and qualified, know how to teach. But each will only know the particular subject matter and teaching methods applicable to the group of students, infants, secondary, tertiary, the gifted or those with special needs, with whom they are trained to work. Presumably, too, people gain something from working within their specialist area. They learn from experience, some more easily than others, and so some become more capable than others. Should the views of those with most experience carry greater weight than those advanced by members with less experience? In any case, are all teachers qualified to reach decisions on educational matters outside their immediate areas of responsibility?

Is it really an efficient state of affairs to expect each member of the staff to debate all matters affecting the running of the institution, and to reach decisions upon those matters, presumably by using the majority vote, before anything gets done? It may be argued that this is neither necessary nor desirable so long as there is an agreed framework within which each works. But who agrees the framework? Is it trade union representatives in negotiations with the government? Or does the government have the right, the responsibility, to define the framework for us? In the case of teachers, a framework for gaining qualifications, hierarchical responsibilities, pay scales, a national curriculum, national standards and means of assessing those standards? Are only some of these properly determined by the government?

It is surely obvious that all of the teachers cannot constantly be debating all of the matters arising in the running of the education system all of the time. We return to the necessity of having different people exercising different responsibilities and may conclude that a team of co-ordinators, the management, should be responsible for ensuring that all parts come together to make an efficient whole.

But, say the enthusiasts for participatory democracy, involving teachers in the making of decisions relating to all matters which influence their working lives, causes them to commit themselves to ensuring that the decisions they have mutually agreed will be efficiently enacted. But is this true?

Is it not more likely that people in general will commit themselves to the upholding of decisions with which they happen to agree while showing only luke-warm enthusiasm, and even hostility, towards those with which they disagree, no matter who made those decisions?

If this is so, is it not only essential to have matters decided by those best qualified to do so, but also to have a system of discipline which ensures that those decisions are properly carried out?

A further factor advanced by the supporters of the participatory type of democratic involvement is the claim that it facilitates the dissemination of information and encourages criticism, particularly criticism of how things are working on the ground. Such a free exchange of views facilitates the adaptation of strategies to needs. But is the establishment of numerous time consuming committees an efficient way of encouraging this participation? Firstly, not every one needs all of the information and secondly, perhaps the most constructive criticism will emerge more easily from the smaller, less formal, meeting between those concerned.

A very significant factor behind all of this thinking is the size of unit in which the members work. It is no accident that much of the change in the ethos of schools has arisen subsequently to their growth in size.

The system which has evolved, based upon the participatory democracy model, is of doubtful efficiency, involving too many people in too great a variety of matters. Expecting them to be involved in matters for which they have neither the qualifications nor experience and yet removing from them authority and responsibility for matters in which they hold expertise has caused great frustration and played a great part in the lowering the morale of the teaching force. We also read reports of increasing stress related illness. Is this caused by the introduction of participatory democratic measures which, because they place people in situations for which they are not trained and take away their authority in places where they have responsibility, breeding insecurity and frustration?

Lay people

Legislation has been introduced which apparently favours the concept of participatory democracy. Teachers and parents were given seats on governing bodies and governing bodies were given greater powers in the running of educational institutions. In reality these actions reduced the professional independence of teachers, for, although they appeared to have gained representation where they thought they had no representation previously, they lost the ability to control their own destinies as assistant teachers working closely with senior colleagues and head-teachers, decisions about the running of the school more and more being reached by a committee comprised of politicians, politically motivated parents and a few politically motivated colleagues. Political sometimes in the sense of party political but just as importantly, politically in the sense of non-political party pressure groups intent on promoting an ideology.

Whereas the head-teacher, firmly placed in a position of authority, informally receives the contributions of each member of staff, evaluating each, absorbing the sensible, rejecting the least useful and, through an on-going dialogue with individuals, providing feedback, the governing body is more remote. The head-teacher, a person with a recognisable personality, is generally accessible to every member of staff every day. The governing body, an institution and not a person, is hardly ever accessible to the classroom teacher, and, if or when it is accessible, access is a formal happening, not a personal face-to-face exchange of ideas. The professional finds his or her working life governed more and more by the decisions of a remote body comprised mainly of untrained, inexperienced people – in reality the exact opposite of what is supposed to happen in a participatory democracy.

Such a state of affairs, where the expertise of the trained and experienced is subordinate to the opinions of a lay body, is bound to be inefficient. The knowledge and acquired wisdom of the professional are either disregarded or adopted via a third party. If disregarded, the situation is absurd. Why ask the plumber how to seal a joint in a water pipe if you are going to ignore the given advice? The result will be a disastrous flood. Why attempt to learn how to do it yourself if you are only going to do the job once and have a thousand and one other things to do? Why is the doctor asked for a diagnosis and remedy when suffering from some malady if you intend to reject the treatment? In serious cases you would end up dead and probably infect all of your friends and relations at the same time.

If the knowledge and acquired wisdom are adopted through a third party, the system is inefficient. Firstly, there is no need for the plumber to be paid to tell everyone how to do the job when he can do it better and more quickly himself. Secondly, in passing knowledge through a third party it becomes distorted, less accurate, less true, and advice becomes blurred, even to the extent of being wrong. Thirdly, wisdom is learned over a long period and cannot be passed on to another in a one off meeting and consequently is lost.

So why do we want to give authority over professional matters to lay people, and then set about trying to train them to do things which the professionals can do better in the first place?

Furthermore, do the lay people, the genuine individuals and not the politically active, want this authority? It is almost certain that they do not. They prefer to leave professional matters to professionals while they carry out their own specific special responsibilities. This principle is demonstrated in two specific ways: the lack of large numbers of people flocking to become school governors and the low proportion of parents taking the opportunity to attend school business meetings. The exceptions in the case of the latter group are when informal pressure groups evolve in order to answer some special question, such as the unpopular decision to close a school or where some other poorly explained unwelcome decision seems to them to be unjust. And in such cases it is likely that the professionals have failed in their duty, and they can fail, and sometimes do.

Pupils

There has developed an attitude that children need to be consulted over matters which affect them and for them to be given authority to influence decisions made which influence their lives.

To be consulted over ALL matters which affect them and given authority to influence ALL decisions which influence their lives? Why? That is not what happens in adult life, where individuals operate within established and generally accepted frameworks. In schools and colleges the established rules of good behaviour, rules which provide a maximum of freedom for each without that freedom impinging upon the freedom of others, make up a part of such a framework. The established curriculum, examination formats and reporting are other examples of established frameworks. If everyone, particularly the young inexperienced members of society, are encouraged to everlastingly challenge these frameworks, they will have no time left to be taught and will not be in the frame of mind to learn.

Nevertheless, pupils and students are provided with school and college councils through which they can air their views and through which, to varying degrees, they can bring about change. But too often they are told their rights without the being informed of the responsibilities which go with them. Emphasis is placed upon questioning what is, often destructively, for they have little knowledge or experience of life and of what, in the accumulated wisdom of centuries, has been found to work.

The traditional view of professionalism

Just as the previous chapters have demonstrated that something has indeed been going wrong with the education since the end of the Second World War, so this chapter has hinted at a loss, or at least a decline, in teacher-professionalism. However, when a more thorough examination of the situation is made, it is not easy to be immediately sure of what has happened. There was an understanding that teachers knew their job and worked those hours over and above class contact time which they felt to be necessary. I remember well taking school parties on historical-geographical trips onto the North Downs and into the Weald of Kent on many Saturdays. During the Easter, Whitsun and Summer holidays I, with colleagues, organised and led school journeys to Dymchurch on the Kent coast, Newquay in Cornwell, Llandudno in North Wales, to Belgium, the Rhine Valley and Switzerland – usually more than one each year, and I think that during one year we actually took three different parties to three different locations, using the general principle that the older the pupils should venture further afield than the younger ones. Other teachers in the sports departments were equally busy, matches took place on Saturday mornings – this was understood to be the norm. Indeed, as a new recruit to teaching I was despatched with a team to some distant playing fields for their match, even though I was never regarded as a sports master. Staff in the foreign language department organised exchange visits with pupils abroad. Science teachers organised their field trips as we organised our geographical-historical expeditions. English and drama departments spent hours training children to take part in the school play and the musicians made equivalent efforts with orchestras and bands. Each of these activities requires much organisation, preparation of material and the encouragement, teaching and supervision of the participants. All of this is work completed in addition to normal preparation and marking for routine classes. Yet this work was carried out by enthusiastic teachers who accepted the duties as an essential part of their professional responsibilities.

There was a general acceptance of the teacher as one who was well qualified, who had studied and learned a subject discipline, who could command the respect of pupils, students and parents alike, and who was a prominent member of the community.

There was a general understanding that the teacher knew about the examinations which the learner could and should work towards, and knew the standards and characteristics of behaviour, for instance application, honesty and punctuality, required by employers.

Under the direction of the heads of schools and colleges the teachers were more or less left to get on with the job. There were the examination syllabi to follow but study programmes, content and methods of teaching, were largely the responsibility of the teachers themselves. I remember well, while working as an assistant teacher in a large London comprehensive school, having the freedom to arrange the subject content of the geography syllabus in such a way as to develop what I regarded as a logical approach to teaching of the subject. I further developed this approach when I became a head of department and used it as the underlying plan for a series of geography text books. Other staff had similar freedoms in their subjects, developing their disciplines along lines which they thought best suited the learners in their care: but within the external framework.

We were expected to be in our places at a reasonable time, ready to receive the students, particularly the younger ones. But we were not expected to sign in. We were expected to take turns with the supervision of youngsters at break, dinner times and after school. These expectances were generally accepted and carried out responsibly, although, by the later 1950s there were teachers with different ideas.

But was there always so much freedom of action among the teachers? A glance at the Education Handbook for a Local Education Authority, in use before the 1944 Education Act, will suggest a different picture. There seemed to be a more rigid approach to teacher discipline and more limitations to what they could do and not do.

"All teachers shall be in their places at least ten minutes before the time appointed for the opening of the school".

"Assistant teachers shall undertake, in accordance with the Head-teacher's allocation, the supervision of children in the playground during playtime, for ten minutes before and for a reasonable time after each school session."

"The school shall ordinarily be open five days each week, from Monday to Friday, inclusive. The school hours shall be as follows: Morning 9.00 to 12.10; afternoon 1.40 to 4.00."

"Children shall not be sent as messengers out of school during school hours."

I also remember, when taking part in student teaching at a North London secondary school, the staff did sign in on arrival, in a book kept for the purpose which was carefully perused by the headmaster each day.

Regulations were prescribed by the Local Education Authority and enforced by the head-teacher, generally without question and certainly without argument.

What is meant by professionalism?

Elsewhere (in 'The Professional Association of Teachers: the first ten years, chapters 8 and 9') I review the development of a broad definition of teacher professionalism as it was seen and developed by a group of teachers who, in the 1970s and '80s, held the view that such professionalism, as they understood it, was in decline.

I referred to Francis Bennion's book "Professional Ethics", which outlines the factors which it is generally understood define a profession. They are relevant to this chapter and consequently, for convenience, I outline them here with some of my own observations.

1. A profession should have an intellectual basis – involving formulation on theoretical lines, requiring a good educational background tested by examination.

    The theory of education exists, a good knowledge of the theory and practice of teaching in surely essential for the teacher, as is the knowledge of the subject matter to be taught, and these disciplines are tested by examination.

2. A profession should be pursued through private practice – so that essential expertise and standards derive from meeting the needs of individual clients on a person to person basis.

   Meeting the needs of individual clients is an essential ingredient of teaching, but can so easily be lost among the narrowness of enthusiasm and dogma of education. It is a paramount objective of the professional teacher.

   The concept of private practice however is not immediately understood to apply to a state education system designed for all. But can the underlying principle here be interpreted as a confidential service given to individuals? If so, does it apply in particular where teaching strategies become more and more student orientated?

   The generally understood requirements of a profession also include the notion that professional remuneration is generated from the fees coming from individual clients and it may be asked how this can apply to any state run system. One answer could be to resurrect the unpopular voucher scheme, where the state provides the learner with a voucher of sufficient value to purchase the courses and modes in instruction which he or she chooses. But perhaps it does not matter in any case. Should the source and means of payment of one's salary determine whether or not you can be described as a professional? Surely there are more significant elements which define professionalism?

3. A profession should have an advisory function, taking full responsibility for the advice given, supervising, negotiating and managing its services.

   Teachers certainly advise and most wish their service to be self governing: the latter being evident from the policies of the various teacher trade unions and resulting in the setting up of a General Teaching Council. (Consultation document "Teaching: High Status, High Standards" published by the Department for Education and Employment in July 1997).

4. A profession has a tradition of service. Teachers agree that service to the client is of prime importance. It has been the different ways in which their trade unions have interpreted how the best this is achieved which has caused a difference of opinion amongst them. The militant trade unionists have argued that it has been absolutely necessary for strike action, the withdrawal of services, to be used as a weapon in order to obtain what is eventually best for those in their care. Non-militants have argued that such actions do not put the interests of

those taught before all else and, indeed, that their use by teachers has led to a de-professionalisation of the service.

5. Lastly, but certainly by no means of least importance, a profession should have a code of conduct.

There remain those who see none of this applying to teachers. They see teaching in the same light as other areas of employment: areas in which employers and employed sit on opposite of sides of some ideological fence and who, from their different standpoints, have to fight for their rights, particularly in the case of the workers fighting for a fair deal in opposition to the management's objective of getting the most for the least out of its workforce. Perhaps it is this very development which most recognise as a decline in teacher professionalism.

The death of the teaching profession

So can it be asked: is the profession of teaching dead? In the Professional Teacher (The journal of the Professional Association of Teachers) of Summer 1987, I reminded readers of the duration of the period of militant disruption in our schools.

"There have been twenty years during which the education service has been disrupted time and time again in one part of the country or another."

In 1970 there was a threat to disrupt the school leaving examinations, surely, a cold and calculated move which would hit young people who have one chance to gain their first qualification, to get their feet onto the career ladder. It surely must have been a calculated move, for if it was not, what was its objective? And it would hardly hurt the administrators of the examinations. Young people were encouraged by teachers to work diligently towards those qualifications. You need them, they were told, in order to get a job and better still to get a good job. In the next breath the teachers were being led into a position where they would deny their students the very chances that they had been promoting a moment before. It is no good saying that when the battle is won we shall give those youngsters the chance we have denied them and that we shall have earned for them far better resources. For young people, it is what happens today which is significant. To study, to make real efforts to learn under the encouragement of their teachers today, only to be told tomorrow that they will have to postpone the climax to these efforts, is demoralising. For them, the day after tomorrow is a different life – they hope to be working by then, earning real money, or moving on to the more grown up world of college.

Strikes, short-term walkouts and the withdrawal from many duties traditionally recognised as a part of the teacher's job are the strategies which were used increasingly by teacher trade unions during the '60s, '70s and '80s.

In 1987, disruption, it was claimed by the militants, was the answer to the then government's imposition of a teaching contract and the withdrawal of negotiating rights. So it could be argued that they were fighting, to use the militant's terminology, to protect the professionalism of the teacher – certainly to uphold an aspect of teacher professionalism. This is a further example of teachers having some clear notion of what professionalism entails, but at the same time attempting to apply non-professional strategies in an attempt to promote that professionalism. It was teacher trade unionism which claimed teachers were not contracted to work out side certain hours in the first place: it was this attitude, taken up by government, which led to the external imposition of a more clearly defined contact of employment, a dilution of professional responsibility.

Clearly a professional work force cannot use both professional and non-professional strategies whenever it feels like it: it is either always professional in its behaviour or non-professional. Although it may be possible for a non-professional to sometimes act professionally, it is hardly a profitably strategy the other way round. Once professionals break professional trust, they lose their credibility.

Due to the following of the policy of militant disruption, teachers lost much of their respect. Government reacted by imposing a closely defined contract of employment, the teacher's status declined and their morale was lowered.

There has been a two sided erosion of teacher professionalism: that instigated by the teachers themselves and also that brought about by government legislation. Subsequent to the initiation of the Great Debate by the prime minister Callaghan, teachers have had more and more imposed upon them and, conversely, suffered a substantial decrease in their autonomy. We have already noted the imposition of a narrow contract of employment, the decrease in the authority of the head-teacher and the increase in statutory influence of governing bodies, where the teachers are in a minority. In addition there has been imposed a National Curriculum. One which experience has shown has had to be modified several times as a result of its inadequacies. How much more efficient it would have been if the teachers had been properly consulted and been both expected and able to provide a realistic input into the formulation of the Curriculum in the first place. The same argument applies to the imposition of Standard Attainment Targets and Standardised Testing; and to the introduction of published league tables to show individual school performance; and to the remodelling of the inspection service.

In spite of these changes, there are those who point to matters such as the increased opportunity for in-service training and the development of an all graduate teaching force as examples of the promotion of teaching as a profession. The fact that such developments have not resulted in improving outputs is overlooked. The criticisms of poor standards have not gone away, although each government tries to show that its particular legislations do bring improvements.

The only way forward, for those who do, no matter how intuitively, recognise the advantages of organising the education service along professional lines, is to seek a new definition of teacher professionalism based upon recognisable and acceptable principles.

A new professionalism

If we agree that the efficient form of democracy is that in which experts, professionals, are to be relied upon to carry out their respective specialised duties on behalf of the rest of us, then it is essential that we identify the principles of professionalism and agree codes of practice which form the bounds within which we trust the professionals to operate. Frameworks of operation are necessary.

Firstly, however, we must seek the elements of professionalism as they apply to the education service: what are the components of the service?

1. The service itself, a definition of what it is and what it embraces

Education involves people of all ages, abilities and attainments and is concerned with very young, immature children, older children, who bring their earlier experiences into schools, adolescents who are beginning to establish themselves as adults, young students who may well have already developed their talents to a remarkable level and mature students already educated to a high level who wish to update their knowledge and skills, or who may wish to learn a new subject discipline. In the rapidly changing world in which we live, it is to be expected that most people will pass through all of these stages in their education.

The education system is concerned with teaching from the nursery, into primary education, through secondary education and into further and higher education.

There will, therefore, be those traditionally known as nursery nurses and nursery teachers, primary school teachers, secondary school teachers and lecturers involved in the service.

In addition, examiners, inspectors and administrators are also a part of the service.

2. The aims and objectives of the service

What is education for? Professional teachers not only need to know what they are doing but also why they are doing it.

A starting point here could be to agree that there exists a body of knowledge, academic knowledge and skills, which is worthwhile passing on to our descendents.

There can be no question that this exists, it is the foundation of present day society, the accumulation of generations of experience, which enables us to live our lives as we do. It comprises of a host of subject disciplines, is used, and is constantly modified and added to through new experiences.

This is such a vast field of experience that it is impossible for everyone to know it all and logically, there will be experts in particular fields of knowledge.

Most of us need to know enough of everything to constitute a general knowledge, a kind of general intelligence which we use in order to react to our world as intelligent beings; and to have a specialist knowledge related to the specific field in which we work, the field from which we earn our living and in which we contribute our bit to the common good.

There is also knowledge associated with the maintaining of civilisation, involving common rules of behaviour which have over many centuries been shown to provide the framework of order in society which enable individuals to live a life of maximum freedom without restricting the freedoms of others. These "rules" must also be passed on to the next generation.

Those entering further and higher education are in a position, by reason of their maturity and previous education, to choose what they want to study. For instance, this will very likely be concerned with the updating or broadening of their specialist knowledge, so that they can maintain and develop their expertise in their work. Some may merely wish to pursue an interest as a part of their leisure occupations.

The younger the recipient, the more the curriculum needs to be presented to them. A choice needs to be made at national level about what is to be taught to the young: knowledge, skills and social behaviour. That is presumably why governments determine a National Curriculum for Schools.

There is, of course, a danger in this. It has been claimed that governments have established education systems for the sole purpose of maintaining an existing class system. The masses shall, as it were, only be taught those things which enable them to carry out the tasks required of their particular strata of society. This will not be the intention of any government which wishes to develop the talents of all members of its society in order to enable them to live a full, useful and happy life; and to contribute fully to the running and further development of their society.

Nevertheless, if people are asked, particularly younger people, what they want to learn, they will say that they need to know those things which will enable them to obtain employment and seek advancement in that employment, consequently earning for themselves and their families the highest attainable standard of living. Idealists cannot get away from this view, they cannot seek some unrealistic curriculum which does not clearly demonstrate that it brings qualifications for life. In any case, it is through this aspect of learning that the individual becomes a useful member of society and you cannot have a society made up of individuals unless those individuals do play a useful part in its everyday business. For those idealists who see the perfect society as one in which each pursues his happiness without reference to any one else, there is no society, there is anarchy.

So there must be structured curricula but those who lay down the contents of them must always be wary of the dangers indoctrination for indoctrination's sake – they must be wary of political ideology overpowering a more reasoned balanced argument.

3. Service to the client

An education system provides a service to those who wish to learn. To state the obvious, without learners there is no need for teachers and no need for an education system. Just as there exists an element which defines what makes up the system and an element which lays down aims and objectives, so there is, in an education system manned by professionals, the element of service to the client.

4. Qualifications

A professional is a person who has followed a recognised course of learning in the field in which he or she practices, and who has qualified by examination at the end of his or her training. Professional teachers will be no exception to this rule. They study the body of subject knowledge which they expect to pass on to their pupils and students, and they learn the variety of methods available for presenting subject matter in a comprehendible and interesting manner.

They learn the basics of psychology which help them to understand the people they teach to recognise difficulties which their students may experience so that they can develop appropriate teaching-learning strategies to overcome these difficulties.

There are some people, because they have been shown to maltreat the young, who, no matter how well they may qualify in the above disciplines, will be unable to qualify as teachers.

It is more difficult to obtain unanimous agreement on other personal characteristics which it may be considered that a professional teacher should or should not possess. For instance, should an individual who openly displays extreme, but not illegal, modes of behaviour be allowed to qualify as a professional teacher? This is an ethical question, a matter of principle, rather than an element of the system and reminds us that underlying the make up of the profession there are also matters of principle to consider. Principles together which make up a professional ethic which can be published together in a professional code.

5. Training and control of entry to the profession

It follows that a profession requires a means of determining the training of its potential members, the methods of examining the success or otherwise of those receiving training, and the means to register those who qualify.

6. Accountability

Teachers in a public education system are public servants and even where they are employed by private corporations, because they work with the public, their responsibilities need to be clearly defined, and their performance be monitored. The professional teacher should be seen to be accountable to their clients.

7. Remuneration

Teachers need to be properly rewarded financially and in their conditions of service in order to make it worth their while entering and remaining in a profession which demands high standards of qualifications and output. People need to feel that their efforts are appreciated and a sure way to show appreciation is to offer them generous financial rewards. Nevertheless, there is also the need to give rewards in other ways. The status of the teacher needs to be high – the member of an elite in terms of the service provided, just as any other professional in any other area of specialisation needs to be a member of that elite. There is nothing wrong with this kind of elitism, where each specialist provides specific expertise in a complex society where all cannot provide everything.

8. The government of the profession

A profession must be self governing. There is no point in paying people to do a job then setting up a body of laypeople to do it for them! Teachers, with the specialist qualifications, experience and appropriate accountability must be left to get on with the task of running the education service – different professional teachers having different professional responsibilities within that service. For instance, university teachers running their sector of the system, teaching at graduate and post graduate level, and carrying out research: infant school teachers specialising in the teaching of the very young and organising that part of the service; administrators carrying out administrative tasks, thus leaving teachers free to do what they are trained to do, to teach, but administrators who are a part of the professional team, not independent outsiders having little or no experience of the profession.

The basic principles of professionalism: the professional ethic

It has already been hinted that, as well as there being fairly easily recognised and accepted elements which make up the structure of a profession, so there is also a need to identify underlying principles which define the professional ethic – a more difficult area in which to obtain agreement.

I outlined and explained my earlier thinking on this question in the Professional Code for Teachers published by the Professional Association of Teachers in 1989 and give further consideration to it here.

The first basic principle: priority shall always be given to the interests of the clients

It will not be difficult for those wishing to have their service recognised as a professional service to agree that the interests of their clients shall be given high priority. It will be more difficult to agree what is meant by putting the interests of those clients above all else.

For instance: professional teachers shall not under any circumstances take any course of action which will harm or corrupt those they teach: at first sight a straightforward and easily accepted item for a professional code. But on further consideration, what is it that harms and corrupts? Does a slap across bare legs harm the young child when it refuses to comply with some quite obviously reasonably request from an adult? Does the teacher with extreme right political views corrupt the student? Does the withdrawal of labour, practiced by the militant trade unionists, do harm by disrupting education and corrupt by reason of its encouragement of disruptive strategies? Clearly, those with different ideals will offer different answers to such questions: and, not only different but opposite!

In my earlier consideration of a professional code, I suggested that the professional teacher should provide a secure framework on which pupils can build their acceptance, rejection or modification of what their life experience puts before them. Security implies the provision of conditions in which the student can follow his or her programme of learning without interruption: without interruption from teachers who decide to withdraw their services and without interruption from other students whose behaviour is disruptive.

This requires a discipline on the part of both teachers and students which places responsibility above unrealistic freedom. In terms of a professional ethic, therefore, the teacher should be expected to uphold a personal discipline and that of the students.

A further aspect of the principle of placing the interests of those in receipt of education first is that it implies a necessary understanding of the unique make up, strengths and weaknesses of each: an acceptance of individuality.

An acceptance of individuality, in turn, implies that the professional teacher holds the belief that pupils and students should be free to choose (within the bounds of their ability to do so) types of education best suited to such individuality, which requires a variety of provision, supported by appropriate objective guidance free from the bias of invested interests.

The second basic principle: professional independent objectivity

Professional strength surely evolves from the application of reasoned argument based upon factual evidence, in so far as this can be achieved, and not upon the ideologies of any one body of opinion which may be fashioned at any one moment. Much of the controversy in the English education system evident during the post World War II years has been due to the entrenchment of political thinking in dogma.

Professional teachers must remain free (and also be sufficiently responsible and consequently trusted) to make professional decisions. The professional teacher, therefore, has the responsibility to actively promote the objective evaluation of evidence, making it possible for lay people to follow genuine reasoned argument which leads to professional judgements.

In this way the professional earns the right to have an overriding say in professional affairs.

The third basic principle: self government and accountability

A professional should be independent, but needs to earn that independence by showing that professionalism can be trusted. Therefore a profession requires a system of appraisal and moderation in order to check, adapt and improve its performance, enabling it to answer complaint and criticism, and to demonstrate that it is accountable.

Professional self-government should be acceptable and it is essential that clearly understood and acceptable methods of moderation, and where necessary discipline, are built into administrative structures and procedures.

The fourth basic principle: co-operation

The application of the first, second and third principles require the professional relationship between teachers, politicians, local government offices, those in receipt of education and others to be carefully considered and defined – with the outlining of expectations in codes of practice.

Teachers need to work together with each other, with other professionals and with those outside the professions; knowing when to listen to and when to consult with others, and when to pass matters to those better qualified than themselves to handle them.

Behind this thinking lies the necessary recognition and acceptance of the much changed role of the teacher since the introduction of the 1944 Act – the new complex role which, for example, embraces responsibilities as counsellor, examiner, administrator and policy maker.

The fifth basic principle: flexibility and adaptability

For co-operation to be possible there must be flexibility and adaptability. Present day life is one of constant change: what is applicable today may not be so tomorrow and what is right in one situation is wrong in another.

The professional teacher needs to be flexible and adaptable rather than narrow and rigid in outlook.

The application of this principle requires that a new look be taken at internal career and management structures and job definitions – looking for example at the ease or otherwise of desirable and appropriate transfers between, and the relative status among, the many varied specialisms within the service.

The sixth basic principle: the positive promotion of professionalism

If professionalism is to succeed, its nature and ideals must be promoted in a positive fashion. Those who use a service provided by professionals must have confidence in those professionals. It is therefore essential for those responsible for the service to define and promote a positive image of the teacher.

There is a need to make clear to the public the ideals, responsibilities, training requirements, skills and other qualifications held by professionals which enable them to provide a high quality of service in which care and dedication are emphasised.

It is consequently also essential that those outside the profession should recognise the methods of qualification, appraisal, moderation and discipline which ensure that professionals are accountable and not merely an uncontrolled and independent body of people intent upon their own objectives for their own sake.

The seventh basic principle: just reward for professional services

This is concerned with ensuring the professionals are justly rewarded in terms of salary and conditions of service without strategies being used which break the first principle.

This is a two sided question because the professionals not only need to show that their service is worth having and worth preserving, the clients, or those who speak for them, need to ensure that a worthy service is rewarded. There is a very significant part for government to play and it is necessary to repeat here the fact that governments have not been interested in promoting professionalism. Perhaps because they like to keep power to themselves or perhaps because they genuinely believe that it is the only way to ensure that the education service delivers high standards. The two sided argument again! Their needs to be a positive initiative designed to promote the value of having a professional service, to establish it and to maintain it.

The application of principles to the structure

Further consideration is required to determine how the professional ethic, the principles of professionalism, should be applied to the structure of the profession through its elements.

Service to those in receipt of education

The most fundamental feature of professionalism is that it requires first place to be given at all times to meeting the needs of those for whom the service is provided, namely those in receipt of education. So, for example, so far as school teachers are concerned, there can be no question of refusing to teach those who wish to be taught; no question of declining to prepare and mark work; no question of refusing to set and mark examination papers; no question of refusing to attend meetings with parents (where these are regarded as a normal part of a particular teacher's work load) and no question of declining to safeguard the safety of the children.

Any one professional teacher cannot do everything: it is necessary to determine the particular professional responsibilities of each teacher. It is also necessary to determine those responsibilities which are properly those of teachers and other duties which are not.

There are responsibilities, properly regarded as those of the professional teacher, which are found outside the classroom or other teaching place and beyond timetabled hours.

There are pastoral responsibilities, as well as those concerned with teaching knowledge and skills. For instance, consultation with and counselling of pupils, students and, where appropriate, their parents.

There are administrative responsibilities such as the keeping of records (mark lists, essay grades and attendance sheets, for example), involving the observance of confidentiality, and the writing of appropriate reports. There is a danger that this work becomes over demanding of time, thus preventing the teacher from carrying out his or her major task, that of teaching. Although there are some administrative responsibilities, relating to any group of pupils or students, which only the teacher in charge of that group can carry out, it is essential that other professionals be given responsibility for those which are not specific-teacher related. For instance, some testing is by definition external to the school or college and papers related to such testing should quite properly be set and marked externally. They are examples of duties over and above those which can be described as the normal responsibilities of the classroom teacher.

The teacher's relationship with those being taught, on the other hand, applies to all those who have contact with pupils and students, and it is the source of serious problems, involving at worse accusations of assaults and the suspension of the teacher, often without justification.

The further clarification of principles governing a teacher's relationship with pupils and students is therefore very significant:

a) The relationship is a professional one and not the same as that of parent-child or family relation-child.

Although the teacher temporarily takes on certain duties of a parent, to various degrees depending upon the age of the child or student, he or she does not have the same close inter-family relationship that a parent has. Consequently, the close physical contact between the child and its family is not generally appropriate to the professional teacher.

This does not deny the need for a physical closeness involving the teacher of the young child. Indeed, where the child is young it may well be necessary to administer to physical needs. It has, until recently, been well understood that a child in the infant school may well expect considerable assistance when visiting the toilet. Equally the young child needs comforting physically when it is upset. The professional teacher should be in a position to help in these cases.

As children do not suddenly become adolescents it is also necessary to understand that sometimes, although it is expected that the occasions will decrease with increasing age, older children will also need similar assistance.

What is to be made quite clear is that the assistance is clearly to be seen to be what it is meant to be and that procedures are in place to ensure that no person other than the proven trusted teacher in the broadest sense of the word, including for instance, teaching assistants, is given such responsibility.

In the secondary school it should not be regarded as proper for a teacher to be in close physical contact with a pupil except for those exceptional circumstances when a youngster is ill or injured and first aid requires such a contact, or in cases where it is proper for the teacher to physically direct the behaviour of child or student.

There was a time in society when it was not necessary to spell out such details of professional behaviour and it is perhaps to be regretted that this time has now gone. Children and young people have been molested and youngsters' awareness of sexual behaviour, intended or innocent, has been greatly enhanced. Although most are sensible enough to know when such behaviour is misplaced there are those who will exploit the innocent or accidental act.

It is not appropriate for the professional teacher, under normal circumstances, to sit close to a pupil or student and it is not appropriate for the teacher to touch that pupil or student – one might say, no matter how well intentioned the comforting arm placed around the shoulders is intended to be!

b) The teacher not only conveys information but also attitudes

This principle follows from the discussion above but also includes the demonstrating and passing on of attitudes in other contexts.

Whenever a teacher, infant, junior, secondary, further or higher education teacher appears in front of a class, he or she demonstrates attitudes which influence, in some way, those people in the class.

This is an extremely difficult matter upon which to give guidance. Some of the most eccentric teachers have demonstrated that they are among the finest teachers. Indeed, some will argue that a little eccentricity actually helps to make a good teacher.

However, there are attitudes which are clearly unacceptable in the behaviour of the professional teacher. He or she should not present subversive or corrupting attitudes.

c) The acknowledgement of the need to avoid indoctrination

Teachers have their own ideals, if not their own ideologies! But the professional is not the promoter of doctrine. Returning to the basic intention of professionalism being an efficient agent of participatory democracy, it is essential for the teacher to provide the pupil-student with all factual information available and the whole spectrum of opinions advanced from different quarters in order to lead people into making their own as near objective judgements as possible.

A complexity in this argument is the promoting of right and wrong behaviour and in this matter there is a need for society to agree codes of what is acceptable and what is not.

d) Recognition that each pupil and student is of equal importance, irrespective of their individual differences

Teachers are human and can, indeed will, be tempted to have favourites among their pupils and students. It is, however, a part of the professional's responsibility to endeavour to make each feel equally wanted and to provide each with an equal part of the teacher's attention – although the equality will also imply the equal value of individual differences.

e) Acceptance of a professional responsibility to prepare thoroughly, teach as effectively as possible and follow up the teaching process conscientiously

Teacher relations with other professionals and parents

Education is such a complex field that it is impossible for anyone person to be expert in all of its disciplines. It is, therefore, important for professional teachers to acknowledge the need to pass students and pupils on to someone better qualified when appropriate.

Procedures for liaison need to be established when pupils and students are the professional responsibility of other professionals as well as other teachers; it is essential to decide how and through what kinds of organisation liaison should take place.

Depending upon the age and maturity of those taught, there will be the need for many teachers to liaise with parents. The teacher's relationship with parents is a critical element in the educational progress in schools. Professionalism calls for an approach which takes account of the following factors:

a) The need to assist parents in understanding and accepting their responsibilities in the education process and for this to be done in a non-threatening and non-condescending fashion.

b) The need for the professional teacher to provide advice and guidance to parents which can be readily understood and carried into effect.

c) An appreciation of the need to establish a constructive partnership with parents, and having regard to the parental contribution to the education process.

Teacher quality: training, qualifications and standards

Professionalism must equate with quality and a large part of educational quality comes from the teachers themselves. They should therefore be seen to be highly and appropriately qualified – recognised as more expert in their work than those outside the profession. Academic or subject knowledge, practical skills and personal qualities are all important.

The individual teacher needs to be appropriately qualified for his or her specific professional responsibilities and different professional teachers may have different qualifications in order to be qualified to carry out different professional responsibilities.

A more contentious aspect of professional teacher qualification is that which concerns character, personality and behaviour. But professionalism does require acceptable teacher behaviour and this must therefore be addressed.

It is possible to recognise those traits which may be expected to help in the teaching situation: for instance, those leading to a sympathetic understanding of the needs and behaviour of those to be taught – particularly significant when dealing with children and young people. All teachers may reasonably be expected to show patience, sympathy, tolerance and imagination and some people may be naturally more gifted in these qualities than others. It is likely that a short-tempered, narrow minded, autocrat would be frequently involved in unnecessary confrontations – providing inefficiency in the teaching situation but also burning up much personal emotional energy and being susceptible to unnecessary stress related illness.

Observing school teachers in the work situation demonstrates that some have the ability to accurately judge the personalities of children and young people while others find this difficult. Those who possess whatever natural abilities make this an easy task, judge behaviour accurately, assess its true significance and produce an appropriate response – one that is neither too easy nor severe, one that invokes the most desirable response from any particular individual in particular circumstances. Experience suggests that there are those adults who have this ability; others who can, to a certain degree, learn to apply strategies associated with it and those who, no matter how much they are helped, cannot make the necessary judgements quickly or accurately enough to help them with assessing and reacting to classroom behaviour. Consequently, they fail to make just demands of their pupils and the class as a whole judges them to be unfair and incompetent, and reacts by displaying rebellion.

There is the question of the relationship between a teacher's private lifestyle and professional conduct. The teacher is a public figure and is therefore subject to public scrutiny and, consequently, his or her behaviour must be acceptable to all. Exceptional negative deviation from an acceptable norm is relatively easy to define, recognise and reject. For instance, there is no doubt in anyone's mind that a proven paedophile cannot be allowed to become a school teacher. There are many other forms of behaviour which are more difficult to judge, not least because different people hold different views as to the acceptability or correctness of the behaviour.

There are, however, some general principles which can be applied to help with this matter.

There is a need for private behaviour, particularly if it is questionable in the eyes of a significant proportion of the population, to remain private – sometimes not easily achieved. A simple and relatively uncontroversial example will suffice. There was a medical doctor who enjoyed stripping to the waist and wearing shorts when following his hobby of summertime gardening. For this reason, he insisted that he live well away from the catchment area of his surgery because he felt that, if this image of himself was to become familiar to his patients, it would erode a very important patient-doctor professional relationship and in turn lower the patient's confidence in the professional. Some may say a silly and insignificant matter in today's broadminded society, but it does have its place. And, of course, this is given as only a minor example of styles of behaviour which include more extreme and more controversial practices.

The close relationship between teacher and taught is one in which the teacher's personal values are easily discerned. Teachers teach not only by what they say but by what they do, and consequently should guard at all times against recommending by word or observable behaviour morally questionable modes of conduct.

A corollary to this argument is that there is such a thing as morally questionable conduct and that conversely there is morally acceptable conduct, a concept which is sometimes denied. But there must be bounds to individual behaviour if each is to live in a society where an optimum freedom is recognised – a freedom in which each individual can only do as he or she pleases so long as this does not take away the freedom of others.

The professional teacher, working within the framework of a democratic society, needs to have defined a code of morally acceptable behaviour, which is generally accepted by the society in which he or she works, as a reference, and to be seen to uphold this code.

To complicate the matter further, it can be argued that a part of a teacher's professionalism also consists of being ready and able to exercise objective judgement as to what is and what is not morally questionable in a particular context. At certain stages in the education process, it will be necessary for the teacher to lead discussion on the substance of morality – to question the validity of the moral code. I remember well, in my naivety, raising with one class of sixteen-year-old school leavers the question of the desirability of marriage, hoping that I was perhaps helping them mature into responsible parents. Everything went well, with a goodly number of traditional points being made in favour of the institution of marriage, until one brave lad shot his hand up and firmly stated his opposition to the whole business. I carefully asked for his reasons for this view. "Marriage has never done me any good!" he exclaimed, with a definite edge of criticism in his voice. What I wondered had a lad of sixteen had in the way of experience of marriage? We waited for him to continue. "My father cleared off when me and me brothers was little, and our muvver 'ad to bring us up on her own. So what's the good of marriage?"

By way of summary, acceptable behaviour at a place of work includes:

a) Effective professional working relationships with those in receipt of education.

b) Trust and reliability.

c) Upholding good order in the classroom or other teaching place, around the premises and in the neighbourhood.

d) Possession and application of a generally accepted and understood philosophy relating to rewards and punishments.

e) Giving time to other than timetabled activities.

f) Covering the duties of colleagues during their unavoidable and unexpected absences in so far as this is reasonable.

g) Appropriate personal turnout: styles generally accepted as usual for the nature of the job being done and, as a general rule, avoiding extreme or bizarre styles which may be interpreted as implying the acceptance of extreme behaviour.

h) Conscientious preparation and marking of work properly, including in one's individual responsibilities.

i) The use of appropriate and acceptable ways of talking with those in receipt of education.

j) The provision of balanced reasoned instruction based upon the best available understood factual knowledge.

k) Remaining neutral when teaching controversial issues: not imposing one's own personal view, providing the student with evidence relating to all reasonable views, but promoting the particular view where such a view is generally accepted by the community (as in an agreed moral code). It is not the case that everything needs to be open to infinite interpretation all of the time.

The management of the profession: A General Teaching Council

A profession should be self-governing and there should be a professional body, with statutory powers, which control standards of entry, and standards of performance and discipline within the profession. Such a body could have the title Professional Education Council.

There have been various initiatives to establish such a council: there now exists the General Teaching Councils for England, Northern Ireland, Scotland and Wales.

In July 1997 the government published the paper "Teaching: High Status, High Standards – General Teaching Council" as a consultation document, eventually establishing the General Teaching Council (GTC) for England by the Teaching and Higher Education Act of 1998.

The functions of the Council are: to maintain a register of qualified teachers in England, to regulate the teaching profession and to provide advice to government and other agencies on issues affecting the quality of teaching and learning.

The GTC is the authority for awarding Qualified Teacher Status and all qualified teachers working in state schools of all types are legally bound to be registered. Many teachers working in independent schools are also included on the register.

The Council has 64 members: 25 are *registered teachers* and are elected every four years; 9 are *nominated by professional teaching organisations and trade unions*; 17 are *nominated through other teacher related organisations* and 13 are *nominated by the GTC's public appointments procedure*. Does such a body satisfy the condition that the profession should be self governing?

With 11 teachers coming from each of the primary and secondary sectors, 1 from a special school and 2 head-teachers, a total of only 25 out of 64, this hardly supports the notion that such a council should be representative of a self governing profession.

Secondly a further 9 members are nominees from teacher associations or trade unions and their main function is to advise and support their members, a different responsibility from governing the profession. They are placed in a situation where there could very well be a conflict of interests: on the one hand registered teachers could be disciplined by the GTC but be legally represented by their trade union.

Of the 17 nominated through *teacher related organisations*, remembering that we are concerned with the management of professional teachers, 7 certainly have direct input into education: the Association of Colleges, the Catholic Education Service, the Church of England, Guild HE, the Independent Schools Council, the Universities Council for the Education of Teachers and Universities UK.

Local Authorities have been the route by which education has been delivered, through Local Education Authorities but this situation is changing and may change further as schools and colleges are established independent of local government. If the trend is to continue, taking the position that it should, if the objective is to establish an independent education system, and in any case questioning the wisdom of local government having any part to play in the management of a professional organisation for teachers, the representatives from local government are not required.

Neither is it appropriate to have representatives from the Commission for Equality and Human Rights nor from the National Children's Bureau and National Governors' Association: these may be interested parties but are not teachers and are not appropriate professionals to be managing an *independent* Teaching Council.

Of the public appointees 8 are directly concerned with teaching; of the others one other is a Forensic Science Manager, another is an accountant, another a parent governor and one is the Chief Executive of the Changemakers' Foundation. With the Secretary of State appointment it is clear that the present Teaching Council is not an independent body for professionals engaged in delivering education.

Professional teachers have different professional responsibilities within the education service: for instance, university teachers teach at graduate and post graduate level, and carry out educational research; those in the field of Further Education bridge the gap between school and Higher Education or employment; secondary school teachers are concerned with the education of the teenager; infant school teachers (and indeed nursery nurses in so far as they teach) specialise in the teaching of the very young; teacher-administrators carry out organisational tasks, thus leaving teachers free to do what they are trained to do, to teach, but they are administrators who are a part of the professional team of educators; and those engaged in preparing national syllabi, setting, marking examinations and granting qualifications. All of these people are engaged in the delivering of education and qualify for inclusion in an independent governing body established to govern the education service.

One last note on the subject concerns governing bodies of individual educational establishments: they are concerned with delivering education but are not included in the above list of educational professionals simply because, in their present form, they are not educational professionals.

The GTC Code of Conduct and Practice for Registered Teachers 2009

The General Teaching Council for England (GTC) describes itself as the professional body for teaching in England and states that its Code sets out expectations of conduct and practice for registered teachers: its purpose 'is to guide teachers' everyday judgements and actions, and provide the GTC with principles to use in regulating the profession'. The Code has been developed through consultation with teachers *and others with an interest in teaching and learning.*

The GTC claims that it has *an important role in strengthening teacher professionalism* and claims to be independent from Government. Following on from previous discussion on the principles of professionalism and the membership of any independent professional governing body for teachers and education, there are both similarities and differences between the GTC approach at that out lined here.

There is great deal of agreement on professionalism between the thinking in this chapter and that behind the construction of the GTC Code Conduct and Practice The first of eight principles of Conduct and Practice given by the GTC is identical in intention to that stated by the Professional Association of Teachers in its Code and continues as a prime principle of its successor Voice the Union for Professionals in Education, but the GTC has a significant problem, the question of strike action.

The withdrawal of services, which necessarily includes the withdrawal of responsibility for the *safety, wellbeing, development and progress* (GTC Code first principle) of children and young people, and the breakdown of *public trust and confidence in the teaching profession* (GTC Code principle number 8), directly undermines its stated intention.

In the third principle of the GTC Code the intention to help children become *confident and successful learners*, cannot be denied but the first two notes of explanation given *(uphold children and young peoples rights and help them to understand their responsibilities and listen to children and young people, consider their views and preferences, and involve them in decisions that affect them, including to their own learning)*, more a statement of a political correctness than professionalism, can be misinterpreted and misused. Children's rights are discussed in previous chapters and relate to the discussion here. Certainly, responsibility needs to be expected and taught more positively but as any mischievous or maladjusted child knows any suggestion that they may make regarding alleged abuse of their rights is given priority consideration without a balanced investigation and at the expense of other's reputations, the question needs careful reconsideration.

There is an element of *children and young people must be consulted about everything* – the principle of participatory democracy again, as opposed to a professional democracy.

In principle 4 of the GTC Code there is again an echo a political correctness in references to equal opportunity, inclusion, access and bullying, and of course, following the requirements of government legislation. The Code is bound by government policy and is an indication of it being not a code compiled by those in the profession but the outcome of too much state interference in the running of the education system. An explanation of the questioning of the concepts of equality and inclusion is discussed in Chapter 4. In the matter of bullying it is somehow unbelievable that a government needs to legislate that each school should have a policy for dealing with it – this over-complicates the matter, even risking the magnifying of the usual into something exceptional. Dealing with the problem should be a matter of teacher training. It is a matter of discipline, a subject considered in chapters 5, 6, and 7.

The determination of pay and conditions of service

Pay and conditions of service should be and now are determined by an independent review body with statutory powers. The former arrangements in which pay bargaining strategies were used were a factor in the diminishing of the professional ethic and are undesirable. But it must be emphasised that society will only have the teaching profession which is really worth having if such a review body is able to ensure the proper and deserved reward for the teachers.

A nation needs to decide the importance which it is going to give to the education of its people and realise that a professional education service in which standards are high can only be achieved by awarding its servants with a comfortable standard of living and decent working conditions.

The **Great** Education Controversy

Bibliography

Bennion, Francis. (1969). *Professional Ethics*. Charles Knight & Co Ltd.

Bryant, R. V. and Leicester, C. R. (1991). *The Professional Association of Teachers - The Early Years*. Buckland Publications Ltd.

Darlington Local Authority. (1938). *Log books of the Eastbourne Schools 1936-68.* Education Committee Regulations.

Gardner, H. (1985). *Frames of Mind: the Theory of Multiple Intelligence.* Paladin, London.

Government Publications.
Consultation document Education in Schools 1977
Consultation document Teaching: High Status, High standards July 1997
White Paper: Your Child, Your Schools, Our Future
 Building a 21st Century Schools system
White Paper: 14-19 Education and Skills February 2005
White Paper Higher Standards Better Schools for All October 2005
Tomlinson Report: Report of the Working Group on
14-19 Curriculum and Qualifications Reform

Ministry of Education
Pamphlet No 9. The New Secondary Education. (1947)

Morris, Giller, Szwed and Geach. (1980). *Justice for Children*. Macmillan, London.

Newburn, Tim. (1995). *Crime and Criminal Justice Policy.* Longmans.

Newsome. (1963). *The Newome Report HMSO.*

Pedley, Robin. (1963). *The Comprehensive School*. Penguin Books.

Professional Association of Teachers (Now known as Voice - The Union for educational professionals)
The Journal of the Professional Association of Teachers
Professional Code for Teachers 1989

Rutter, Michael. (1979). *Fifteen Thousand Hours: Secondary schools and their effects on children.* Harvard University Press.

Turner, Barry. (1973). *Discipline in Schools*. Ward Lock Educational.

Vernon, P.E. (1971). *The Structure of Human Abilities*. Methuen, London.

Wringe, Colin. (1984). *Democracy, Schooling and Political Education*. George Allen and Unwin.

Index

11 plus examination 125
14- to 18-year-olds, Education of 8

academic learning 24, 37, 49, 116, 118, 121, 123
accountability 126, 141, 142, 205, 223, 225
Accredited Schools Groups 204
accusations 2, 101, 184, 228
age of criminal responsibility 71
Aggression 60, 97, 98, 100, 174
Aims and objectives of education 220
Anglesey School 21
Anglican National Schools 6
antisocial behaviour 1, 59, 63, 68, 82, 84, 85, 86, 87, 92, 172, 187
Applied Learning 196
Apprenticeships 120
aptitudes 27, 41, 50
Assessment, internal 138, 141, 142
Assessment of a general level of education 126
attitudes towards children 55
authority 2, 6, 7, 21, 34, 45, 47, 51, 52, 57, 58, 59, 63, 64, 65, 68, 71, 72, 73, 77, 80, 82, 83, 84, 86, 87, 88, 89, 90, 93, 95, 97, 98, 99, 100, 101, 132, 144, 149, 164, 189, 191, 200, 204, 207, 208, 209, 210, 211, 212, 213, 214, 219, 234

Baldwin, Stanley 9
Balfour Education Act 7
basic skills 30, 149, 169, 171
behaviour 1, 5, 26, 38, 40, 43, 44, 45, 46, 48, 49, 50, 51, 52, 53, 55, 57, 58, 59,

61, 63, 64, 65, 66, 68, 69, 73, 74, 77, 78, 79, 80, 81, 82, 84, 85, 86, 87, 88, 89, 91, 92, 93, 94, 95, 96, 97, 98, 99, 100, 103, 119, 161, 171, 172, 173, 174, 175, 177, 182, 186, 187, 189, 203, 204, 214, 215, 219, 221, 222, 224, 229, 231, 232, 233
  behaviour in school 48, 93
Bell, Andrew 6
Beloe Report 163
Bennion, Francis 216
beyond parental control 81
Binet, Alfred 35
Board of Education 7, 149
body of knowledge 56, 58, 209, 220
Boyle, Edward 159
Boyson, Rhodes Sir 58
Branksome School and Science College 195
Break in learning at age sixteen 142
British Association of Social Workers 74
bullying 50, 51, 66, 91, 99, 103, 174, 236
Business Apprenticeship Centres 200
Butler Education Act 1944 10

Cambridgeshire Schools 21, 194
Care Order 67, 75
Carmel Roman Catholic Technology College 195
Carpenter, Mary 69
carrying of weapons 98, 99
Central Council for Recreative Physical Training 179
Centres of Vocational Excellence 121
chalk-and-talk 104, 105, 106
Chief Executive of the Changemakers' Foundation 235
childcare 151, 183
Children's rights 86, 236
Children and Young Persons Act 1933 76
Children and Young Persons Act 1969 67, 73
Children and Young Persons Act of 1969 67, 72, 73, 76
child rearing 53, 81

Index

Child Welfare 86
Christian faith 175, 188, 189, 193, 194
Church of England 175, 192, 193, 194, 234
City and Guilds 133, 151, 158
Clarke, Kenneth 76
classroom furniture 103
class size 11, 96
class system 7, 221
cleanliness 176, 177, 178, 179
Clerk to the Justices 67
codes of practice 220, 225
Code of conduct 95, 99, 218
  General Teaching Council (GTC) Code of Conduct and Practice for Registered Teachers 2009 235
code of ethics 176
code of values 58, 59
cohesive society 194
Commission for Equality and Human Rights 235
communities 21, 22, 76, 192, 207
compulsion 172, 203
Computers in learning 112
Continuous Professional Development 196
contract of employment 54, 219
controversy in education 112
counselling 39, 40, 41, 60, 120, 121, 126, 173, 183, 202, 210, 227
Countesthorpe Community College 58
County Council 6, 24, 160
  The London County Council Comprehensive Schools 24
Court Orders 70, 73
Criminal Justice Act of 1948 71
Criminal Justice Act of 1982 75
Criminal Justice Act of 1991 67, 76
Criminal Justice and Public Order Act 1994 76
Crossland, David and Anne 193
Curriculum 147
  14-19 Curriculum 160

academic 21, 197
alternative 148
broader aspects of, 153, 171, 172
condensing 143
hidden 14
in Faith schools 193
in Specialist schools 195, 196, 197
Lack of variety 107, 108
National 2, 120, 167, 168, 184, 191, 192, 211, 219, 221
post-1940 13, 150, 155, 159, 162
pre-1940 150
Primary/stage 1 169, 170, 171
Secondary 7, 169
secondary school 7, 55, 162
senior school 152
Technical and Vocational Initiative of 1980s 2

Darlington Church of England Academy 192
Darlington Education Village 196
Darlington Training College 179
delinquent/cy 43, 48, 49, 51, 55, 63, 66, 67, 69, 71, 72, 73, 77, 78, 79, 80, 81, 82,
    83, 84, 85, 86, 88, 91, 92, 93, 95, 101, 120, 172
democracy 18, 45, 207, 208, 209, 210, 211, 212, 213, 220, 229, 236
detention 67, 71, 73, 75, 99, 100
detention centres 71, 74
De Gruchy, Nigel 44
diagnostic tests 126
diet 178, 181
differences in learning ability 116
   academic and practical learning 116
different schools 10, 11, 12, 16, 18, 19, 34, 41, 129
diphtheria 5, 181
diplomas 117, 118, 126, 140, 142
Discipline, Just - see Chapter 5 43
discipline - see Chapter 7 91

Index

discovery method 112
disruptive pupil/s 43, 44, 48, 158
diversion
  of young offenders 77, 88, 90
diversion
  and social control 89
dogmatic 34, 55
Duke of Edinburgh's Award 154, 172
Durham Diocese of the Church of England 193
dysfunctional families 94

Eastbourne Schools, Darlington 150, 172, 178, 179, 180
Eccles 159
education, purpose of - see Chapter 12 177, 182
Education Act 1870 149
Education Act 1899 7
Education Act 1918 8
Education Act 1921 149
Education Act 1944 4, 21, 38, 152, 216
Education Act 1945 115
education and behaviour 187
education and the economy 187
education and the national culture 188
education service 59, 209, 218, 220, 223, 227, 235, 237
egalitarianism 33, 147, 163
Elementary Education Act 1870 6
elitism 6, 21, 33, 34, 107, 125, 147, 148, 163, 223
Employment Programme, Entry 93
employment prospects 115, 185
Entry to Employment programme 93
Environmental Studies 165
equality 2, 22, 33, 133, 140, 230, 236
Equality and Individuality - see Chapter 4 33
equal worth 39, 118
        in Academic and Vocational Qualifications 118
ethics 189

multi-cultural 176
ethos 1, 13, 14, 21, 34, 41, 46, 47, 48, 49, 50, 51, 55, 63, 80, 93, 94, 172, 175, 192, 193, 194, 195, 199, 204, 212
Examinations
    Eleven-plus 23, 24, 51, 157
    Certificate of Secondary Education 2, 118, 133, 136, 159, 163, 166, 167, 170
    General Certificate of Education 118, 133, 157, 166
    General Certificate of Secondary Education 2, 136, 167
    General School Examination (GSE) 147
    Schools Certificate Examination 7
    School Certificate Examination 132
    School Leaving Certificate 152
    School leaving examinations 16, 29, 134, 137
exclusion 93, 98, 99, 100, 101
Executive Advisors 204
Executive Head-teachers 204
extended schools 198
extra-curricular 99, 143, 144, 155, 171, 172, 198, 199

Factories Act 1833 68
factor analysis 36
failing schools 43
failure 15, 16, 18, 34, 39, 45, 46, 47, 50, 58, 59, 64, 66, 73, 85, 87, 88, 91, 92, 103, 109, 127, 128, 133, 136, 139, 140, 152, 164
faith schools 175, 176, 186, 189, 193, 194, 195
family responsibilities 172
fees 6, 7, 217
financial assistance 92, 155
First, middle and high schools 29
Fit Person Orders 71
frameworks of operation 220
freedom 46, 50, 54, 64, 78, 79, 87, 92, 95, 119, 172, 191, 194, 203, 204, 214, 215, 216, 221, 224, 232
functional English and maths 169
Galton, Francis 36

Index

Gardner 37, 38
general knowledge 30, 170, 221
General Teaching Council for England (GTC) 234, 235, 236
Glaisdale School 43
Goddard 36
Great Debate, The 3

Hadow Report 10
hallucinatory education system 191
Hard Federation 196
Haughton Community School and Arts College 195
health education 181
Hebburn School, South Tyneside 43
Her Majesty's Inspectors of Schools 159
His Majesty's Inspectors of Schools 181
Home-School Agreements 201
Home Office 69, 70, 75
housecraft 150
Humanities Project 165
human rights 40, 47
Hummersknott School and Language College 195
Hurworth Maths and Computing College 195

idealism 16, 162
ideology 86, 106, 125, 165, 192, 213, 222
individual differences 6, 12, 33, 34, 39, 40, 52, 53, 230
individual needs 41, 158, 184
individual personalities 52, 157
indoctrination 13, 222, 229
infectious diseases 180
Intelligence
    Body-kinaesthetic intelligence 38
    General intelligence (g) 37
    Mathematical-logical intelligence 37
    Multiple intelligence 37
    Musical intelligence 37

　　　　Quotient IQ 35
　　　　Tests 35
inter-personal relationships 97
intermediate Treatment 73, 75

juvenile courts 67, 70, 73, 77
juvenile delinquency 63, 68, 70, 71, 74, 76, 77, 85
　and the school 63
　appropriate responses 85
　causes 74
　early responses 68
　need for principles 77
Juvenile Liaison Schemes 66

knowledge,
　　　general 30
　　　and skills 3, 50, 58
　　　of results 126, 127, 142

Lancaster, Joseph 6
leadership 18, 45, 52, 57, 156, 158, 173
league tables 50, 132, 136, 142, 205, 219
learning for vocational goals 116
libraries 12
linguistic intelligence 37
Local Education Authority 43, 216
London County Council 24, 160
　London County Council Comprehensive Schools 24
Longfield School Sports College 195
lowering of standards 46, 133, 134
low ability 50, 128
lunchtime supervision 45

Magistrates Association 74

maladjusted pupils 46
Manton School 43
mathematics 23, 150, 192
mental age 35
meritocracy 17
mixed ability teaching 46, 106, 107, 109
modern technology 13
monitorial scheme 6
Mortimore, Peter 57
multi-cultural 176, 194
multicultural society 95, 175, 188, 189, 193

National Association Union of Women Teachers NASUWT 43, 44
National Children's Bureau 235
National Council for Civil Liberties 74
National Curriculum 2, 120, 167, 168, 184, 192, 219, 221
National Governors' Association 235
National Standardised Attainment Tests STATS 131
National Strategy
  Secondary 169
National Workforce Agreement, The 141
neighbourhood schools 22
Neill, A.S 58
Newburn, Tim 75
Newsome Report 1963 159, 160, 162
New Secondary Education 11, 17, 30
Non-conformist British and Foreign Schools Societies 6
normal distribution hypothesis 128, 135
nutrition 181

objectivity in testing 125, 127, 225
Ofsted 44
one school for all 125, 191
out of school activities 171
parent-child relationships 84

Parents Guarantee 201
Parkhurst Act 1838 69
participatory democracy 45, 209, 210, 211, 212, 213, 229, 236
Pedley, Robin 17, 18, 19, 21
peer group pressure 109, 158
personal, social and health education (PSHE) 168
personalised learning programmes 121
personal and social development 161
physical fitness 171, 179, 180
police 63, 64, 65, 66, 74, 75, 79, 87, 89, 98, 99
politicians 13, 45, 147, 208, 213, 225
practical subjects 138, 150, 151
Prevention of Cruelty to Children Act 1879 69
principles of professionalism 220, 223, 227, 236
private practice 217
Probation Orders 71
professionalism 207, 214, 216, 217, 218, 219, 220, 223, 225, 226, 227, 229, 231, 232, 236
professional democracy 18, 236
professional independent objectivity 225
profiles
  Student/Pupil Profile 144
programmed learning 112, 113
provision for learning difficulties 120, 121
psychological reports 7, 83, 112
punishment/sanctions 1, 22, 48, 58, 60, 68, 69, 76, 85, 86, 88, 93, 95, 96, 99, 100, 101, 233
Pupil Guarantee 201

qualifications 6, 27, 31, 50, 53, 55, 59, 116, 117, 118, 121, 125, 126, 133, 134, 135, 140, 141, 125, 151, 142, 148, 161, 162, 163, 167, 171, 174, 184, 191, 201, 202, 208, 211, 212, 218, 221, 223, 226, 230, 231, 235
Qualifications and Curriculum Development Agency (QCDA) 167

reasoning 37, 38, 49, 73, 81, 82, 113, 130, 164, 166, 209

reasons for testing and examining 126
records of achievement 3, 16
rejection 18, 28, 60, 224
religious education 148, 175, 186
remedial teaching 169
remuneration 8, 164, 182, 217
Residence Order 82
residential school 82, 93
Ridings School, The 43
rights and responsibilities 71, 99
Royal Society of Arts 27, 158
Rutter, Michael 47, 48, 49, 63

Schools Council 159, 167, 234
School Admissions Code 192
school attendance 48
school boards 6
school buildings 17, 28, 196
school ethos 51
school houses 154
school leaving age 6, 10, 28, 119, 135, 137, 142, 150, 160, 161, 162, 163
  1911 7
  1918 8
  1945 115
  1973 55, 160
school leaving examinations, disruption of, 218
school processes 47, 48, 49, 63
school report card 201, 205
school uniform 154
science 7, 8, 12, 15, 22, 23, 30, 131, 135, 148, 158, 170, 172, 184, 192, 195, 202
secondary school population 55
Simon, Theodore 35
Simon-Binet test 35
slow learners 109, 156
social background 94, 125, 136

social disadvantage 6
social education 172
Social Enquiry Report 67
social justice 17, 38, 92, 93, 173, 178, 191
social services 63, 64, 67, 73, 74, 75, 76, 77
Spearman 36, 37
specialisation 148, 223
special educational needs 35
special places scheme 7
speech, music and drama 156
Spens Report 10
sponsors 191, 192, 193, 195, 200, 201
staff turnover 53
Standardised Testing 219
Standard Attainment Targets 219
Stenhouse Project 165
streaming 16, 107, 128
strike action 43, 217, 236
subjective assessment of learning 127
Summerhill 58
supervision order 64, 66
support 7, 16, 20, 44, 49, 55, 70, 75, 92, 93, 95, 99, 103, 111, 113, 121, 179, 183, 189, 196, 198, 202, 208, 234

teacher-pupil contact time 108
Teachers
  morale 132, 212, 219
  personal characteristics 222
  qualifications 222
  responsibilities 31, 54, 60, 211, 214, 215, 223, 226, 227, 228, 231, 233, 235
  stress 2, 44, 108, 212, 231
  with industrial experience 7
  militancy 54
  training 57, 198, 237
Teaching and Higher Education Act 1998 234

Index

Teaching and Learning Centres 196
Teaching Council 217, 234, 235
teaching machines 112
teaching methods 2, 3, 12, 16, 41, 53, 57, 103, 111, 116, 163, 209, 211
teaching profession 23, 164, 218, 236
  accountability 223
  aims and objectives 220
  a definition 220
  basic principles of professionalism 223, 224, 225, 226
  determination of pay and conditions of service 237
  government of, 223
  qualifications 222
  regulation of, 234
  training and control of entry 222
The National Workforce Agreement 141
The Welfare Principle, of 1989 Act 82, 86
Times, The 46, 57, 63
Times Educational Supplement 46
Tomlinson, Mike 43, 118, 137, 139, 140, 145, 160, 170, 171, 172
Tomlinson Report 118, 137, 139, 140, 160, 171
trade unions 2, 91, 159, 172, 217, 218, 234
traditional classroom 35, 40, 104
Training and Vocational Education Initiative (TVEI) 115
tripartite system 16, 17, 21
truancy 26, 50, 91, 93
Turner, Barry 58
tutors 40

uncontrolled deviant 50
underprivileged 6, 40, 55, 63, 73, 107, 108, 169

values 4, 47, 58, 59, 79, 95, 174, 208, 209, 232
Vernon, P.E 37
vocational courses 7, 10, 40, 94, 118, 119, 121, 123, 140, 157, 185
vocational courses 7, 10, 40, 94, 118, 119, 121, 123, 140, 185

vocational education 41, 116, 121, 122, 123, 139, 185, 188, 197, 200, 201 - see also Chapter 9
Voice (the Union for Professionals in Education) 236

Watts, John 58, 59
weaknesses in the system 137
White Paper
  14-19 Education and Skills 91
  1970 74
  Children in Trouble 1968 72
  Education and Skills 2005 90
  Higher Standards, Better Schools for All 91
  Supporting Children and Parents 183
  Teachers: High Status, High standards 1997 217
  The Child, Family and Young Offender 1965 72
  Young Offenders 1980 75
  Your Child, Your Schools, Our Future 2009 201
Wilkinson, Ellen 11
Wilson, Tim (Detective Inspector) 64
Wringe, Colin 210

Young Apprenticeships 120
youth hostels 155

www.ingramcontent.com/pod-product-compliance
Lightning Source LLC
Chambersburg PA
CBHW022004160426
43197CB00007B/262